A Literate South

A Literate South

Reading before Emancipation

Beth Barton Schweiger

Yale

UNIVERSITY PRESS

New Haven & London

Published with assistance from the foundation established in memory of
Amasa Stone Mather of the Class of 1907, Yale College.

Yale University Press books may be purchased in quantity for educational, business,
or promotional use. For information, please e-mail sales.press@yale.edu
(U.S. office) or sales@yaleup.co.uk (U.K. office).

Set in Bulmer type by Tseng Information Systems, Inc.
Printed in the United States of America.

Library of Congress Control Number: 2018961530
ISBN 978-0-300-11253-5 (hardcover : alk. paper)

A catalogue record for this book is available from the British Library.

This paper meets the requirements of ANSI/NISO Z39.48-1992 (Permanence of Paper).

10 9 8 7 6 5 4 3 2 1

For Tom and Marcus

Contents

Preface

Culture is ordinary: that is where we must start.
—Raymond Williams

THE ORIGINS OF THIS BOOK ARE IN A small hand-stitched journal bound in homespun linsey-woolsey. When I pulled the acid-free paper from around it at a table in the Virginia Historical Society, I found the pages crowded with Amanda Jane Cooley's handwriting. Begun in 1842, when she was twenty-two years old, so that she might "compare one day with another and see the difference in my feelings," the journal ended a dozen years later when she died of consumption. "The writer of this journal is now no more," her younger sister wrote on the final page. "She died this morning at 8 o'clock . . . in full hope of inheriting a crown of Glory."[1]

The journal tells of life at the Cooley farm in Virginia, a few miles off the present-day Blue Ridge Parkway, in extraordinary detail. Amanda recorded not only her feelings but also the movement and labor of her busy household: yards of fabric woven and hanks of thread spun, coats and dresses stitched, pigs slaughtered and soap made, church meetings and funerals attended, three-month school sessions convened. But the journal's revelation is in her list of what the family read: English novels, newspapers from Virginia, Philadelphia, and Missouri, Maine humorists, the Bible, biographies, religious tracts, grammars, songsters, advice literature, and several national magazines, including *Godey's Lady's Book,* to which Amanda subscribed, carefully sewing the issues together for safekeeping. Not long after this, I found Allen Speer's account of his ancestors who lived about fifty miles southeast of the Cooleys in the Yadkin River valley of North Carolina. Methodist tanner Aquilla Speer's family were also avid

Front cover, Journal, Amanda Jane Cooley Roberts. Courtesy of Virginia Historical Society.

readers. His daughters Jennie and Ann read New York newspapers, magazines, eighteenth- and nineteenth-century English and American poetry,
histories, advice literature, and biographies. Of the memoir of Margaret
Fuller Ossoli, Jennie pointedly observed, "I like many of her thoughts and
opinions, and *some I do not.*"[2]

The writings of the Cooley and Speer sisters—Amanda Cooley and
her younger sister Betsy, and Jennie and Ann Speer—form the spine of this
book, for they offer a preliminary bibliography of the variety of print that
was available to rural people in the 1840s and 1850s. More people could
read in the southern states than almost anywhere in the Western world in
1850 and they had many things to read.[3] Schoolbooks told them how little
of their native tongue they understood, hymnbooks taught them poems and
tunes composed across the Atlantic, novels offered visions of fog-shrouded
moors, and testaments gave their speech a biblical cadence.

In *A Literate South* I argue that print permeated the rural South, co-

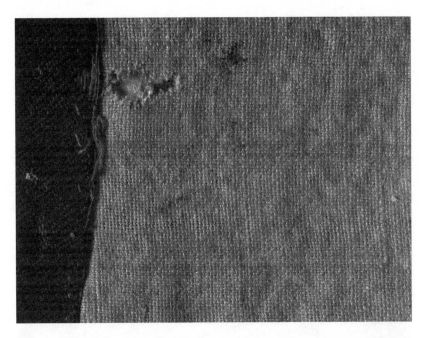

Front cover detail, Journal, Amanda Jane Cooley Roberts. Courtesy of Virginia
Historical Society.

existing with oral tradition in a rich give-and-take in which printed texts
reflected speech and speech incorporated texts. Print insinuated itself into
every life in the nineteenth century; there was simply no escape, even for
those who could not read at all. Speech and writing are always in relationship, never entirely separate things. Musicologists have discovered, for
example, that slave spirituals spread through Richard Allen's hymnbook,
printed in Philadelphia in 1801 and revered among black Methodists.[4] Literate and illiterate people read or were read to from texts that circulated
across the Anglo-American world. Some of these were memorized and
entered the oral tradition off the printed page; others became the inspiration for new work scribbled in journals and commonplace books or spontaneously voiced aloud. Examining the ways in which print flourished alongside speech among rural people will help us better understand the poetics
of everyday life in the nineteenth century.[5]

In this story of cultural change and persistence, readers in the rural

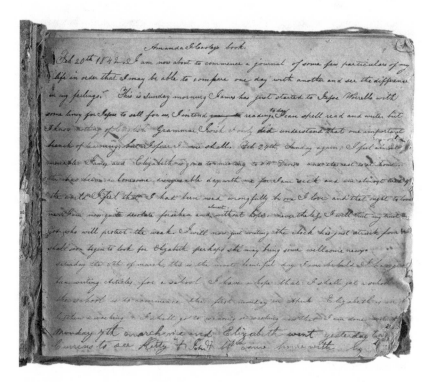

First page, Journal, Amanda Jane Cooley Roberts. Courtesy of Virginia Historical Society.

South were American readers. Regardless of where they lived, the language, intellects, and imaginations of people in the early United States were shaped in part by the same schoolbooks, the same poems, and the same sacred songs. Yet the ideology of literacy that developed in the nineteenth century effaced these southern readers, veiling them even to their own generation. This ideology imagined readers as a single undifferentiated mass, who embraced liberal ideals and had learned to read in school. Neither of these assumptions characterized most American readers before the Civil War, but they were particularly poor descriptions of people in the southern states, where millions of slaves were barred by law or custom from learning to read, and few communities had free public schools or publishing firms. By 1860 the ideology of literacy seemed to divide the United States just as surely as slavery did.

All of this has encouraged the view that people in the northern states lived in a modern literate society while those in the slave states languished in a premodern ignorance, with little desire and even less opportunity to read.[6] Slavery and literacy still seem somehow incompatible, a view that accords with that of the great North Carolina polemicist Hinton Rowan Helper. "Slavery is the parent of ignorance," he wrote in 1857, and it is "inevitably hostile to literary culture." While recent studies have corrected the view that the Old South was a premodern society, it continues to be characterized as a broadly illiterate one. More than thirty-five years ago, Michael O'Brien argued that there were "varieties of modernity" in the nineteenth century. His history of intellectual life in the southern states described one of these, while recent histories of slavery and religion describe others. This book describes yet one more. People in both the northern and southern states nurtured market capitalism, vibrant religions, and vigorous racism. Most were also profoundly literate.[7]

When I read the diaries of the Cooley women, I was intrigued to find a modestly educated household reading British novels in a county without a printing office or railroad. I began to look for more readers, eventually finding evidence of much more print — mainly magazines, newspapers, handbills, and pamphlets — circulating in the rural South than I expected.[8] The artisan families at the heart of this book were avid readers, but they were unexceptional; they did not have to go to extraordinary lengths to find reading material. While the Cooleys were self-educated slaveholders of Quaker lineage and mixed Methodist/Baptist inclinations, the Speers were stout antislavery Methodists who sent their children to an academy across the county and later grieved a son who died for the Confederacy. Both families lived far from the main transportation routes of their day, yet both were devoted readers. In the case of the Cooleys, this included their young slave Jincy, who for a time sat with the family on Sunday afternoons rehearsing her speller.

During a year in Cambridge, I read the British cultural critics Richard Hoggart and Raymond Williams, whose work with and about the working classes after World War II became a foundation of cultural studies.[9] They helped me gain a critical perspective on nineteenth-century reading that lifted the veil of the ideology of literacy. One striking anecdote told of how the undergraduate Williams arrived in Cambridge from rural Wales to find people who insisted that the rural culture in which he grew up had disappeared a few years before he was born. When the bewildered student began reading to find out why and how this Old England and its "timeless agricultural way of life" had disappeared, he found himself on a sort of escalator that kept sliding further and further into the past, he said. One writer asserted that the rural way of life "handed down from the days of Virgil" had ended fifty years earlier, while another maintained that it had happened during the generation before that. Eventually, pastoral Britain declined back to a time long before Virgil, and from there continued falling away back to Eden itself. What Williams called the "problem of perspective" was sustained by each generation's nostalgia for an imagined past.[10]

The broad themes of Williams's work rest on his insight into how modern culture effaced what preceded it. He showed me that writers such as John Clare, George Eliot, and Thomas Hardy—who described the making of a new order in rural capitalism—resonated deeply with developments in the early Blue Ridge. Williams also taught me that, because all writing is a "way of seeing," critical readers are obliged to look for what is not seen.[11] This is how rural southern readers became blindingly obvious to me. The liberal orthodoxy that a reading people would embrace liberty was the form that Williams's "problem of perspective" has taken in American history.

At the same time that Hoggart and Williams were writing in the late 1950s, scholars in the United States were recovering the history of slavery. Slave narratives figured largely in this task; their central theme, critics have explained, was the search for literacy. They told of enslaved people who sought a voice and freedom in reading and writing. Slaves could intuitively equate literacy with power and liberty from the earliest days of the Atlantic trade because nearly all of those who held them in bondage could read and write. Their sense of literacy's power was only reinforced by their conversion to Christianity in large numbers by the late eighteenth century, when they celebrated a gospel propagated in books that told them the truth would set them free. By the 1850s it had become a commonplace among slaves, free black people, and their white allies that reading was a basic human right, suggesting that the most important truths were read, not spoken.

Illiteracy, then, became another name for slavery at the same time that the ideology of literacy was being created. This ideology declares that the ability to read is necessary for human progress, freedom, happiness, and prosperity—what Harvey Graff famously called "the literacy myth."[12] In an era of republican revolutions, the ancient convention that justified the rule of kings and the illiteracy of their subjects was upended. Slaves and masters, workers and industrialists, colonists and imperialists all declared that the ability to read was a vehicle of modernity and human freedom. While Western empires colonized illiterate peoples around the world in the name of progress, Americans wrote a national history that reimagined the purpose of New England Puritan reading as the basis of nationalism and justified the establishment of free common schools to spread liberal individualism—something that would have horrified the Puritans.[13] Meanwhile, slaves who thirsted for freedom and schooling—seemingly in equal measure—took it for granted that a reading people could break human chains. This powerful conviction hardened into a universal truth even as it was starkly contradicted by daily life in the society that embraced it, one in which literate slaves remained in bondage, literate Indians were brutally disinherited, literate poor people remained impoverished, and literate women sometimes shunned legal equality with men. Their experiences continue to sit uneasily in a liberal narrative of American history that hopes freedom and equality are within reach for all who can read, for they show that the power of literacy alone cannot set people free.

This is a book about what rural people read in the Old South, what they did with their reading, and why they have been so hard for historians to see. People in the nineteenth century created the ideological meaning of reading just as surely as they invented stereotyping, steam presses, and lithography. The late invention of the term "literacy" itself—coined in the pages of an American magazine only in 1880—heralded the maturity of the liberal consensus on reading that endures as one of the most powerful ideologies in the modern world.[14]

This book has four goals. The first is to show that print was freely available to readers who lived at some distance from a printing office or publisher. The geography of production did not correlate with consumption.

Aside from cheap steady-sellers like schoolbooks, Bibles, and hymnbooks, books were expensive. Rural readers read mainly ephemera—broadsides, magazines, newspapers, tracts, pamphlets, and almanacs—which for the most part were never intended to survive, and predictably did not. These offered a rich variety of news, fiction, history, book reviews, poetry, jokes, toasts, and songs. As time passed and more print was produced by heavily capitalized firms in northeastern cities, printing offices continued to produce ephemera and a few inexpensive books. Historians still know little about how the enormous output of power presses made its way across the country, but the evidence offered here shows that print of all kinds found many rural readers.[15]

The book's second goal is to place reading and writing in the context of nineteenth-century pedagogy. Most people learned to read and write outside of school by methods that were set aside long ago, but these shaped how people used language and understood what reading meant. To assert that someone was literate meant something different in 1750 than it did in 1850. Nor did it say much about the reader, as reading and writing skills varied enormously between neighborhoods and even within households. The method by which students learned to read and write also changed dramatically between the eighteenth and nineteenth centuries. Understanding the norms of pedagogy, as the book historian Robert Darnton has suggested, can help us better grasp how and why people read, especially those whose voices are silent in the archives.[16]

A third aim is to show that rural people, including those who could not read, used print to create and circulate ordinary culture. Most scholarship on nineteenth-century reading has turned on two questions—how reading created a public sphere and how it nurtured a private self. Even at this late date, the history of readers is largely uncharted territory. Analyzing them is a daunting task, as most of what their reading meant to them has been lost forever. A reader closed her book two hundred years ago, rose from her chair, and walked out of the room, leaving no trace behind. Yet the history of readers can be written as a study of cultural formation.[17] "Culture" became one of the most complicated words in the English language in the nineteenth century as its meaning shifted dramatically from tending crops and livestock, to the nurture of human minds, to an abstraction pointing to "the best that has been thought or said in the world," in the words of the critic Matthew Arnold.[18] This study pulls on a single strand of culture—printed texts—to show how sacred songs, jokes, stories, and religious doctrines were learned and passed on both by those who could read and those who could not.

Women are central to this project. Historians are undecided as to whether nineteenth-century women read differently than men did, but they have nearly all concluded that reading liberated women, both individually and collectively. This book offers another angle from which to view women's reading. Just as they made cloth and coats, and cured hams, women also wrote songs, poems, and stories that they passed along, often to children or others who could not (yet) read.

Oddly, the sources used in this study only rarely show people reading the Bible. Its omnipresence for all people, enslaved or free, is beyond question. It was the foundation on which all other Anglo-American culture rested, although this hardly indicates consensus about its meaning or whether it was true. The tendency of nineteenth-century writers to overlook this crucial text underscores how pervasive it was. But it also offers a sharp reminder of the limits of reading even in the age that invented the steam press. Biblical culture remained largely oral, especially for those of modest or no education, as enslaved people remind us. The Bible was memorized off the page, of course, but most people learned it by heart listening to three-hour sermons, singing sacred tunes and hymns, and hearing myriad allusions to its language and stories in conversation, jokes, and tales that circulated freely among the learned and unlearned alike.

A final goal of *A Literate South* is to challenge the nineteenth-century perspective that literacy and slavery were incompatible. The ideology of literacy declared that reading spread the light of knowledge to darkened minds, that it was a gift of the gods that left freedom and prosperity in its wake. Such optimism about reading's potential continues to shape the history of the United States. American historians stand virtually alone in their confidence that literacy promotes liberal ideals and that print is an unequivocal good; those who study other places and times know well how easily it can foster oppression. High literacy rates in repressive societies such as Nazi Germany or contemporary Zimbabwe demonstrate that reading can be an efficient means of social control. It can close minds as easily as open them.

As reading is one of the most complex of human activities, this book rests on insights from fields ranging from anthropology to bibliography, literary studies to rhetoric, and folklore and musicology to social history. I have written mainly for historians, but I have been inspired by Raymond Williams's understanding of ordinary culture, Roger Abrahams's poetics of everyday life, Shirley Brice Heath's ethnography of language, Donald McKenzie's sociology of texts, Donald Mathews's study of religion as mood and social process, David Whisnant's politics of culture, and Eileen Southern's African American musicology.[19] I assume, like Lawrence Levine, that intellectual history is not "the history of thought, but of people thinking," and, like Daniel Wickberg, that narrowing analysis of culture to questions of power impoverishes our understanding of the past.[20]

The eclectic list of subjects covered here is based on the tastes of the Cooley and Speer families and other readers I found in the archives. In this sense, this book resembles the miscellanies favored in the nineteenth century. It is intended to open a conversation by suggesting fruitful avenues for further work.

On a Sunday in March, 1847, seventy-two-year-old Benjamin Franklin Cooley suddenly took ill. His daughters rushed home from visiting a neighbor to find their father "nearly dead! I think it must be a stroke of the palsey for he has no use at all of his right side and hand, and but little of his left," Amanda wrote. "When we lift him up he is perfectly limber and cannot even hold up his head—Lord have mercy on us."[21] For two and a half weeks, Ben Cooley lay nearly motionless in his bed, taking nothing but a little milk. The house filled with neighbors who came to pay their respects to a man who had been at the center of the county's affairs for more than four decades.

At first, the dying man refused to send for a doctor, but when he relented, the physician could offer little hope. The grieving family finally sent a hired slave to town for the white cotton that neighbor women stitched into shrouding. Five days after he lost his ability to speak, still prone in his bed and in great distress, Ben Cooley died at 9 o'clock on Thursday, March 25. He was buried next to his eight-year-old daughter Eliza on the hill above the farm. "My dear father is no more on earth—we have just finished the sad office of consigning his remains to the earth—Oh! What a task," Amanda wrote. "Last night about twenty persons staid here and of all the singing I ever heard it beat—they sang all night long."[22]

Two months later, Cooley's will and probate inventory were recorded in Carroll County, Virginia.[23] A committee of "three impartial men" appointed by the probate judge—neighbors Joshua Hanks, Silas Ward, and Thomas Tharp—carefully inventoried the family's possessions, including furniture, livestock, crockery and silverware, bed linens, carpeting, spinning wheels, pounds of wool, and carpentry and blacksmithing tools. In all, the family's possessions filled two and a half pages and were valued at $808.05, which was "more than we expected," Amanda said.[24] Listed between the $45.00 debt of Ben Cooley's son-in-law and two pairs of sheep shears valued at $1.75, was a single line: "1 lot of books, 4.00."

A few strokes of a pen are the only witness to the Cooley household's reading in the public record, and it is a wonder that the committee saw fit to list the books at all.[25] If any of the volumes had leather or stamped cloth bindings, the "lot" probably numbered four or five books at most; if they were schoolbooks or other volumes cheaply bound in paper boards, it might have included up to ten titles. Importantly, neither the magazines, newspapers, almanacs, and pamphlet novels, nor the Cooley sisters' handmade journals and commonplace books, were included. Most of what the family read and wrote, then, literally had no value. This brief line—"1 lot of books, 4.00"—bears witness to how hard it can be to see people reading in the rural South even when you are looking for them. This book begins to tell their story.

Acknowledgments

IT IS MY PLEASURE TO THANK THE many people and institutions who helped me with this project over the years. I would not have been able to write about the Cooley and Speer women without the generosity of Ellen Carpenter, the late Love Worrell Cox, Allen Paul Speer, and Janet Barton Speer. They and other generations of the Speer and Cooley families have lovingly preserved their family histories. I am also indebted to local historians of the Blue Ridge who shared their time and expertise, particularly Charles Mathis, Lewis Brumfield, and the late Frances Harding Casstevens. The late John Perry Alderman's patient recording of the history of families in Carroll County, Virginia, was invaluable. It will be evident to those who persevere through these pages that this study rests on the fine work of many people, both living and dead.

For research support, I thank the National Endowment for the Humanities for a Research Fellowship and a semester fellowship at the American Antiquarian Society, the Spencer Foundation, the Yale Institute for the Advanced Study of Religion, the Library Company of Philadelphia, the Historical Society of Pennsylvania, the Huntington Library, the Virginia Historical Society, Calvin College, and Wolfson College of Cambridge University.

The librarians and staff at Mullins Library at the University of Arkansas; Sterling Library and the former Seeley Mudd Library at Yale University; Alderman Library and the Albert and Shirley Small Special Collections Library at the University of Virginia; Cambridge University Library; the Southern Historical Collection at the University of North Carolina; the Historical Society of Pennsylvania; the Library Company of Philadelphia; the Center for Appalachian Studies at Brock Library of East Tennessee State University; Wytheville Community College; Galax-Carroll Regional Library, Hillsville; Boonville Community Library; Yadkin County Public Library; the Library of Virginia; the Virginia Historical Society; North Carolina State Archives; the Museum of Early Southern Decorative Arts; Brock Historical Museum of Greensboro College; the Eury Appalachian Collection at Belk Library, Appalachian State University; Special Collections at Mercer University; the Harry Ransom Center at the University of Texas at Austin; the Public Library of Cincinnati and Hamilton County, Ohio; and the Rubenstein Rare Book and Manuscript Library at Duke University were unfailingly helpful.

I have presented these ideas to many audiences, including the Centre for the History of the Book at the University of Edinburgh, the faculty of history at the University of Leicester, the American History Seminar at Cambridge University, the American Studies Seminar at Sussex University, the Rothermere American Institute at Oxford University, the annual meeting of the British American Nineteenth-Century Historians, the Center for the Study of Southern Culture at the University of Mississippi, the American Antiquarian Society, the Library Company of Philadelphia, the St. George Tucker Society, the Institute for the Advanced Study of Religion at Yale University, the Seminar in American Religion at the University of Notre Dame, and the Southern Intellectual History Circle.

The original roots of this study lie in Ed Ayers's graduate seminar on Southern history at the University of Virginia. I returned to Charlottesville in July 2010 to spend an unforgettable week in Michael Winship's course on nineteenth-century books at the Rare Book School. Michael's support has been crucial. The late E. Jennifer Monaghan was a model of scholarly generosity; she supported this work from our first correspondence. I am especially grateful for how she and Charles Monaghan freely shared their exhaustive knowledge and love of early American schoolbooks and pedagogy with me.

Karen B. Carroll and Beverly Michaels superbly edited the manuscript and Erin Greb beautifully rendered the map. Portions of this book appeared as "The Literate South: Reading before Emancipation," *Journal of the Civil War Era* 3 (September 2013): 331–59, and "A Social History of English Grammar in the Early United States," *Journal of the Early Republic* 30 (Winter 2010): 533–55.

At the University of Arkansas, my work was generously supported by the Office of the Provost, the William J. Fulbright College of Arts and Sciences, and the Department of History. I thank former colleagues in the history department and beyond, especially Melinda Adams, Caree Banton, Liang Cai, Vivian Davis, Ben Fagan, Brenda Foster, Jim Gigantino, Laurence Hare, Greg Herman, Jim Jones, Elizabeth Markham, Leo Mazow, Jeanne Short, Josh Smith, Julie Stenken, Patrick Williams, and Rembrandt Wolpert. I also relied on a cohort of gifted graduate students, especially Michael Bohlen, David Boozer, Tammy Byron, Nate Conley, Susan Dollar, Dan Fischer, Ron Gordon, Michael Hammond, Louise Hancox, Chelsea Hodge, Liz Kiszonas, Anne Marie Martin, Laura Smith, Sonia Toudji, and John Treat.

Friends and colleagues in Fayetteville and beyond offered encouragement, research tips, critical readings, conversation, libations, and nourishment of all kinds over the long life of this project. I thank them all, especially Margaret Abruzzo, Christy and Steve Adams, Kurt Berends, Emily Bingham, Bill Blair, Lynda Coon, Susan Donaldson, Paul Erickson, Sarah Gardner, Richard Godden, Jim Greene, Chris Hager, Mike Hamilton, Paul Harvey, Cole Hutchison, Richard John, Cheryl Fradette Junk, Don Krummel, George Lewis, Anita Marino, Donald Mathews, Deborah Dash Moore, Adam Nelson, Mark Noll, Ted Ownby, Michael Pierce, Lloyd Pratt, David Rawson, Lou Sanders, Kathy Sloan, Caroline Sloat, Elisabeth Sommer, Tricia Starks, Steve Stowe, James Turner, Elizabeth K. L. Vukman, Jon Wells, Charles Reagan Wilson, and S. J. Wolfe.

The Southern Intellectual History Circle has been an unrivaled pilgrim home for me for two decades of conversation and friendship. The circle's founder, the late Michael O'Brien, was a kind and generous mentor and friend. For their encouragement and interest I especially thank Ray Arsenault, Tony Badger, Al Brophy, Vernon Burton, Jim Farmer, Mary Kelley, David Moltke-Hansen, Tricia O'Brien, James Peacock, Dale Reed, John Shelton Reed, Mitchell Snay, Doug Thompson, Mills Thornton, Anne Wyatt-Brown, and the late Bert Wyatt-Brown.

I am most thankful for Tom and Marcus. This is for them.

A Literate South

The Presence of Print

N. I. King had a book here.

—Betsy Cooley

BY THE 1840S PRINT WAS A COMMONPLACE in the rural South. Schoolbooks, Bibles, testaments, hymnbooks, songsters, tracts, newspapers, magazines, pamphlets, broadsides, and almanacs poured into post offices and general stores and out of peddlers' packs, making their presence known even to those who lived a day's journey or more from a printing office. Almanacs, tracts, and pamphlets were modest things, stitched together in thin paper covers. Newspapers were clumsily inked and roughly stashed in pottery crocks to be consulted again or shared with a neighbor. Hymnbooks, testaments, and schoolbooks were bound in simple paper boards. Receipts and ledger books recorded orders from wholesalers or purchases on credit. Handbills and paper currency in a bewildering variety circulated from hand to hand. Handbooks offered templates of legal documents to copy. Printers produced hundreds of pamphlet editions of Baptist association minutes annually. Broadsides on shop walls announced the sale of a farm or the date of a revival meeting. Old print wrapped purchases and filled book bindings, images and verses were torn out of newspapers and magazines to be tacked onto cupboards and window frames, schoolbooks were ripped apart and the pages stuffed into hats or pockets. Holes were punched into almanacs so they could hang by the fireplace.

When bound books were listed in probate inventories, as they only rarely were, they often appeared as a "lot," the same term used to describe farming tools, barrels, or beehives. A lot of books typically included simple volumes of little value, but most of what rural people read was not valued at all. Almanacs, one of life's necessities, could be had for a nickel and were the most mundane of productions. But print could also be marvelous in the nineteenth century. In its finest forms, it inspired the kind of adulation paid to minor deities or to lovers; the English critic Charles Lamb was known to kiss his books. Occasionally, books appeared in remote places clad in bright cloth bindings stamped in gilt or half-bound in calf leather, with colorful endpapers and hand-colored plates that cost more than a week's wages. When such books did appear, they became events in themselves. Betsy Cooley visited a neighbor's house in the Blue Ridge in November 1843. "There I found a book entitled Biglands History of Animals and Birds. They lent it to me and I have been reading it," she wrote. John Bigland (1750–1832) was a British schoolmaster whose two-volume *Natural History of Animals* (Philadelphia, 1828) featured a dozen hand-colored plates; a leopard prowled the frontispiece. Two weeks later, the Cooleys were still reading from it.[1]

Even in modest guise, print drew attention to itself. People talked about it, thought about it, and remembered it, whether they could read or not. They parted ways with friends over what was in the newspaper. They used images from two-hundred-year-old English Puritan texts to describe their days. They carved verses from Shakespeare onto tombstones and named their children (or horses) after characters in eighteenth-century novels. When a newspaper arrived, people gathered to hear the news, and store owners piled magazines on counters to lure customers. Printers had to reprimand those who seized upon "copy, written or printed" and peered over the compositor's shoulder as he worked. People deciphered shape-notes in singing schools, read their testaments aloud, worried over the weather forecast in their almanacs, and recited spelling books to distracted companions.

Print was the great technology of the nineteenth century. The best authority for this extravagant claim was print itself, which repeatedly declared that it had revolutionized the whole world. It had not, of course. Writers, printers, and publishers had much to gain from such claims, but people knew many things that were not in print. "Book learning" had never been necessary to acquire the skills that kept people alive. Instead, people learned how to shoe a horse, slaughter a pig, weave a coverlet, birth a child, or till a field through years of practice. Elders warned against sowing turnips in the dark of the moon or beginning a journey on a Friday. But print's power to persuade people of its importance only grew over time, as books and pamphlets began to co-opt skills that had long been learned by oral tradition. Handbooks and manuals explained the best recipe for lye soap or how to lance a boil, while grammars convinced readers that they knew nothing of their native tongue. In this way, more and more of what seemed important in everyday life was drawn from the page in the nineteenth century, a time in which people learned to depend on print.

This chapter surveys the abundance of printed material available to readers in rural southern communities before turning to describe the women in two Blue Ridge families who have provided the bibliography at the heart of this book. Their reading offers a glimpse of how the words of an Elizabethan viscount—"knowledge is power"—became meaningful to a tanner's daughter a continent away and two and half centuries on.[2]

Torrents of Print

In the span of a generation, print moved from scarcity to abundance. Those who study print after about 1830 face the same problem as readers have ever since: there are too many books. The mass of print grew at an astonishing rate in the early nineteenth century, and it has never let up. Librarians and archivists seem to have the universe of eighteenth-century print well in hand, but turn to the nineteenth century and their schemes begin to go awry. To scroll through the pixilated titles only begins to skim the surface; whole buildings of books still wait to be catalogued. Production began to outpace even the most avid reader; where it was once possible to absorb or at least to glance at an entire field of study, by 1850 it became impossible to be familiar with a tiny corner of it. In 1750, 11,000 books were published; in 1850, 50,000 titles appeared. In 1750 the cumulative bibliography was approximately 700,000 titles; by 1850 it was 3.3 million. The bewildered response to all of this is recorded in books themselves. In her great novel *Middlemarch*, George Eliot's antiquarian Edward Casaubon labored in his study for the "key to all mythologies" in a futile attempt to integrate all knowledge in the age of the steam press.[3]

Meanwhile, newspapers, handbills, broadsides, magazines, almanacs, pamphlets, and tracts appeared in numbers beyond calculation. Along with cheap copies of the Bible and hymnbooks, schoolbooks seemed to be everywhere, such modest things that they hardly counted as books at all. Copies circulated for decades until they were completely worn out. Most of the print rural people encountered has not survived. A leading bibliographer estimated that four-fifths of what was produced in the small printing offices in the early United States is forever lost.[4]

Many of these publications were broadsides. The hundreds of surviving specimens of broadside verse printed between 1850 and 1870 are a fraction of what was produced and distributed gratis or for a few pennies a copy; these have survived against all odds, offering a glimpse of the satire, humor, and doggerel that circulated freely both by spoken word and in print. During the Civil War, some of these sheets were printed in military camps on portable presses. Occasional copies survive, along with the wartime letters and diaries in archives and attics, only because they recalled an extraordinary time.[5] Sometimes even ephemera became vessels of readers' memories as they pressed flowers and newspaper clippings between pages that bore the names and marginalia of earlier readers, to be passed on to the next generation.

Printed and handwritten texts were particularly important to religious people. Word of revival meetings and church gatherings was spread in newspapers, handbills, and broadsides to be amplified by word of mouth. Religious leaders kept lists of mourners and converts so they could invite penitents to join their churches or subscribe to their denominational organs. Careful records were kept of any monies collected and the biblical texts of the sermons. On revival grounds, Bibles, hymnbooks, and songsters were plentiful. Meetings were governed by rules that were solemnly signed and posted. Campgrounds drew pious seekers and irreverent hucksters in equal number. Politicians passed through with handbills, and ped-

Caleb Taylor, *Spiritual Songs* (Lexington, KY, 1804). From the Collection of the Public Library of Cincinnati and Hamilton County, Ohio.

Caleb Taylor, *Spiritual Songs* (Lexington, KY, 1804). From the Collection of the
Public Library of Cincinnati and Hamilton County, Ohio.

dlers and book agents sold newspapers and printed sermons among their
many wares. At one meeting, a man bustled "from tent to tent, thrusting
into the faces of the occupants a printed notice promising speedy and gra-
tuitous relief from the headache." Meanwhile, compilers of sacred songs
used camp meetings both to gather material and to sell their broadsides
and songsters.[6]

By the 1840s much of what people read came from the cities that were
emerging as the great publishing centers: Philadelphia, New York, Boston,

and Cincinnati. Rural readers who learned about new publications in news-paper advertisements or publishers' catalogues regularly wrote for "speci-men" copies. Heads of schools ordered quantities of books from merchants on the East Coast.[7] The number of post offices grew fivefold in the 1840s and 1850s in many rural areas as the volume of letters, newspapers, and magazines grew along with the number of rural readers. While bound vol-umes were technically barred from the mail until 1851 and were sent by publishers via express or freight companies, books sometimes squeaked through.[8] Printers and publishers worked around this rule by printing book-length works as pamphlets, and many books first appeared as serials in the magazines piled in the corners of rural post offices. Thus, when rural people lamented a lack of books, they did not mean print. Finely bound books may have been relatively rare, but ephemera had ceased to draw much notice at all.

Book agents, newspaper agents, colporteurs, and peddlers crowded the roads. These were nearly all young men who were eager for a chance to leave the plow behind. Editors recruited agents in the pages of their publications. Once enlisted, their names were printed so that anyone who read the paper or magazine might track one down. These lists also certi-fied agents' legitimacy, for there were many imposters combing the back roads collecting monies from credulous people. Agents earned a percentage for each subscriber; many worked for several publications at once. There were also agents for national benevolent societies such as the American Bible Society, the American Sunday School Union (ASSU), and especially the American Tract Society. Reverend John McCullagh, a Presbyterian who had emigrated from Scotland, arrived in western Kentucky in 1839 to work for the ASSU. "Who can estimate the power and influence of a good book?" he asked. "On the day of Pentecost three thousand were converted by Peter's spoken sermon; but who shall tell us of the tens of thousands who have been blessed by reading the printed report of that remarkable discourse?" The Louisville superintendent for the ASSU paid him a dollar a day. By 1846 he was hired by the Sunday School Missionary Association of Second Presbyterian Church in Louisville to work for two hundred days for three hundred dollars.[9]

Peddlers were usually men (and occasionally women) with a literary bent. Aquila Johnson Peyton was a newly baptized schoolteacher with pretensions to expertise in English grammar, poetry, and the pulpit.[10] Forced to give up teaching in Piedmont Virginia after contracting a fever, he was soon asked to become an agent for a new Fredericksburg weekly, the *Virginia Baptist*. "I think I ought," Peyton wrote. "It would probably suit my health better than teaching and would be improving." An aspiring author, he was pleased to see his article in the pages of that very paper a few weeks later. "The printing is very well done. There are, however, several alterations in the spelling which I don't like," Peyton complained. "Printers have no more right to alter the spelling than the grammatical construction—I want everything I write to be printed literative."

In the fall of 1859, Peyton set out with a bundle of newspapers, a new songbook to read on his journey, and a forty-dollar horse named Crockett. He did not have an auspicious start. "I had considerable vexation and trouble this morning in getting ready for starting. My saddle bags ripped in two places, and two straps, tacked to the rear of my saddle, failed to hold my overcoat. I finally left it, taking another coat in its place." A few days later, in a terrible downpour, he came upon a tobacco field and a "handsome villa." "I dismounted, and went under the stable shelter, and after a little brushing and adjusting of my garments &c., I advanced to the house, a stately mansion approached by a neat graveled walk, and surrounded by a yard very tastefully ornamented. After standing in the porch a few moments, and making a signal by thumping on the floor with my umbrella, a benevolent looking lady appeared and bade me enter. In a short time, a gentleman descended a flight of steps, and in accordance with my request that I might have an opportunity of taking off my wet garments, conducted me up stairs, where was a young gentleman lying on a low bed with a volume spread before him. Entering into conversation with him, I learned that his name was Terrill. I then knew that I was in the house of Dr. W. Terrill," Peyton wrote. The doctor was not well-disposed toward teetotalers, and Peyton was obliged to leave without a sale. He did manage, however, to get the man's slaves to wash his clothes for him.

Peyton traveled for six days before he signed his first subscriber, and across six more counties before he dejectedly turned toward home just a month after he had begun. It turned out that most people already subscribed to papers they considered far more interesting than the *Virginia Baptist*. He tried a variety of methods to sell papers, but seemed to have little inclination for sharp dealing. At a church meeting in Albemarle County, "I put up a number of the paper near the door, but it attracted little attention," he complained.

A detour to the Piedmont Female Academy at Cobham offered him a vision: the windows were full of young women, one of whom invited the transfixed young agent to get off his horse and go to the door. "I accepted the invitation," Peyton remembered, "although I knew it was but a saucy speech from some pert damsel." In Charlottesville, he mustered the courage for some solicitation on the street, but "after walking and talking until fairly worn out, and almost sick," he returned to his hotel with the names of but three, none of whom had paid him. He visited the courthouse, but the busy crowd could not be bothered. His horse fell ill, and he had to borrow another. He met a woman who agreed to take the paper, but only if her husband permitted it. One man agreed to take it because he felt that the Baptist *Religious Herald,* published in Richmond, was not suitable for children. A deaf and dumb man who wrote a beautiful hand paid him promptly at the store at Free Union. When approached by a man who tried to hire him as an agent for the *United States Journal,* Peyton recoiled in disgust, as that was "one of the poisonous kind," he said. The last straw came at a Mrs. Grayson's. She "expressed a preference for the [*Religious*] *Herald,* and I could not urge upon her instead to take so inferior a paper as the *Baptist*." As he turned toward home, he concluded that if he were to be a paper agent, it would be wise "to give a wider scope to my labors by circulating at least half a dozen different papers."

Nearly any preacher, or aspiring preacher such as Peyton, could be counted on to provide something to read. Many were formally enlisted as agents of a denominational publishing house or a national benevolent society. More often, pastors sold subscriptions to denominational newspapers and magazines or religious books. Itinerant Methodists were particularly well known for their bookselling. With their well-oiled system of rural itinerancy, they helped solve the most persistent problem of publishing by incorporating book distribution into the structure of their denomination. From the time that they established their Book Concern in 1789, Methodists were better at it than almost anyone else. In 1800, ministers were formally deputized by the Annual Conference as book agents for denominational publications. As the work of Methodist publishing grew to include newspapers, magazines, tracts, and pamphlets, these too became part of the preacher's wares. Dunning in this manner could be quite wearisome. Preachers' diaries are filled with notations about changes of address, and monies collected and owed, suggesting that more people were interested in reading a newspaper or magazine than were willing to pay for one.

Allen Turner, a ten-year veteran of the Georgia Conference, received regular shipments of books in the early 1820s as an agent of the Methodist Publishing House in New York. Known as a "rough hewn and stern featured man" who once tried to get the conference to censure a peer for shaving on the Sabbath, Turner operated a thriving business among patrons scattered along the Broad and Little Rivers to the north and west of Augusta, Georgia. In 1826 he recorded the sale of more than seven hundred books in at least thirty different neighborhoods.[11]

Most of these were religious works, particularly those favored by Methodist preachers, but Turner also sold schoolbooks, including primers and Hugh Blair's *Lectures on Rhetoric and Belles Lettres* (1783), and books of poetry by writers such as John Milton and Edward Young. A large part of his trade was in ephemera. He sold subscriptions and individual copies of at least three Methodist periodicals, the *Methodist Magazine* (New York), the *Wesleyan Journal* (New York), and *Zion's Herald* (Boston). His pamphlets and tracts bore titles like *Youth's Pattern, Stranger's Offering,* and *Christian's Manual.* He also sold Sunday school books, Scripture tickets that featured Bible verses and images, and "cards of approbation" that rewarded Sunday school pupils for memorizing Bible verses.

Turner sold Methodist works by authors such as John Wesley, Francis Asbury, John Fletcher, Thomas Coke, and Richard Watson. He ordered eleven sets of Francis Asbury's journal, published in New York by Nathan Bangs in three volumes, and Johann Mosheim's four-volume *Ecclesiastical*

History, also published in New York. He sold quarto Bibles, hymnbooks bound in calf leather, songbooks, sermons, theological treatises, biographies of eminent ministers, and church histories. There were commentaries by Adam Clarke, Bible dictionaries by James Wood and Miles Martindale, and John Brown's Bible concordance. Turner often left books with customers to sell on his behalf, allowing them to keep a small amount for each one they sold. In July 1826 he left seventeen books with Mary Wright, only to take them all back—no doubt a bit worse for wear—when he returned on October 1. Turner was also a source of money in a cash-poor neighborhood, loaning one, five, or even fifteen dollars at a time. Some customers paid for their books with chickens.

Turner's interest in selling books was not remarkable. Methodist preachers understood this to be part of their calling. They carried boxes of books, saddlebags stuffed with magazines and newspapers, and pockets of tracts across the continent. Freight costs were prohibitive—approximately five to ten dollars per hundred pounds by wagon—so Methodists created a depository for books and other printed materials in Pittsburgh in 1835. Itinerants were allowed, under agreement with the Methodist Publishing House in New York, to claim a small profit on their sales. Growth in the numbers of books distributed paralleled the astonishing growth of the denomination itself. Between 1808 and 1848, Methodists sold approximately $600,000 worth of printed materials to 650,000 customers. Profits were distributed among the conferences, providing a significant source of support for pastors in those like the Holston Conference of southwestern Virginia and eastern Tennessee. In the early 1840s, Holston received $700 from the Book Concern.[12]

The thriving itinerant system also demanded books. Methodists did not require college degrees for ordination until the twentieth century, but early conferences examined aspiring ministers in grammar and rhetoric, the Bible, church history, and other subjects. Those who could not pass were turned away. In 1836 the Holston Conference of the Methodist Episcopal Church, which included the Blue Ridge, printed "A Course of Reading and Study" for those who wished to be ordained. The first year included the Bible and various commentaries; John Wesley's *Notes;* several biblical and theological dictionaries; Richard Watson's *Life of Wesley;* John Wesley's *Sermons;* and "Murray's, or some other approved system of English Grammar." They were also required to take penmanship, and write "at least one composition on some literary, moral or religious subject." In the second year they had to study the *Methodist Discipline* and other theological works, along with Hugh Blair's *Lectures on Rhetoric,* and produce "one sermon written out at full length." "It is expected of all to give satisfaction respecting their knowledge of the above subjects, embraced in this plan, before they are received into full connexion," Rev. Thomas A. Morris of Madisonville, Tennessee, wrote. Four years later, the two years of self-study had been expanded to four. Similar expectations were adopted by the Methodist Episcopal Church, South after it was created a few years later.[13] All of these requirements assumed the ready availability of books.

Rural readers could nearly always find a schoolbook. Historians, bibliographers, librarians, and collectors have all paid schoolbooks little mind for a single reason: so many were printed that, even two centuries on, they remain commonplace objects of modest value. Some libraries have destroyed old schoolbooks and even the best institutions stopped collecting them long ago, if they ever did.[14] Noah Webster remains one of the few textbook authors with a credible, if incomplete, bibliography, and his case underscores the difficulties this genre presents. Not even Webster, who famously pioneered early copyright laws and kept elaborate records of his publications, could keep track of all the editions attributed to him during his lifetime. There were simply too many to count.

Estimates of how many schoolbooks were in circulation in the early nineteenth century are impossible to make not only because so many were produced, but also because old books were circulated until they literally fell apart.[15] All but the least popular of these "steady sellers" appeared in several editions, while the most popular were printed in hundreds of thousands of copies, or in some extraordinary cases, millions of copies. The reformer and educator Henry Barnard compiled the most comprehensive list of American schoolbooks for the first half of the nineteenth century and printed his list in the *American Journal of Education* between 1863 and 1864. It included almost 10,000 separate titles in more than 190 columns of print.[16] These numbers probably fall far short. Samuel Griswold Goodrich, the best-selling author of the Peter Parley schoolbook series, estimated that, in the two decades after 1820, schoolbooks increased from 30 percent to 40 percent of all publishing business at a time when the numbers of books produced was rising sharply. Schoolbooks circulated in greater numbers than religious materials.[17]

Even slaves had little trouble finding them. When Frederick Douglass began teaching Sunday school under an oak tree, he found it was "surprising with what ease" his students got spelling books.[18] Spelling books were the featured texts in Sunday school classes for free and enslaved students, and occasionally they became the basis of the odd sermon.[19] Although they ran to almost two hundred pages, spellers were so cheap that they seemed more like pamphlets than books. Sought after by those who did not have them and scorned by those who were obliged to study them, the surviving copies are nearly always scuffed, faded, stained, scribbled in, and torn. Many, including entire editions, have disappeared completely.

By the 1840s most schoolbooks were produced by large publishing firms in eastern cities, although scattered copies continued to be made in rural printing offices. These often bore the name of the state where they were produced. Imprint lists from early Tennessee show three schoolbooks printed in that state before 1830, including Thomas Eastin's *Tennessee Spelling Book* (1810). In Lexington, Kentucky, Samuel Wilson printed the *Kentucky English Grammar* in 1812. Printing offices produced English grammars in the early decades of the nineteenth century in Montgomery, Alabama; Louisville and Frankfort, Kentucky; Richmond, Virginia; Raleigh, North Carolina; Baltimore, Maryland; Macon, Georgia; and Chattanooga, Tennessee. Imprint lists, however, were compiled in major libraries that never seriously collected these volumes and are likely incomplete. When these are compared to copyright lists, bibliographies, and catalogued copies, it is clear that many schoolbooks have escaped notice. The *Kentucky Copyright Ledger* for 1800–1854, for example, lists schoolbooks of all kinds produced in that state, of which only a few appear to be extant. Not all copyrighted books were printed, but the disparities seem to be too great for this to explain.[20]

Those who could not borrow schoolbooks could buy them cheaply at mercantiles or printing offices; even the most modest stores offered the odd speller, grammar, or reader. Preachers and colporteurs sold schoolbooks and academy principals ordered quantities to sell to their students and others in the neighborhood. As many learned basic literacy skills into their teens and beyond, readers of all ages sought these books. Booksellers liberally advertised in small newspapers and almanacs, where they usually described their stock as "a fine selection of [undifferentiated] schoolbooks." Regardless of title or author, their sales were assured.[21]

A nationwide count of establishments that sold books by publisher O. A. Roorbach in 1859, one of the few such lists compiled in the period, listed 555 merchants in the slave states in more than 200 towns and cities that sold books. Of these, only 204 shops in eighty-four towns and cities sold books exclusively, the rest were general stores. Bookstores were virtually unknown in rural places.[22] Prices of these works varied, but they were always low. In the 1850s, spellers could be had for ten cents in Grayson County, Virginia, twice the price of an ordinary nickel almanac; prices remained steady from earlier decades.[23] Stores in the Blue Ridge and across the southern states also handled accounts for slaves and the odd storekeeper may have sold schoolbooks to them.[24] Merchants purchased books at a discount from booksellers in Lynchburg, Raleigh, or Richmond, who in turn ordered them from booksellers in Philadelphia or New York. In 1838 Turner & Hughes, proprietors of the North Carolina Bookstore in Raleigh, advertised a stock of more than five thousand schoolbooks in the *Raleigh Register,* claiming that number represented only a part of the store's inventory. The firm probably had patrons who purchased at wholesale and retail prices across the state.[25]

Advertisements listing schoolbooks appeared in nearly every newspaper issue, regardless of how small the community was. The Cooleys, who regularly read a variety of papers, saw ads from booksellers and publishers in eastern cities and those closer to home like Raleigh and Lynchburg. The dearth of printers in their own and neighboring counties meant that most of these papers came from cities that were scores, if not hundreds, of miles away. Few readers could afford to be choosy about which edition of schoolbooks they used, but merchants probably tried to accommodate them. Webster and other schoolbook authors seemed to be obsessed with creating new systems that might catch the eye of potential buyers, but they misread their customers, as tastes nearly always ran toward proven authors.

In the early 1840s, books arrived in the Blue Ridge by horseback or wagon. Although there had been plans for a railroad to the region from the 1830s, the Lynchburg and Tennessee Railroad was not incorporated until 1848, and the line from Lynchburg to Bristol, which passed through Wythe County about thirty-five miles northwest of the Cooley farm, was not completed until 1856. Before 1845 the nearest transport to Grayson was via the James River and Kanawha Canal from Richmond to Lynchburg, from where books would be sent on to Roanoke and then complete the journey on the Wilderness Road. Completion of the canal to Lynchburg in 1840 made that town the "focal point of Southwest Virginia's trade."[26] In this way, readers and merchants in Grayson, Carroll, and other counties in the area obtained books from Lynchburg, Richmond, Raleigh, or points further east.

The Diffusion of Knowledge

Print was a tool of empires in the nineteenth century, and like them, its logic bent in a single direction, from capital to periphery. The printed page decreed entire societies and regions primitive and in need of reform. It colonized the provinces several times over, declaring them uncivilized, pastoral, and unspoiled in turn. Rural people collaborated in this subjugation, welcoming the imperial forces of education and literacy as genuine allies. The print that arrived in saddle and mail bags came not as a missive from an alien world as much as something exciting and useful. Most people did not expect to find themselves in their books; they understood that to be educated was to learn about more cosmopolitan places.

Armstrong "Strong" Thomasson (1829–1862), a farmer and sometime teacher who lived in northern Iredell County, just south of the Speer farm, was an avid reader. Born in a nearby county, he never left western North Carolina. A devout Methodist, he disapproved of slavery. By the time he married, he owned a farm of seventy-one acres. He read a wide variety of poetry, histories, religious works, and biographies, and was known to read while driving his wagon. His great obsession, however, was periodicals, including magazines and newspapers from North Carolina and other parts of the country. He read no fewer than twenty periodicals during the late 1850s, and fancied that he might become an editor of a magazine himself one day. He subscribed to the *North Carolina Planter, Spirit of the Age, Old Rip's Pop Gun,* the *Georgia Blister & Critic, Youth's Cabinet,* and *American Eagle,* among others. Book peddlers and agents of benevolent societies regularly stayed with him, often finding the stop worth their time, as Thomasson frequently bought their wares. While engaged to be married, he ordered a copy of the *Young Bride's Book* from New York to present to his wife on their wedding day.[27] He had regular custom with New York publishers, including George Cooledge. He read widely in Shakespeare and Milton, anatomy, geology, and a history of the Reformation, and regularly commented on the quality of his reading materials. "I like it tolerably well and regret that it is not better bound," he wrote of Sears' *Pictorial History of the U.S.,* for which he paid $2.50. "Book binders, like some of the other trades, greatly slight their work at times."[28]

Broad reading like Thomasson's was not a new impulse. Readers in neighborhoods bereft of print's institutional allies such as libraries, printers, bookshops, and publishers had long found a cosmopolitan perspective in their reading. Those in Thomasson's generation continued the patterns of what has been called the "village enlightenment" that flourished in British North America. In the nineteenth century, New England women used their reading to envision their villages as timeless and idyllic places, while in the upper Connecticut River valley, readers devoured books, magazines, and newspapers. By comparison, little is known about rural readers in the southern states.

There is no doubt that town and city residents had more reading matter from which to choose, but the geography of print's production did not correlate precisely to consumption. Those living far from the rapidly concentrating publishing industry in northeastern cities were hardly beyond the reach of print. Nor were illiterate people, who heard texts recited and talked about every day. By mid-century, print propagated its customs and expectations everywhere.[29]

Print carried an authority that outweighed its fragile form. In rural places, most of it was literally ephemeral, lasting in some cases for a single day, like mayflies or fevers. Even in its brief life it offered notions that lodged in people's heads and were intriguing enough to repeat in the churchyard or report in a letter or journal. Much of what drew notice — scientific discoveries, election results, battles, bizarre crimes, tragic deaths, or world events — was actually news. The pages of newspapers and magazines heralded human progress that left readers marveling at the pace of change. Just as often, however, print rehearsed what had long been known for a new group of readers. Local printers could only afford to invest in the surest of the steady sellers, which were often two centuries old. Newspaper editors desperate to fill columns seized on long-winded accounts of the English Civil War or a few lines from Edward Young or John Milton. Each generation had to learn again the story of the Battle of Hastings, the Ninety-Five Theses, or the Wife of Bath. In this way, print spoke of old things to new readers. They learned stories and poetry by seventeenth-century Puritans and memorized letters written by first-century Christians. The rules in their English grammars were modeled on those applied to Latin in the ancient world; those in their rhetorics were decreed by eighteenth-century Scottish philosophers who drew on classical conventions of language. Pamphlets and broadsides repeated stories and songs that were centuries old.

This is what people meant when they marveled at the "diffusion of knowledge" in the early nineteenth century. They were not thinking about college lecture halls or laboratories as much as what had just arrived at the post office. Newspapers and magazines coupled two-hundred-year-old events with what happened yesterday. This is how culture worked. Arbitrary knowledge of the past and present gleaned in their reading mixed with remembered and imagined experience to shape what people thought about, talked about, and the language they used. In earlier generations, most of this knowledge had been transmitted orally. In the age of the steam press, even the most modest productions became vessels of language and cultural memory.

Print did not destroy tradition in the rural places it came to. On the contrary, it offered readers perspectives, ideas, and language that built on tradition. It reflected its readers' ambivalence toward progress and uncertainty about the future. Its pages evoked past heroes or older ways even as it dismissed them as antiquated, sometimes in the same sentence. Change was not especially welcome in the nineteenth century; people did not resist it as much as embrace it warily. It often portended financial misfortune, illness, or death. Print could persuade readers of the thrilling power and attractions of novelty; a new word like "telegraph" seemed to change everything at once. Yet the steam-driven presses that grabbed damp sheets of paper with iron fingers and churned out twelve thousand impressions an hour still reproduced texts that were centuries, or even millennia, old. Like Gutenberg's press, the steam presses made old ideas accessible to large numbers of people, who were eager to weave what they learned from books into what they already knew.[30]

Counting Readers

For most of the nineteenth century, the meanings of the terms "literate" and "illiterate" were far from settled. Reading and writing continued to be taught as separate skills in many communities, and neither dictionaries nor census queries indicated clearly whether both skills were necessary for one to be considered "literate," or just the ability to read. In light of this inconsistency, the words were used differently in different places.

Federal census queries show dramatic changes in how government officials defined illiteracy between 1840 and 1870. Illiterate adults were counted for the first time only in 1840, in itself a sign that the meaning of reading was changing. That year, census marshals asked the heads of households how many white people aged twenty or above could not read and write, a question that reflected two assumptions: that most people continued learning basic literacy skills into their teens and beyond, and that all African Americans were probably illiterate. But the meaning of the conjunction "and," which some historians have mistakenly reported as "or," was not clear.[31] Were people who could read but not write literate or illiterate? In 1850, marshals asked individuals, including free black people for the first time, whether they could read and write. These queries remained the same in 1860.

They changed dramatically in 1870, however. First, marshals were told to ask individuals whether they could read and whether they could write, recording responses in two separate columns headed "cannot read" and "cannot write." "It will not do to assume that, because a person can read, he can therefore write," marshals were told. "Very many persons who claim to be able to read, though they really do so in the most defective manner, will frankly admit that they can not write." This suggested that people who could not write were illiterate, even if they could read, a change from earlier usage.[32]

Second, marshals were instructed for the first time to count all of those above the age of ten who could not read and write, a marked change from the earlier practice of counting those aged twenty or above. This change reflected a striking new norm: at a time when state-sponsored primary schooling was spreading, federal officials assumed that people learned how to read as children. Historians have puzzled over why literacy rates fell in 1870 (nationally the rate of illiteracy rose from 7 to 9 percent between 1860 and 1870), alternately blaming the effects of the Civil War or the counting of freedmen and women (with their generally high rates of illiteracy as a legacy of enslavement) for the first time. In fact, it is likely that the decision to significantly lower the age in the query accounted for much of this change. The influence of public primary schooling can also be seen in the instructions to marshals to exclude Sunday schools and night schools from the definition of "schools" for the first time; only those enrolled in state-sponsored or private day schools were to be counted as students. This count thus poorly reflected practices in rural neighborhoods where informal education was still practiced, dismissing those who continued learning to read and write as adults as "illiterate."[33]

The shifting meanings of literacy are also apparent in county-level census data. Most histories cite rates of illiteracy for the state level, and these seem straightforward. At the county level, however, the numbers fluctuate wildly over time. For example, in the 1840 census, Grayson County,

Virginia, listed 93 percent of its white adult population as literate. Ten years later, Carroll County, created out of Grayson in 1842, counted only 59 percent of white adults as literate, a decline of more than 30 percent.[34] It is mathematically impossible for this change to be accounted for by demographics in the county. Part of the disparity may have come from blundering census marshals or careless copyists, but if so, such mistakes affected the numbers for counties across the country. Several scholars have speculated to me that people across the southern states probably lied to census marshals, claiming to be able to read when they could not. If a regional penchant for lying could be demonstrated among people who have been dead for generations, this might be a credible point.

Instead of catastrophic demographic change or an epidemic of mendaciousness, these variations at the county level suggest at least two things. Scholars have long known that there are many errors in the census, and these likely are the reason for some of the erratic numbers. More strikingly, they suggest a lack of consensus about how to define illiteracy. The meanings of "illiterate" and "literate" were created in particular historical contexts and these changed over time. Reading and writing had been learned as separate skills—first reading and then writing—from ancient times. It was only with nineteenth-century pedagogical reforms that the two began to be taught concurrently, as composition became valued as a part of primary education for the first time. E. Jennifer Monaghan's definitive history of reading and writing in early America has explained why learning these two skills separately mattered.[35] Men were far more likely to benefit from writing instruction than women or free people of color into the nineteenth century, leaving a higher rate of illiteracy among the latter as the two skills merged.

Throughout a period marked by growing numbers of readers, expansion of state education, and dramatic pedagogical reform, the standard by which a person was judged to be literate was in flux. This shift will be examined more closely in part 1. Was someone who knew how to read but not to write an illiterate? Neither the instructions to census marshals, social practice, nor histories of the period offer a clear answer for a period in which the meaning of reading was changing. Yet it is clear that by 1870, "illiterate" was beginning to refer to one who could neither read nor write. The meaning of illiteracy finally appeared to be settled only about 1880, when the term "literacy" was coined in an American magazine. In sum, the generation in which Jincy, Amanda and Betsy Cooley, and Jennie and Ann Speer learned to read and write witnessed significant changes in the understanding of what these skills meant.[36]

Learning to Read and Write in the Blue Ridge

The writings of four young women — two sets of sisters born in the 1820s and 1830s in the Blue Ridge of Virginia and North Carolina — form the bibliographical spine of this study. Their journals and commonplace books offer a rare and beautifully detailed record of the print that made its way into the Blue Ridge before the Civil War.

Like Appalachia and the greater South, the Blue Ridge region has been perceived to have a strange relationship with modernity. Accounts of the region estimate that time was somehow warped there, yet its story mirrors that of much of the United States. As the ancestral home of the Cherokees, the Blue Ridge became a backcountry upon early European coastal settlement. It gained a reputation as remote even as it lay at the busy crossroads of early migration routes that transformed it from backcountry to frontier and then to backcountry again as settlers pushed further west. Men with money eventually turned up to exploit the mountains' potential as a stage for industry. Missionaries followed, determined to redeem people who were already deeply Christian from the backwardness that the capitalists could not cure. By the twentieth century, folklorists had arrived to safeguard what they regarded as traditional culture, which was in danger of destruction by modernization. Government agencies declared a war on the region's poverty in the mid-twentieth century, although they could not decide whether its backwardness or its exploitation by modern industry was to blame. Finally, environmentalists tried to repair the damage imposed by progressives of all kinds whose schemes had failed not just the people but the land as well.[37]

Print was present in the Blue Ridge all along. Its existence predated all but the Cherokees, who soon learned how to read once it arrived. Reading fanned the ambitions of people in the mountains, fostering their creativity in ways that we have yet to account for. They began to write and speak in light of what they learned in their spellers and grammars. They sang songs, many of their own making, with texts or tunes learned off pages printed in New York; Lexington, Kentucky; or London. They listened to humorous stories by writers from Maine and Alabama and repeated them to neighbors. They stitched bonnets inspired by the latest European styles they had seen in their magazines. When Phoebe Palmer's holiness doctrines colonized the hearts of Blue Ridge women, they altered their prayers and rituals to conform with them. In all these ways, those who could read and those who could not used print to create ordinary culture. These developments will be discussed at length in part 2.[38]

The journals at the heart of this study were written by young women in two artisan families who lived in neighboring counties that straddled the state line along the eastern boundary of the Blue Ridge. The steep escarpment of the mountains fell away more than twelve hundred feet from the Cooley farm on the New River plateau of Virginia to the Speer farm in the Yadkin River valley of North Carolina. Travelers making their way along the road through Surry County northwest into the mountains and over the state line to Grayson County passed the ancient knob called Pilot Mountain, which soared more than 2,400 feet. (Jennie Speer climbed Pilot Mountain in 1854.) The counties had been linked via Indian trading paths from time beyond memory. European settlers first trekked northward onto the New River plateau in the late eighteenth century.

Neither Grayson County in Virginia nor Surry County in North Carolina had a printing office in 1840 or even in 1850.[39] The nearest printer to the Cooley farm was about thirty-five miles north in Wytheville. The nearest printer to the Speer farm was about thirty miles east near Salem. Even in the early 1850s, neither county published a newspaper. By 1859 there were printing offices within reach but still no bookstores. Neither family, then, had easy access to local print. Their news—at least the printed kind—came from other places.

In late winter of 1842, twenty-two-year-old Amanda Cooley and her younger sister Betsy sewed together some pages and bound them in a cover

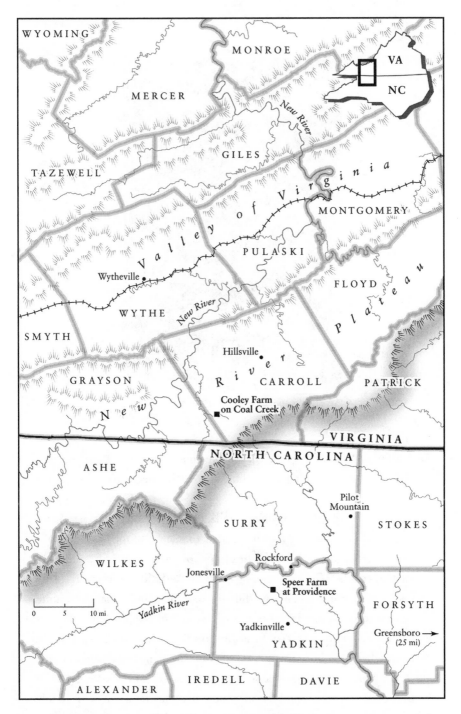

Yadkin River valley and New River plateau, c. 1855. Map by Erin Greb.

Amanda Jane Cooley, c. 1851. Courtesy of
Ellen S. Carpenter.

made of their own homespun. They wrote almost weekly in these journals
until their deaths; Betsy's grieving husband carried hers back to the family
on Coal Creek after she died from a fever in western Missouri. The journals recorded yards of cloth woven, hanks of thread spun, candles dipped,
coats cut and stitched, along with allusions to matters of the heart, news of
the neighborhood, poetry, and a brief note of what the women and their
households read. "Mother is reading the Bible and Elizabeth is reading the
western songster and Julian is reading the testament and father is listening
to mother read," Amanda wrote in the summer of 1843.[40] A few months
earlier and about fifty miles south as the crow flies, thirteen-year-old Jennie
Speer stitched together some pages, took up her pen, and described how
she had attended a camp meeting the previous fall. At Hickory Grove in
Surry County on the second day of September, "my father with his family
tented," she wrote soberly. "And from that time I have dated the greatest

Nancy Jane "Jennie" Speer, c. 1850. Courtesy of Allen and
Janet Speer.

event that ever occurred in my life, for at that Camp Meeting the Lord convicted & converted my soul."[41]

Jane (mother of Amanda and Betsy) and Elizabeth (mother of Jennie
and Ann) could both read. We know Elizabeth could write, although it is
not clear that Jane could.[42] Jane Dickey Cooley (1788–1869) grew up in
Grayson County, where her parents were prominent in the county's early
history. Married at age seventeen, she bore seven sons and four daughters
over the next twenty-six years. She buried two children on the hill above the
farm, and in 1841, she began to care for her four-year-old grandson Stephen
Isaac "Ika" Smith (1837–1858) after the death of her daughter Mary, who
was also buried on the hill. Elizabeth Ashby Speer (1804–1890) married at
age twenty and bore seven children, five of whom she buried.

Both Jane's husband, Benjamin Franklin Cooley (1774–1847), and

Jane Dickey Cooley, c. 1862. Courtesy of
Ellen S. Carpenter.

Elizabeth's husband, Aquilla Speer (1804–1888), were artisans. Cooley was
a cabinetmaker, farmer, and self-taught silversmith, clockmaker, and occasional slaveholder who moved to Grayson County when he was twelve years
old. Of Quaker heritage, he served two terms in the Virginia legislature
in the 1810s and later served as sheriff, justice of the peace, and member
of the county court. Speer learned the trade of tanning from his father.
He was also a farmer, a justice of the peace, a devout Methodist, a sabba-
tarian, and an ardent temperance man. An antislavery Whig who admired
Horace Greeley, he saw one of his sons die for a Confederate cause he
opposed. Neither of his daughters lived to see their brother buried. The
young women at the heart of this book were all dead by 1858, three of them
wasted by consumption, the most common killer of their day. Betsy Cooley
was the first to die, killed by typhoid fever at age twenty-two in 1848. Ann,

Julia Ann Cooley, c. 1851. Courtesy of Ellen S.
Carpenter. Julia began keeping a journal about
1846; it is now lost.

or Annis, Speer was the last when she died of consumption at age twenty-
three in 1858.

   These women left behind a remarkable record of the kinds of print
that made its way into the Blue Ridge in the 1840s and 1850s. Their diaries
show that two households of similar status, living just fifty miles apart, had
strikingly different tastes in reading, testimony to the variety of print that
was available to them. The Cooleys preferred novels, humor, songbooks,
magazines, newspapers, schoolbooks, histories, and, of course, the Bible.
They read novels by the British writers Edward Bulwer-Lytton and Frederick Marryat, and the popular American T. S. Arthur. They favored humor
by the Maine writer Seba Smith, who created the well-known character Jack
Downing. They read the famous humorous magazine *Brother Jonathan,*
and newspapers from New York, Philadelphia, Greensboro, Wytheville,
and western Missouri. They knew J. G. Pike's *Persuasives to Early Piety,* the
Free Mason's Monitor, and the *Moral Instructor.* They memorized Samuel

Annis Melissa "Ann" Speer, c. 1850. Courtesy
of Allen and Janet Speer.

Kirkham's and Lindley Murray's grammar books and read widely in a dictionary and the *Parlour Letter Writer.* They studied Joseph Ray's *Arithmetic,* a book on hydrostatics, and John Bigland's *Natural History of Animals.* They read about the lives of Generals Andrew Jackson and Francis
Marion, and *Miss Leslie's Magazine.* They sang from the *Western Songster.*
They read John Wesley's sermons and a pamphlet on Universalism. They
read the *Saturday Evening Post* and subscribed to *Godey's Lady's Book* and
Graham's Magazine. The household occasionally included enslaved men
and women, at least one of whom sat with the family as she learned from a
blue-back speller, so named because spelling books were generally bound in
blue paper boards. Called Jincy, she featured in both Amanda's and Betsy's
diaries, although neither noted that she ever advanced beyond spelling.

 Jennie and Ann Speer's taste ran to biography, poetry, prescriptive
literature, religious works, and history. Their white farmhouse—which sat
some distance away from the family's tanyards at the creek—was full of carefully chosen books. These included poetry by the English writers William

Cowper, Edward Young, Caroline Norton, Felicia Hemans, and Lord Byron, and the Americans William Cullen Bryant and Nathaniel Parker Willis. They knew the Bible, Homer, Milton, and John Bunyan. They read Jonathan Edwards's *History of Redemption*, histories of the Middle Ages, the Reformation, Ferdinand and Isabella, and Madame Roland. Jennie read the *Eclectic Magazine of Foreign Literature, Science, and Art*, Eliakim Littell's *Living Age*, the New York *Christian Advocate* and early issues of the *New York Times*. She read the *Young Lady's Mentor*, Samuel Mason's *Spiritual Treasury*, Mrs. Phelps's *Fireside Friend*, and the musings of the Virginia Presbyterian and colonizationist Joshua N. Danforth. She studied Hugh Blair's *Lectures on Rhetoric and Belles Lettres* and Joseph Butler's *Analogy of Religion* several times over. She knew the biographies of the missionaries Harriet Newell and Elizabeth Boles, the journalist Horace Greeley, and Margaret Fuller Ossoli.

By any calculation, all these women—Jincy, Amanda, Betsy, Jennie, and Ann—were literate. Yet this says little about them. They had different habits of thought, vocabularies, reading skills, and motives for their reading. These differences were rooted just as much in the different contexts of their lives as in the level of learning they had attained. The basic texts of English literacy—the drab succession of speller, grammar, and rhetoric book that initiated all formal learning in their generation—replaced the "ordinary road" of hornbook, primer, Psalter, testament, and Bible of earlier centuries.[43] Few people in the early United States ever mastered, or even read, all three of these books, but nearly everyone knew at least one. Slaves and the scions of Boston Brahmins recited the blue-back speller, daughters of weavers and bankers memorized English grammar, children of farmers and senators learned the elements of taste in their rhetorics. In the long years before graded primary schooling became the norm, and when only a tiny number of people could attend secondary schools, books were the most important teachers for all students, whether schooled or not.

These scuffed, unremarkable volumes laid out the progression of an "English" education. Each shaped the ways that students used language and their habits of thought. Self-taught readers like Jincy usually stopped with the speller; they memorized the alphabet before stumbling through

columns of haphazard syllables. Those who progressed to the end of the
two-syllable words—known as "spelling to ba-ker"—were understood to
have achieved something important. Many never even finished the book
and most did not learn to write fluidly, if at all. Those few readers with the
means to attend secondary schools (usually known as academies or semi-
naries) worked through spelling and on to grammar. The Cooleys never advanced beyond their grammar books, while the Speers studied rhetoric and
composition, a privilege offered only to a few women of their generation.

A close reading of the Cooley and Speer women's writing suggests
some of the differences between those who learned grammar and those who
were apprenticed to the art of rhetoric. The Speers learned to appreciate the
sublime from the eighteenth-century Scot Hugh Blair. They were partial to
abstractions, recording their observations about the sky, the beauty of the
seasons, and the meaning of a virtuous life. The Cooleys, meanwhile, taught
themselves how to write in the pages of their journals with the aid of their
grammar books. In contrast to the Speers, their writing was strikingly concrete, focused on counting out the yards of cloth they had woven, visitors
to the cabin, and the likelihood of marriage to men in the neighborhood.
They also had the delightful and unusual habit of recording what was happening while they were writing.

The Cooley sisters were weavers and tailors, but that hardly touches
on the skills they used to support their household. They raised sheep,
farmed, and sold cloth and coats to neighbors and local merchants. They
worked alongside Jincy and other hired workers and slaves. Jincy may have
been born on the farm or in the neighborhood about 1831; her grandmother
still lived nearby in 1848. It is unlikely that she learned to write even though
she studied spelling. She married Joshua, a slave from the neighborhood,
in December 1847, when she was about sixteen. Amanda and Betsy found
many occasions to remark on Jincy's work, her movements, her socializing,
her punishments and whippings, and especially what they considered her
saucy attitude. They also wrote about her to their Missouri kinfolk, report-
ing on her wedding and the welfare of her friends in their neighborhood.

The Cooleys complained routinely to their journals (and probably
to each other) that they never accomplished anything, but the suggestion

is absurd. They worked long days to keep the large household healthy, fed, and clothed. The household's livelihood depended on skills handed down for generations and learned by patient practice. Occasionally, there was an opportunity to learn something new. "Last Wednesday Robert I. Bell came here and learned Amanda & myself to mark out coats," Betsy Cooley wrote in the summer of 1844. "I glory in the system he practices."[44] Jane Cooley, her daughters, Jincy, and the occasional hired hand spun wool and flax, wove yards of cloth, dipped candles, sheared sheep, kept bees, cooked, gardened, washed, cleaned, knitted, quilted, and embroidered. The women sent their cloth to be fulled and dyed before stitching it into dresses, bonnets, and coats. They also used store-bought cloth to make clothing for the family and to sell to neighbors. They sold their linsey and blankets to the mercantile in Hillsville or at the lead mines across the county. A days' work at the loom meant throwing the shuttle thousands of times to make about three yards of closely woven woolen or linsey-woolsey cloth. A day of spinning twisted a pound of wool into thread. "For sometime I have not wrote any," Betsy admitted one afternoon. "I have been very busy spinning and weaving. All the wool is spun up. Of course I read of Sundays. I have read Marriatts novel and most through Bullwers."[45] Like the Cooleys, Jincy knew how to spin and weave. She sewed her own dresses from homemade and store-bought cloth. Most of her days were spent in the kitchen or in the fields, where she tended livestock, sheared sheep, cleared wheat stubble, and planted in the meadows, threshed wheat, hauled wood, washed, built cow pens, and cleaned out fencerows.

Time for pleasurable reading was hard to come by in a household preoccupied with work. As the women worked, they were surrounded by evidence of reading and writing—slates and slate pencils, foolscap, steel pens, handmade journals and commonplace books, newspapers and magazines, almanacs, songbooks, and bottles of homemade ink. These, too, were tools that helped the family earn its living. Ben Cooley's offices in the county and state required written notices of meetings, correspondence, and writing and signing legal documents. Amanda and Betsy copied out documents for their father, perhaps because his eyesight was failing or they had a finer hand. There were receipts for items purchased at local stores and for newspaper subscriptions, ledger books that recorded sales of the family's crafts to neighbors—furniture, cloth, and coats—and deeds and promissory notes. Their frequent letters regarding business and family matters contributed to the huge expansion of the postal system in the 1840s and 1850s.[46] The Cooley daughters both taught school and their fees supported the family, although there is some suggestion that they also kept their own separate accounts. Amanda taught at least twelve brief school sessions over twelve years at various locations in Carroll and Grayson Counties. Betsy taught in Virginia and later in Missouri, where she moved with her school-teacher husband. They kept careful records of students and fees paid in their commonplace books and spent their Sundays studying grammar and mathematics to stay ahead of their best students.

At home and in school, the Cooley sisters read aloud. In their generation, "to read" most often meant "talking from a book," as it had since ancient times."[47] Even as the Romantic ideal of the silent and solitary reader lost in a book came into view, the Cooleys continued to practice social reading. For them, time to read for pleasure was determined by a rhythm of work and rest; they read aloud on Sunday afternoons as Protestants had for centuries, in the midst of family in a room full of noise and activity beneath their father's tall walnut clock. Their journals are filled with voices, work, and visitors whom they welcomed to their table. Piety did not seem to be their main motive for reading, although they read the Bible, religious works, and hymns. Instead, they seemed to read mainly to discover the world beyond Coal Creek, as Amanda put it. They did not expect their books to tell them how to live so much as to tell them about how other people lived. Their writing bears the influence of sentimental forms, but they seem relatively unmoved by their generation's association of reading with moral improvement and social reform.

Things were different in the Speer household, where Jennie and Ann used their books and journals to "improve the time." Jennie's diary documented neither the voices in the room nor the menial tasks of her days, but instead recorded her spiritual ambitions and aspirations. She was a firm antislavery Whig like her parents and sister; and like them, she was horrified that "a man, one that God created, endowed with rationality and possessing feelings" could be "chained like a brute."[48]

Aquilla and Elizabeth Speer saw to it that all their children were formed by Methodist schoolmasters at a small academy across the county. Their daughters went on to Greensboro Female College, Jennie as a teacher and Ann as a student. As a favored protégé of the college president, Jennie traveled north to attend Mount Holyoke Female Seminary in Massachusetts for a year in the early 1850s in order to report on the methods used in the famous school. She briefly was head of Rockford Female Seminary, six miles from her parents' farm, but was forced to resign as her consumption worsened. Her brother Aaron taught school and edited a newspaper in Tennessee before returning home to die of consumption less than a year before Jennie's death. Two of her uncles were pastors—one Christian, the other Baptist—and her neighborhood counted many Quakers, including at least one Speer cousin. While Jennie was in Greensboro, she attended Quaker meeting to hear a woman preach, and briefly wondered whether she should be a preacher herself. Quaker preaching was to her "a feast of fat things" and she praised them when she was sixteen years old as "the only people who acknowledge the rights of women."[49]

The habits of mind Jennie formed in her reading traveled well. When she arrived in western Massachusetts to begin a year of study at Mount Holyoke Female Seminary, the bitter winters stunned her and she longed for her mother's hot corn pone and chicken pie. Even so, she found the carefully regulated world of Mary Lyon's school reassuringly familiar. She seemed, in many respects, entirely at home there. She knew the assigned books, admired the manners, and emulated the earnest piety of her teachers. The place suited her so well that she told her mother, that when she married, her home would "be in some respects a northern home."[50] The seminary's bookshelves were lined with the same authors—Cowper, Pope, Bunyan, Edwards—that she pulled from her parents' shelves in North Carolina.

In sharp contrast to the Cooleys' journals, the Speers' writing was empty of other people and full of universal truths. Their thinking seemed to be unencumbered by the physical world; it flowed freely in the categories of providence, hope, love, and immortality. It is virtually impossible to learn what they did every day, even as the Cooleys offered quotidian detail. While the Cooleys seemed to live in the present, time was burdened with eternal consequences for both Jennie and Ann. Jennie looked up from her book out on "a world that presents such a vast field for usefulness," carefully balancing self-denial and humility with her conviction that she would accomplish something extraordinary. "From an early period of my childhood I have felt a strong desire to be employed in something that would be beneficial to mankind. That desire has increased with my years until it has become so strong as almost to render me uneasy," she wrote. "My prayer is that Heaven may direct me aright."[51] Jennie routinely begged her books to make her better. She spent her Sabbaths working to gain eternity, learning the life of women like Harriet Newell by heart. Newell was newly married when she died at nineteen as a missionary on a strange shore, perfectly composed and secure in her hope of heaven. Like nearly everything Jennie read, Newell's memoir laid out an unattainable standard of piety.

Ways with Words

To begin to trace what reading meant to people in the past, we need to know not only what they read, but also what they did with their reading. Although few people recorded what they read in detail, they wove what they learned from printed texts—the content, the vocabulary, and the turns of phrase—into their own experience and oral traditions to make something new. The linguist and anthropologist Edward Sapir called language "the most massive and inclusionary art we know, a mountainous and anonymous work of unconscious generations." By this reckoning, the same creative impulses apply to writing poetry, composing songs, and even to everyday speech. What reading meant, then, can be traced in how people used language and what they made with it, what one linguist has called "ways with words."[52]

Strong Thomasson, whose farm was just south of the Speers', read more than usual in early January 1856. Shortly after he wrote to New York for specimen copies of three new magazines on New Year's Day, about a foot of snow fell in his neighborhood. A week later, another storm brought even more snow, leaving it knee deep with a fat coating of ice. "I don't recollect its equal in the snow line," Thomasson wrote, "and am in my 27 year."

Finding that the snow kept the rabbits in their beds and made travel nearly impossible, Thomasson put aside his gun and took advantage of a fresh stack of firewood to read during the long cold nights. "I have, to night, been reading Byron and Moore, and see the effects above," he wrote, pointing out the fourteen lines he had inscribed. His poem was inspired by the Irish poet Thomas Moore and Lord Byron, and complained about "the fowls of the air," scolding them for laying waste to the wheat, oats, and rye stored in his barn. "How proud would be the farmer / If some kind friend, or charmer / Would teach those birds a lesson / And learn them how to reason / To reap, and sow, in season."[53]

Like Strong Thomasson, Amanda Cooley was inspired by her reading to compose original poems. The spring of 1843 was a long time coming in the Blue Ridge, and the snow lay in sad piles by the Cooley cabin until late March, leaving people short of food and patience. When spring finally arrived, it was a fine season, with a bumper crop of strawberries and bright Sunday afternoons for strolling by the New River "viewing much of the sublime beauties of nature." By early June, when Amanda celebrated her twenty-third birthday, the garden was full of columbine, mayflowers, and sweet William, and the moss roses were just about to bloom. In those weeks, Amanda tried repeatedly to write a poem. One Sunday evening, she succeeded in drawing and writing "some little verses," but she remained frustrated with her efforts. "In vain I strive my thoughts to bind in some poetic strain," she sighed. "The more I try the more my mind inclines to prose again." Finally, after a long week of picking wool, weaving thirteen yards of cloth that she felt was "very ugly indeed," and cutting a coat for her neighbor, she found inspiration on Sunday evening, and recorded a poem in her commonplace book. "While I write the sweetbriar is waving at the window in full bloom as if to win me from my sad meditating & while I see it my thoughts are something like this. How fair the sweetbriar grows / Beside the window here / I grieve to think how soon / These lovely flowers fade / And wither ere the noon / To sink in death's dark shade. Amanda."[54]

The impulse of farmers and weavers to write poems in common meter about "fowls of the air" and "death's dark shade" was something new in the nineteenth century. This creative expression set them apart from earlier generations. Strong Thomasson's mother Leah Hauser Thomasson was born in 1807 and Amanda's mother Jane Dickey Cooley was born in 1788. If either had been moved by the sight of a blossom outside of her window, she might have composed a few lines in her head and perhaps hummed them to a popular tune as she washed clothes or worked at a loom. But by the 1840s and 1850s, their children were inspired by their reading to compose their own poems and carefully record them. Strong and Amanda's generation did more than shoot rabbits, slaughter pigs, and make cloth and coats; they also employed paper and ink.

Texts circulated in rural neighborhoods both on paper and by word of mouth. Strong and Amanda penned couplets that built on the meter and metaphors familiar to them from the Bible, Shakespeare, eighteenth-century English hymns by Isaac Watts or William Cowper, and verses by the contemporary poets Lydia Sigourney and William Cullen Bryant. Readers were inspired both by countless anonymous poems or toasts printed in newspapers, magazines, or almanacs, and by the many attributed verses in magazines and books. These works, in turn, rested on compositions that were centuries old — often handed down by oral tradition — suggesting the complicated layering of texts and memory that created ordinary culture. Just a few days after he read Byron's poetry, Strong Thomasson copied passages from Satan's speech in Milton's *Paradise Lost* into his journal.[55]

Print was also crucial to the creation and transmission of sacred song in the southern states. I will address this further in chapter 4. Spirituals depended on images and stories slaves heard repeated from childhood in the early modern English of the King James Bible. They learned these by heart, ingeniously rendering them into an entirely new genre that combined European and African forms. Musicologists have shown how spirituals relied on printed hymnbooks for transmission, notably the one compiled by Richard Allen in Philadelphia in 1801. Shape-note singing, sometimes called "Sacred Harp" singing, relied on print in a different way. Widely recognized as a traditional southern form, the genre's very existence depended on print because it demanded that singers learn four-part harmony from books that featured printed shapes for each tone. Itinerant teachers roamed the countryside, conducting informal singing schools for several days at a time and earning money from tuition fees and sales of tunebooks. The most famous of these, the *Sacred Harp*—compiled by two Georgians who published their collection in Philadelphia in 1844—is still in print.

To ignore the print that circulated in the Blue Ridge and other rural places, then, is to misunderstand how nineteenth-century culture worked. And how it continues to work. Scholars have called readers' responses to the Internet "vernacular creativity," something most of us know as a commonsense part of our daily lives.[56] Stories, jokes, videos, memes, and news circulate through our screens, to be passed on, talked about, argued over, and used as the basis for more jokes, videos, and memes. Like printed media, digital media is an inherently social endeavor, offering readers connections to people beyond their own horizons, inspiring and exasperating in equal measure, and often sparking a creative response.

In the 1940s the folklorist Richard M. Dorson argued that "stories in the United States travel interchangeably through the spoken and the printed word."[57] He explained that print was more important to American folklorists than to their European peers. The peculiar circumstances of the birth of American culture—among a people with unusually high rates of literacy at a time of remarkable innovation in printing technologies—underscored the importance of printed texts. The spread of stories, songs, and poems flourished through both oral and printed transmission in the early United States. In many cases, these entered the oral tradition only after appearing in print. In this way, printed texts were important even for those who could not, or did not, read.

Jincy, Amanda, Betsy, Jennie, and Ann all made many things in their brief lives: school lessons, poems, and compositions, as well as cornbread, butter, soap, bonnets, quilts, and counterpanes. What they made with their reading offers only one angle of vision on their world, and it can be easy to overestimate the power of reading in lives that often found their significance beyond books. Lettered people are too quick to make reading the most important work of the world.[58] Yet these women exploited their reading for their own benefit and the benefit of others, enlarging both what they knew and how they voiced their thoughts and desires as they made things with paper and ink.

PART ONE

A Good English Education

While at school [in Norfolk, Virginia], Mary acquired a good
English education, and, in addition to this, a knowledge of
various kinds of needle-work, and also dress-making.

—Lewis C. Lockwood, *Mary S. Peake, the Colored Teacher at
Fortress Monroe*

He did not enjoy the benefits of classical learning, but possessed a good English
education, which he greatly improved by subsequent reading and study.

—James Barnett Taylor, *Virginia Baptist Ministers*

For centuries, a good English education was the only kind to which
most people could aspire. Classical learning—based on Greek and
Latin—was available only to the wealthiest of people, nearly all
of whom were men. Mastery of the classics was compulsory for any who
wished to be called learned; it was the key to all knowledge in the Western
tradition. People of more modest resources were left to study their Bibles
and testaments or the odd primer that might come their way. Schooling was
hard to come by and books were scarce.

This changed dramatically in the nineteenth century, as is evoked in
an essay by the Charleston classicist Basil Gildersleeve in 1854. In "The
Necessity of the Classics," he lamented the influence of Romantic lin-

guists who celebrated the vernacular tongues. No, he declared, the classics were "eternal norms."[1] Perhaps. Yet the city in which he wrote was already knee deep in schoolbooks—spellers, grammars, and rhetorics—that were teaching the formalities of the vernacular to the daughters of tanners, blacksmiths, and slaves. Gildersleeve's impulse to defend the classics only showed how much ground they had already lost.

In part 1, "A Good English Education," I examine the easy availability of cheap spellers, grammars, and rhetorics in the rural South. The spread of education is an abiding theme in the history of the nineteenth century, but it is not well understood what all this learning actually accomplished. In the main, it taught people a new way to use language, offering a formal idiom that informed their habits of thought, speech, and writing.

All people, regardless of their status or where they lived, learned formal English expression from the same succession of books: speller, grammar, and rhetoric. In the decades before graded public schools became the norm, only a few students were able to study all three subjects. Some stopped a few pages into their spelling book. Others went on to study English grammar, sometimes learning the subject in night classes because it was not taught in common schools. A few went on to study rhetoric and learn the art of composition, a new subject that was particularly important for women.

In chapter 1, I explore the importance of spelling and trace the production and distribution of Webster's spelling book in the southern states. Chapter 2 recovers the importance of English grammar to many self-taught readers, including African Americans, and chapter 3 describes the uses of rhetoric, a subject that was accessible only to the few who could afford to attend private academies and colleges, including increasing numbers of women. Students learned from each of these drab books habits of speaking, writing, and thinking that shaped not only their everyday conversation, but also their creative efforts like poems, songs, and stories.

Spellers

Father reading geography, Mother Bigland's History, Julian dictionary,
Amanda journalizing, Ika is gadding about the house, Jincy spelling.
— Betsy Cooley

IN WHAT HAD BECOME A RITUAL FOR MORE than a year,
eighteen-year-old Betsy and her older sister Amanda took up their journals
as their father's tall walnut clock kept time on a Sunday in 1843. Betsy often
paused before continuing to describe what was happening while she wrote.
On this particular Sabbath afternoon almost everyone in the household was
reading, including their young slave Jincy.[1]

Jincy was not yet thirteen years old. She may have been born on the
Cooleys' 117-acre farm. Her grandmother lived in the neighborhood and
her mother had probably been taken by other family members to Missouri
a few years earlier. Her master and mistress were aged sixty-nine and fifty-
five. Jincy worked with them and the four Cooley children who remained on
the farm—Amanda (b. 1820), James (b. 1822), Elizabeth (b. 1825), and Julia
Ann "Julian" (b. 1831). Her days centered on the Cooley's two-story log
house.[2] It had four rooms running east to west, with an ell on the north side
at the western end. There was a large porch with a small room on it along
the south side at the east end. Two staircases, one from each end room,
led to an upper story, also divided into rooms. The ell housed the large
kitchen with an immense fireplace. Between the house and the creek were
a flower and vegetable garden, a small summer house, two one-room log
outbuildings, and a large two-story barn. Jincy slept in one of the outbuild-

ings; the other was a shop where Ben and his sons made furniture, clocks, timepieces, and the occasional pair of shoes. An oft-told family story celebrated Ben's skill as a self-taught clockmaker; the Cooley men were known in the neighborhood for their joinery, blacksmithing, and silversmithing. Ben probably made the Stilliard scale that regularly measured the weight of every family member, including Jincy.

Jincy moved with the freedom that was generally granted to mountain slaves; the Cooleys often admitted they did not know where she was.[3] She performed a variety of tasks, ranging from running errands, working in the fields and with livestock, cooking, and washing to weaving, sewing, and quilting, sometimes for herself. When the family dog Growler died, she helped bury him. She made cloth for her dresses and, on at least one occasion, bought some cloth in town for a new dress along with what Betsy called "a heap of finery."[4]

Jincy's family had ties to Surry County, south over the North Carolina line. Regular travel between Surry and Grayson Counties began in the mid-eighteenth century with the first Moravian settlements at Wachovia, later called Salem.[5] Jincy accompanied the Cooleys when they traveled down the mountain to trade at the Surry Courthouse in the village of Rockford (originally White Rock Ford) on the Yadkin River, or farther east at Salem or Greensboro. She sometimes spent Christmas and other holidays in Surry County.[6] She also traveled with the family to trade at the county seats of Hillsville and Independence.

The farm was a lively place. Relations, friends, and visitors, enslaved and free, came and went almost daily. Neighbors stopped to inquire after a tailoring job or about a legal question, relatives and friends periodically returned from the western states to visit, preachers and peddlers appeared at the door needing dinner. Someone traveled to town almost every week to go to court, to trade, or to pick up the mail. Jincy carried notes and letters around the neighborhood, and was regularly sent to neighbors to work or to help care for the sick. In the spring of 1847, she nursed her pregnant friend Fanny, who gave birth later that summer to "a white boy."[7] She went to Sunday meeting almost every week, usually with the Cooleys but sometimes by herself. She also attended "singings," weddings, and burials with the Cooleys and other slaves, and entertained friends and kinfolk at the farm on Sunday afternoons. Some Sundays, Amanda reported, the family had "no white visitors." The Cooley farm was less than two miles from the Mt. Pleasant Monthly Meetinghouse, established in 1801, and the household attended meetings there and services presided over by Baptist and Methodist ministers.[8] In December 1847, when Jincy was about sixteen, she married Josh, a slave from a nearby farm. Unable to establish a household of their own, the young couple often spent weekends either at the Cooleys' or at his master's place. Five years later, perhaps with her husband in mind, Jincy balked when the family agreed to hire her out in the new year. "Jinsy has been mean and says she don't want to go to Mrs. Paul's and went off yesterday to hunt herself a home & came back today just before dinner and said Billy Hanks would hire her." The young woman prevailed, for within a few days, she was living at the Hanks's place.[9]

For at least some of her young life, Jincy was the only slave living on the Cooley farm. Southwestern Virginia never had many slaves, but their numbers increased more than three times faster than in the state as a whole during the 1850s. In Carroll County (created from eastern Grayson in 1842), the tiny slave population grew by 70 percent between 1850 and 1860, outpacing the more than 50 percent increase in white residents.[10]

Like most slaveholders in their neighborhood, the Cooleys did not earn a living from farming alone.[11] They also practiced cabinetry, weaving, and tailoring, raised and sold livestock, taught school, and held public office. Household income in the Blue Ridge was unstable in the best of times, dependant on fickle weather, bodily health, and market prices. This was one of the main reasons that the Blue Ridge filled up in Ben and Jane Cooley's generation only to begin emptying in the next. Jane watched many of her children and grandchildren leave to seek their fortunes in the West. After her oldest son died, her daughter-in-law took their children to settle in the Willamette valley in Oregon. Other Cooley children settled in western Missouri, near Independence, the destination of many settlers from the neighborhood. The migrants regularly posted letters and newspapers back home. Ties between the Blue Ridge and Missouri were close enough that when a new county seat was established in Grayson County, it was called

Independence, perhaps after the town where many of its native daughters and sons had gone.

As family moved west, the critical mass of bodies needed to support the large family, farm, and shop was depleted, leaving the household in some peril and making the work done by Jincy and other hired help more critical than ever. Ben Cooley died in 1847, leaving his twenty-five-year-old unmarried son James as head of a household that included his aged mother, two younger sisters, a nephew, and the young slave. Betsy had gone to western Missouri with her husband the previous year. The shrinking number of skilled hands meant the family was becoming too small to sustain itself. James compensated by buying a slave named Jerry at the Carroll courthouse for six hundred dollars.[12] He also paid fifty dollars for the labor of his neighbor's slave named George and began to trade horses and cattle on long trips out of state.[13] Amanda, meanwhile, left home more often to teach three-month school terms. The Cooley women continued to weave and sew, selling their cloth to local merchants and at the lead mines. They made clothing and tailored coats for their neighbors weekly. Two years after his father's death, James bought a daguerreotype camera from a traveling photographer in hopes of making some money.[14]

In the fall of 1850, James tried to take advantage of the region's mining boom by investigating the prospects of a copper mine "below Hillsville," where he thought he might invest and "make something," Amanda reported. No fewer than twenty-five mines opened in a five-county area straddling the Virginia–North Carolina border, including Carroll County, in 1853. Within six years, more than 2,700 tons of ore had been extracted.[15] It was shipped by wagon down into the Great Valley to the depots of the Virginia–Tennessee Railroad at Christiansburg and Wytheville. Before the line between Lynchburg and Bristol was completed in 1856, coal, copper, lead, iron, tobacco, and wheat had been shipped to eastern markets along the Great Valley Road to Roanoke, on to Lynchburg and then further east via the James River and Kanawha Canal. Wagons had traveled the Great Road laden with furniture, silver spoons, china plates, books, port wine, combs, and snuff boxes to stores in the southwestern part of the state since the eighteenth century. Most of these goods were bought up by the people in the valley, some of whom Amanda and Elizabeth considered to be rich. But the opening of new mines stimulated interest in building new roads into the mountains. It was even suggested that a railway should be constructed south from the trunk line in the valley into Carroll County.

In this chapter, I examine what reading meant to people like Jincy, whose education began and ended with a spelling book. First, I describe how white attitudes toward slave literacy changed by the early decades of the nineteenth century in the context of changing ideas about pedagogy, as well as the fears of slave revolts. Second, because most self-taught readers, enslaved or free, never progressed beyond their spelling books, I describe how they used those spellers. Finally, using the example of Webster's "blueback" speller, I investigate the hints offered in the archives as to how spellers were produced and distributed to readers in the southern states.

Spelling and Whipping

Jincy's reading merited the attention of the Cooley sisters only three times in more than twelve years of surviving diary entries. Just seven words tell that Jincy could read—"Jincy is spelling"; "Jincy spelling"; and two years later, "Jincy reading." Many more words describe the young slave's disobedience; the sisters regularly noted her "pouting" and "roguery." One April morning, there were more than complaints. "Yesterday morning James whipped Jinsy for stealing and this morning again for saucy talk," Amanda wrote.[16] It is not clear how severe the whipping was, but later that afternoon, Jincy was sent to clean out a fencerow with Ika, Amanda's nine-year-old nephew. The rare mention of the whipping in the journals may suggest that it was unusual. Even so, it was neither the first nor the last time Jincy was whipped.

The journals are silent on Jincy's motive for learning to read. Her immediate concern may have been to communicate with her mother, who had been taken to Independence, Missouri, with the family. As people scattered across the continent, cheaper postal rates encouraged a wave of letter writing by the 1840s.[17] Slaves wanted to write letters for the same reason free people did: to maintain contact with their far-flung family members.

After his enslaved mother and sisters were hired away, John M. Washington (1838–1918) of Fredericksburg, Virginia, asked two young white men to help him learn to spell, but they would not teach him to write. One day his uncle "noticed me trying to copy the writing Alphabet as shown in Cowley's Spelling Book." His uncle seized the pen from him and wrote out a passage in the manner taught in letter-writing manuals. "My Dear Mother, I Take this opportunity to write you a few lines to let you know that I am well," he wrote. " 'Now,' he said, 'when you can do that much you can write to your mother.' " Washington bought a twelve-cent copy book and began to copy out letters from his uncle's example.[18]

Alternatively, Jincy may have labored over her speller in the hope that reading could be, in the words of Frederick Douglass, her path to freedom. Yet her reading could not protect her from James Cooley's whippings. In this, her experience was more representative than that of Douglass. Jincy learned to read in an era marked by confusion among white people over whether slave reading was a threat or a boon. Stories tell time and again of slaves whose reading was alternately approved of by masters or considered grounds for punishment. Some white people scoffed at antiliteracy laws while other masters brutally punished slaves even in places where slave reading was not legally prohibited. A slave in Mason County, Kentucky, born in 1840, remembered another slave on his plantation whose sole task was to teach slaves to read, write, and figure. Yet if any slave was tardy when called by their master and used the lessons as an excuse, he whipped them. "He would near beat the daylights out of us—after getting somebody to teach us!" the man marveled.[19] Another master owned two preacher slaves. "Mitchell was a Hardshell Baptist and Andrew was a Missionary Baptist." A patroller found some letters addressed to the two and demanded whether the man knew that his slaves could read. He apparently approved enough of their "spunk" that his will provided each one a home.[20] Slaves were often taught to read for religious reasons, sometimes under fearful circumstances. "There was an old white man used to come out and teach Papa to read the Bible. Papa said, 'Ain't you 'fraid they'll kill you if they see you?' The old man said, 'No, they don't know what I'm doing, and don't you tell 'em. If you do, they will kill me.' "[21]

White people's confusion over slave literacy highlighted the contradictions inherent in a slaveholding republic. It also showed that the meaning of reading was changing in the final decades before emancipation. White attitudes toward slave reading changed markedly between the colonial and early national periods. Some slaves could read from the earliest days of the Atlantic trade, yet during the colonial period, slave reading was not deemed a threat to white power. No colony in British North America had prohibited slaves from learning to read and only two barred them from learning to write. In the notorious South Carolina Slave Code of 1740, slaves were barred from writing, and in 1770 Georgia began to fine those who taught slaves to write, "or to read writing," specifically not mentioning printed type. After 1830 it is well known that white people began to openly fear the prospect of literate slaves. Why did white people's attitudes toward slave reading change, especially given the constancy of their racist estimations of black people's intelligence?

In premodern society, learning to read was a conservative act. This was particularly true for people of modest status, for whom reading was envisioned by rulers as yet another means of social control. Any text they had ready access to demanded submission to both divine and earthly rulers and underwrote social hierarchy. It was believed that ordinary readers could only passively imbibe a few (primarily sacred) texts, and perhaps learn to write their names. Such people were assumed to be unable to comprehend abstract thought; complexity of any kind was considered to be beyond their ability.[22] In this context, to learn meant to reproduce the wisdom of the ages, always in the vernacular rather than in the learned languages of Latin and Greek. Thus, even after people were educated in ways appropriate to their low status, they remained illiterate, meaning unlearned. Those who could not read Latin or Greek were never considered truly literate or learned. In fact, ordinary readers were not always bounded by such expectations, and reading has always been potentially subversive. Nevertheless, the norm that considered reading a passive act for ordinary people prevailed for centuries.[23]

These assumptions began to change in the eighteenth century. The critic Raymond Williams has called this the "third revolution," that is, a revolution in culture that accompanied those in politics and economics. Republican revolution, rising expectations among people who enjoyed a higher standard of living than their parents, the growth of a liberal market economy, the new interest in state-sponsored schooling, and education's role in citizenship, all contributed to this shift. Education in the early United States and Western Europe was no longer instinctive, safe, and reliably accomplished by the family and the church.[24]

In this new era, the thinking went, even ordinary people needed to learn to think in some abstract and complex ways. Pedagogical reform was demanded, and new ideas upended customs of teaching and learning that had been settled for millennia. There was much debate to determine the best methods. Above all, citizens needed to be able to appropriate and apply knowledge so that they could contribute to the good of the republic. In premodern eras, a common education at best taught people only to recite, copy, and do simple figures. Many students never learned to write at all. Writing instruction was offered only after students had learned to read, and importantly, instruction was gendered, as writing was considered to be a skill suited for the marketplace.[25] Composition was never taught in premodern common schools nor learned by the self-taught; students learned only to memorize their books and to copy passages from them. This kind of learning emphasized acquisition of skills even more than students' comprehension. The expectations for education were raised markedly in the nineteenth century, fostered by a new class of professional educators invested in public schooling. Primary students began to be expected not only to be able to read and write fluently, but also to compose original texts, a remarkable change that will be addressed in more detail in the next two chapters. Students also began to learn to read and write concurrently instead of sequentially. This shift took decades to accomplish, but gradually, the two skills were merged into a new concept known as "literacy."[26]

These new readers were surrounded by texts that proclaimed the virtues of republican citizenship. In the colonial period, popular texts were likely to urge obedience to the king, the church, parents, husbands, masters, and other social superiors. By the late eighteenth century, some popular texts advocated republican values, subverting deference and obedience.

Even the Bible was reinterpreted in light of republican ideals. Writing from early national Virginia, Reverend Devereux Jarratt marveled at the change from his childhood, when "we were accustomed to look upon, what were called gentle folks as beings of a superior order." He was bewildered at behavior in the present "high republican times" in which "there is more levelling than ought to be."²⁷ Jarratt did not say so, but the leveling he condemned was promoted in much of the print that circulated in the early republic.

One of the best-known examples of the difference this literature made is cited by Frederick Douglass. He famously attributed his political awakening to reading Caleb Bingham's *Columbian Orator,* a popular schoolbook first published in 1797. In it, he found speeches by the Irish and British leaders Daniel O'Connell, William Pitt, and Charles Fox which argued that slaves should be freed.²⁸ Douglass, of course, was an exceptional mind who experienced an exceptional freedom. Many slaves who read the *Columbian Orator* or similar texts never gained the freedom that Douglass attributed to his reading. As E. Jennifer Monaghan explained, it was writing, not reading, that offered slaves like Douglass the possibility of freedom, by giving them a voice.²⁹ Nevertheless, Douglass read abolitionist speeches in cheap and widely available schoolbooks, something slaves in earlier eras would never have been able to do.

Schoolbooks, however, also continued to proclaim older values. If Douglass found abolitionist speeches in his primer to be a revelation, little in Webster's speller or any other schoolbook suggested that learning would undermine the social order. The editor of a 1998 edition of the very book Douglass read was compelled to warn contemporary readers that most of the book was extremely moralistic and religious.³⁰ This was hardly an anomaly; schoolbooks remained authoritarian. The cover of Webster's spelling book touted his credentials as Noah Webster, LLD. The frontispiece of some editions featured a sandal-clad Minerva holding the hand of a child and pointing to a Pantheon-like building inscribed with the words "knowledge" and "fame." Although something grand was afoot in this modest book, readers were expected to understand that their learning would not disrupt the status quo.

Jincy's spelling book intervened, then, in her daily fare of scrubbing, thrashing, sweeping, and washing, but like her master and mistress, it demanded submission, deference, and obedience. Like the Bible and the preachers she heard, the speller taught that "God will destroy the wicked" and the "Bible is the Holy Book of God." The admonition to "be good and learn one's book"—a phrase taken from Webster—was repeated endlessly, and importantly, assumed that the book in question taught goodness. Elizabeth Keckley, whose parents were enslaved, found a message addressed to her in nearly every letter her father wrote to her mother. "Tell my darling little Lizzie," he wrote, "to be a good girl, and to learn her book." In this sense, it could be said that a literate slave simply submitted herself to a new master when she learned to read, the authoritative voice in her book. All students understood (and still do) that schoolbooks demand obedience.[31]

By the 1830s slaveholders were all too aware of how the meaning of reading and the content of popular texts had changed from the colonial period. Their dread of literate slaves was dramatically heightened after the murderous rebellion led by the strange literate prophet Nat Turner in 1831. By 1834 seven states had legally restricted the teaching of slaves and free blacks to read or write. Some of these laws were vague—Virginia, for example, banned only teaching groups of slaves, not the teaching of individuals—while in other places slave literacy was prohibited by custom, albeit often enforced with violence.[32]

Why, then, were literate slaves deemed a threat in 1840 but not in 1740? For a slave in 1740, to read was to hear again what was proclaimed from the pulpit and by the whip: the nonnegotiable submission to divine and earthly rulers. But as common education moved to appropriate republican ideals, and as the skills of reading and writing began to be taught simultaneously, literate slaves became a threat. By 1840 schoolbooks and other print gave enslaved readers access to the liberal ideals of the revolution, including individualism and human liberty.

This is why some slaveholders awkwardly attempted to teach slaves to read only the Bible, or alternatively to catechize them without teaching them to read at all.[33] Learning was being redefined from an act of reproduction to a process of creativity even for primary school students, a subject that will be more fully addressed in the next chapters.[34] As nineteenth-century readers began to be seen as active agents, the restrictions on slave learning were a quixotic attempt to keep slaves as passive learners who would merely memorize texts that underwrote slavery. At a time when free minds were expected to read critically and to compose their own thoughts, rote memory was deemed good enough for slaves.

All of this takes us back to Jincy, spelling on a Sunday afternoon in 1843. In households like the Cooleys', a literate slave was a boon. Slaves who could read, write, or figure were useful in a society in which printed texts were becoming commonplace; they also brought a higher price at auction. The Cooleys also tolerated Jincy's reading because they believed their mastery over her was guaranteed. In places where the institution of slavery was thought to be secure, such as early Baltimore, slaves and free blacks were customarily afforded some freedom in learning to read.[35]

In the end, the Cooleys saw no contradiction between their power to whip Jincy and her ability to read because they assumed that she was being educated for servitude alone. They, like many slaveholders, imagined that literacy would confirm rather than challenge slavery. In this, they understood "literate" in its ancient sense. The whole apparatus of learning bent away from human liberty not just for slaves in the early United States, but for most of human history. Texts and reading were a means of social control; they were proxies for kings, preachers, parents, and masters. These norms did not change suddenly, nor were new ideas about learning adopted everywhere at the same time, sweeping across the landscape like a weather front. Instead, it took time for the liberal ideology that proclaimed reading to be the handmaiden of human freedom to fully take hold.

The new ideology of reading, which imagined it would spark freedom, progress, or uplift, was intuited by slaves, even those for whom freedom remained out of reach. "Oh this book," a young slave woman cried to a European visitor, "I turn and turn over its leaves, and I wish I understood what is on them!" The ideology that proclaimed reading to be a tool of social progress and human liberty cruelly burdened those with little hope of either. "'Missus, what for me learn to read,'" another slave told Fanny Kemble, "with a look and a manner that went to her very heart, 'me have no prospect.'" Even Frederick Douglass despaired that his reading had "opened his eyes to the horrible pit, but to no ladder upon which to get out." He would learn that his ability to write, not only to read, would make his ladder.[36]

Autodidacts and Old-Field Schools

Whether they were tutored in a great house, or stole away with a speller to a hayloft, everyone in the early United States learned to read the same way: they memorized their spelling book. Of the three books that comprised a good English education, the speller offered competency only in the most rudimentary components of written language — syllables, words, and a few sentences and short paragraphs. Those who persisted toward the end of the book would find Bible verses and moral lessons, many of which were familiar, but which might be difficult to learn to recite off the page. Even illiterate people knew what it was "to spell." "When me and my brother was learning outen the blue-black speller," one slave remembered, his illiterate grandmother would say, "'How's that? Go over it.' Then we would laugh and answer, 'How you know? You can't read.' 'Just don't sound right,' she would say. 'The Lord tell me when it's right. You-all can't fool me, so don't try.'"[37]

When Jincy picked up her spelling book, she already spoke two dialects fluently, one with her masters and another with fellow slaves, a skill that linguists refer to as code-switching. This practice was widely shared and not just among slaves; its most famous practitioner was perhaps Abraham Lincoln, whose legendary eloquence was rooted in his ability to move fluidly between vernacular and formal speech.[38] Yet the mastery of language had heightened importance for slaves. They had to be especially careful with their speech around white people and they were skilled eavesdroppers. "I would catch words from the white people and retain them in memory until I could get to my dictionary," Lucius Holsey remembered.[39] Slaves were beaten for speaking in displeasing ways, such as calling a young black woman "Miss."[40] Linguistic custom was especially complicated in a slave society, for many house slaves were compelled to speak grammatical English to please their owners. "My association with white folks and my training while I was a slave is why I talk like white folks," Mary Anderson said.[41]

In nineteenth-century parlance, spelling and reading were two separate skills taught from two different books, the speller and the primer. Spellers taught by the "alphabet method," which dated from before the invention of printing and was rooted in classical practice. A seventeenth-century schoolbook author explained that a child was first taught his letters "backwards and forwards, until he can tell any of them, which is pointed at. . . . The greatest trouble at the first . . . is to teach them how to know their letters one from another, when they see them in a book together."[42] This method had hardly changed by the time Jincy picked up her speller three centuries later. School reformers had to learn repeatedly the hard lesson of how much people revered tradition in matters of learning; their reforms were routinely spurned. Their attempts to weaken the alphabet method's hold came to naught for self-taught readers and those in rural places, as it remained a popular method of reading instruction into the twentieth century.[43]

People harbored enormous affection for Webster's spelling book. Small and plainly made, it was the size of a modern-day paperback, bound in blue paper–covered boards (hence a "blue-back"). It could fit easily in the hand, a generous pocket, or a hat. Like other schoolbooks, spellers were routinely scribbled in or ripped apart. One young slave cut the board covers from the pages and stuffed it into his hat, as he had no pockets. There, "it was safe unless a rain came up then cap, book, and all suffered."[44] A fifteen-year-old slave folded a single page torn from a spelling book, "so that two or three of the lessons were on the outside as if printed on a card." This he put into his pocket, pulling it out while waiting in a carriage, walking, or hoeing, to "catch a word and commit it to memory." In the evening, by the light of a pine knot, he would review his lesson.[45]

For Jincy, as for many before her, to read was to read aloud. As she sat with the Cooleys, she called out letters and syllables from her book. Webster's definition of language—"the expression of ideas by articulate sounds"—was standard. Pronunciation, he said, was "the most important and difficult part of grammar."[46] In this, he followed the centuries-old convention of reading instruction that defined reading as speaking from a book.

THE

AMERICAN

SPELLING BOOK,

CONTAINING

THE RUDIMENTS

OF THE

ENGLISH LANGUAGE.

FOR

THE USE OF SCHOOLS

IN THE

UNITED STATES.

BY NOAH WEBSTER, ESQ.

THE REVISED IMPRESSION, WITH THE LATEST CORRECTIONS.

MIDDLETOWN, CONN.
PUBLISHED BY WILLIAM H. NILES.
STEREOTYPED BY A. CHANDLER.

1827.

Noah Webster, *American Spelling Book* (Middletown, CT, 1827). Courtesy of The Louis Round Wilson Special Collections Library, University of North Carolina at Chapel Hill.

The goal of the student was to pronounce uniformly and accurately off the page.[47] The importance of recitation made the disadvantages of self-study clear, as students needed someone to hear their lessons. In this context, Elizabeth Cooley's lament made sense. "I have not a teacher and how can I learn," she wrote.[48]

By the 1840s the speller was an iconic product of American printing. As E. Jennifer Monaghan explained, spellers were the first reading texts in the eighteenth and nineteenth centuries. Although the book's form originated in early modern England, spelling remains a peculiarly American preoccupation. The annual Scripps National Spelling Bee is rooted in the lively competitions that marked the end of rural school terms. In January 1846 Amanda Cooley had a full school of students who were preparing their speeches and dialogues. "The girls beat [the boys] and gained the cause," she wrote. The final examinations were lively community events, full of cheering students, parents, and neighbors who reveled in the public speaking and the perennial favorite—the spelling competition.[49] "At school we spelt aloud and read aloud; sometimes we could have been heard two hundred yards away, especially on Friday evenings when we had a spelling match, which was an evening of great excitement," John Carroll (b. 1841) recalled of his school in west Tennessee. When the spelling started, "everything went with a roar," another student remembered. "Just as loud as you pleased. You might spell baker or circumlocution or anything else and the people going along the road were happy to know that the children were getting their lessons." Betsy Cooley wrote on a March Saturday, which was "the last day of E. Davis's school. I have quit head. I have had a close race for it. I have been spelling for three days."[50]

Gideon Lincecum (1793–1874) recalled his early days at school in Georgia. "Whenever Mr. Gill would storm out 'Mind your books,' the scholars would strike up a loud, blatant confusion of tongues, which surpassed anything I had ever heard before. . . . I soon accustomed myself to this method of studying aloud and felt very much at home," he wrote. "I had one of Dillworth's spelling books at first, but there was so much talk about the new spelling book—Webster's—that father got me one." After five months, he could read "very well, write a pretty fair hand by a copy," had progressed in arithmetic to the double root of three and had committed the speller "entirely to memory, besides many pieces of poetry." Lincecum later became a self-taught physician, planter, and naturalist.[51] This method of learning persisted, especially in rural schools. In the 1880s a missionary teacher in a school in the Kentucky mountains heard about what the locals called "blab schools" in which students opened their books only to commence shouting the syllables from the pages.[52]

Following the spelling book's title page, preface, and a long section called "Standard of Pronunciation" with instructions in a tiny font, was a page covered with large letters of the alphabet in three different fonts. Arabic numerals were listed at the bottom, while the facing page featured three columns. The first offered the letters, upper- and lowercase, in Roman font. The second listed them in italics. The third listed "the names of the letters." "A" was "a," "B" was "be," "C" was "ce," and so on. Students began by saying aloud the names of the letters, learning to recognize them on the page.

Once Jincy had mastered the letters and their sounds, she moved on to the "syllabarium," the longest and most complex part of her book. She quickly learned that writing was not the same as speaking, for the words she began to pronounce were not words at all—they were nonsensical single syllables. People in her generation learned to read by decomposing and reconstituting language, one syllable at a time.[53] These syllables became notorious in English from the early modern period, becoming the basis for rhymes and songs. The well-known speech of the giant in "Jack and the Beanstalk," for example, was taken from the syllabary—"fee fi fo fum." If Jincy studied as far as page nineteen, she worked down the column of single-syllable words to find the word "slave."

The book itself measured the student's progress. One learned to spell to the "a-b-abs" or to the "b-a-bas." Learning to spell to "ba-ker," the first of the two-syllable words, "was a great triumph," one former student remembered, "but it seemed like a long road."[54] This meant the student had worked through less than one-fifth of the book. The syllables became so well-known that how "to spell to baker" became shorthand for mastering basic knowledge. Slaves took every opportunity to rehearse what they had learned. "When they reached 'baker' in the old blue-back speller, it was b-a ba, k-e-r ker, baker; l-a la, d-y, lady; s-h-a sha, d-y dy, shady," one student

Lesson III.

Brake	glare	brave	hence	mince	bleed
drake	share	crave	fence	since	breed
flake	snare	grave	pence	prince	speed
spake	spare	slave	sense	rinse	steed

Lesson IV.

And	ill	age	his	rich	less	duke	life
act	ink	aim	has	held	mess	mule	wife
apt	fact	aid	hast	gift	kiss	rule	safe
ell	fan	ice	hath	dull	miss	time	male
ebb	left	ale	add	till	tush	tune	save
egg	self	ace	elf	will	hush	mute	here
end	else	ape	pen	well	desk	maze	robe

Lesson V.

Glade	snake	tract	clank	clamp	black
grade	glaze	pact	crank	champ	crack
shave	craze	plant	shank	cramp	match
wave	prate	sang	plank	spasm	patch
quake	slate	fang	clump	splash	fetch
stage	shape	rang	thump	crash	vetch

Lesson VI.

Mine	sire	strife	bride	brick	strive
spine	quire	fife	chide	kick	spike
vine	spire	trite	glide	chick	splice
gripe	mire	quite	pride	click	strike
snipe	smite	squire	vice	lick	ride
stripe	spite	spike	trice	stick	wide

Lesson VII.

Examples of the formation of the plural from the singular, and of other derivatives.

name,	names	camp,	camps	slave,	slaves
dame,	dames	clamp,	clamps	brave,	braves
gale,	gales	lamp,	lamps	stave,	staves

"Slave" in Noah Webster, *American Spelling Book* (Middletown, CT, 1827). Courtesy of The Louis Round Wilson Special Collections Library, University of North Carolina at Chapel Hill.

recalled. "At the wash tub, over the cook pot, in the kitchen, at the mule lot and in the cotton patch, it was 'baker,' 'lady,' 'shady,' from sun-up to sunset, and way into the night."[55]

Jincy learned that formal English had little to do with her own life. If she advanced in her book to the section of dialogues, she would recite sentiments utterly foreign to her experience. "Come, my sweet girl. . . . But stop, let me see your work," the speller said. "Your little fingers are very handy with a needle. Very pretty indeed; very pretty work. What small stitches. You shall hem and mark all your papa's handkerchiefs." When had this young woman ever heard someone address her in this way? Slaves learned to read texts that threatened to make them invisible, so foreign were the language and experiences they sometimes found in their books.

The yearning of enslaved people to attend school suggests how quickly schooled literacy became the norm. This was new. For centuries, most people learned to read by themselves, from parents or other family members, in apprenticeships, or from their peers. People expected to learn reading skills even at advanced ages. Amanda and Betsy Cooley had probably mastered spelling beginning about the age of five, and their journals show them learning the more advanced subject of grammar in their late teens and early twenties. Jincy was not likely to progress beyond spelling. For people of means, spelling was something for children to learn. For everyone else, especially the enslaved, learning to spell was a luxury that could only be stolen from weeks burdened with work regardless of their age.

"Old-field" schools such as Amanda and Betsy taught in, so named because they usually met in buildings built in fallow fields, were much maligned by education reformers. Yet they were a vital and enduring part of rural communities. Free children whose families could afford to send them attended these schools to learn their lessons—usually described as "reading, writing, and ciphering to the rule of three." Amanda Cooley taught school for all of her brief adult life and by the time she died had gained a good reputation as a teacher in much demand. She probably began teaching in her late teens. Between 1842 and 1852, she convened a dozen different schools in Grayson and Carroll Counties. "I have just been writing Articles for a school. I have hope that I shall get a school," she reported in the spring of 1843. A few days later, "yesterday I went out with my school Articles and have now got 12 scholars signed." Such schools were not free, neither were they expensive, although they were beyond the reach of some families who could neither afford the modest tuition nor spare the labor their children provided.[56]

The articles Amanda wrote served as a contract that announced the length of the term (usually three months), the location, and the fee. She kept careful records in her daybook and generally had twenty to thirty students on her roll, although attendance varied widely. In the winter of 1848, she had almost forty students, and she complained that her school was "very full and troublesome." Students probably brought whatever books they had on hand, along with slates and slate pencils. Although she was occasionally challenged by more advanced students to offer English grammar, cursive writing, or advanced arithmetic, she was hired to teach the common subjects of spelling, reading, and arithmetic. In the spring of 1852, she successfully bargained for a dollar a month per student rather than settle for the seventy-five cents that was offered. Amanda taught in varied settings — sometimes near her family's farm, other times boarding with kinfolk or in the household of the school's sponsor. In 1852 she reported that Colonel Stephen Hale of Grayson County, who owned twenty slaves, had invited her to teach a school on Elk Creek. He charged her eight dollars per term for board.[57]

Amanda built a fine reputation that earned her more opportunities to teach than she could accept. In 1846, she was approached by a neighbor, J. Hanks, to begin teaching immediately after her current session ended. "I do not approve of his plan," she wrote the next evening. "I am resolved to tell him when he comes this evening that it will not do (I do not wish to be a tool for any person)." In 1851 she agreed to teach two consecutive sessions at Independence, the Grayson County seat. The schoolhouse was in such poor shape that she threatened to quit, but eventually it was repaired and she continued. By 1852 she was juggling several requests: "everyone almost is wanting me for a teacher." She could apparently teach as much as she wanted to, although she continually affirmed her desire to marry and give it up altogether.[58]

The federal census of 1840, the first to count schools, students, and illiterates, shows that schools like Amanda's flourished in the Blue Ridge. Scores of schools convened in Grayson and Carroll Counties. Nationwide, census figures show that many more students in rural areas attended common schools than did students in cities and towns.[59] In 1850, about 33 percent of the white school age population in Carroll County attended forty-five separate schools, while in Grayson County, 17 percent attended ten schools. In Surry County, North Carolina, 33 percent of the school age population attended sixty-eight schools; while in Yadkin County, state education records show that, in 1854 and 1857, teachers taught at forty-two different sites for sessions ranging from one to five months. They earned from eleven to sixty-three dollars per session.[60]

Students disliked school for good reasons. They were cold in the winter and hot in the summer; they were full of uninspired students, tedious rules, and harsh discipline. Students bent over their books practicing recitation until they were asked to come forward to say their lessons at the teacher's desk, or were drilled as a group. Common school teachers did not lecture, they simply directed their students (with encouragement from a ferule) to learn their books. Books exerted intellectual authority while the teachers enforced discipline. The system rewarded only the most motivated self-learners. Teaching routinely involved plenty of beatings and shamings. Halting recitations or forgotten sums were repaid with blows in front of the other students, sometimes until the blood ran. At times, Amanda called her students "numbskulls," and reported scolding them and "knocking them about." In the spring of 1851, she said she was "compelled to whip Louisa Bolin."[61]

Blue-Back Spellers

Jincy may have studied a spelling book made in part by slaves. Enslaved people routinely worked in paper mills and printing offices. They worked in a paper mill in Fayetteville, North Carolina, as early as 1809.[62] Gottlieb Schober's paper mill at Salem, North Carolina, a town where the Cooleys traded, used slave laborers from its founding in the spring of 1791.

By 1795 Schober sold paper to towns across the state and beyond, including Halifax, Fayetteville, Morganton, Charlotte, and Salisbury; Lynchburg, Virginia; and Lancaster, South Carolina. The mill was known for its high-quality product, and it had established enough local custom that it was able to compete with firms that adopted new paper-making machinery in the 1830s. In 1836 the Salem printer John Christian Blum bought the mill. Until he sold it in 1844, Blum's mill used primarily enslaved laborers who lived nearby.[63] His printing office was well-known to people in the Blue Ridge. In 1847, for example, Blum printed copies of the Fisher's River (Surry County, North Carolina) Primitive Baptist Association Minutes.[64] Blum's paper mill was one of only a handful in North Carolina; mills in the southern states were scattered across the Upper South, especially in Tennessee and Kentucky. During the 1830s, paper mills were established in Knoxville and Nashville. By 1840 there were six paper mills in Tennessee and several operating in Kentucky. But over time, the manufacturing of paper, like publishing, became concentrated in highly capitalized mills. By 1861 just fourteen mills were operating in the states that would join the Confederacy, while the Northeast had become a hub of paper manufacturing.[65]

Slaves also worked in printing offices. Patsy Mitchner's master, Alex Gorman, printed the *Spirit of the Age* in Raleigh. "He had a lot of printers, both black and white. The slaves turned the wheels the most of the time, and the white mens done the printing," she remembered. In 1937, when her interview was recorded, the old two-story printing office still stood. In Mitchner's day, the press was on the ground floor; type was set upstairs. Although her master printed a newspaper, his enslaved workers were not allowed to read it. "You better not be caught with no paper in your hand; if you was, you got the cowhide."[66] Ananias Davisson, a printer in the Shenandoah Valley, saw his *Kentucky Harmony* (1816) and *Supplement to the Kentucky Harmony* (1820) gain wide influence among later compilers of popular songbooks. He employed at least one slave in his printing office in the 1820s and perhaps several more in the decades before his death in 1857.[67] Slave labor in printing offices was common enough to be mentioned in antiliteracy legislation in the 1830s. The Georgia Penal Code of 1833, for example, prohibited any person who owned a printing press or type to

Blum's Paper Mill, Salem, N.C., undated. Collection of the Wachovia Historical Society; photograph courtesy of Old Salem Museums & Gardens.

allow slaves to set type or perform any task that required a knowledge of reading.[68]

Noah Webster died in New Haven, Connecticut, in 1843, just six months before Jincy sat with her spelling book. Webster offers the best account of the production and circulation of schoolbooks in the southern states, as he is the only schoolbook author with a credible, if incomplete, bibliography. Although it is not known which speller Jincy used, it is likely that she learned from Webster's book. Between its first appearance in 1783 and Webster's death six decades later, almost thirteen million Webster's spellers were printed in shops across the country at a time when the nation's population was just over seventeen million.[69] Even these figures, however, underestimate the number in circulation, because steady demand led many printers to pirate the book, printing copies far in excess of the licensed number. In spite of Webster's attempt to prevent it, the incentive for such piracy clearly lay in the book's profitability.

Webster had many rivals in the southern states, but his speller was particularly favored by slaves. The enslaved poet George Moses Horton of North Carolina, for example, taught himself to read from "old parts" of a Webster's speller.[70] Its reputation among freedmen and -women only grew after emancipation, when its annual sales of one million spiked by 500,000 in a single year.[71]

Three major editions appeared in Webster's lifetime; many copies of the second and third editions were produced in the southern states. Few copies survive from Webster's first edition, *A Grammatical Institute of the English Language* (1783). When his first copyright expired in 1804, a new edition appeared as the *American Spelling Book, Revised Impression.* Webster's final major revision appeared in 1829 as the *Elementary Spelling Book.* Jincy may have read the *Elementary Spelling Book* in one of its multiple reprintings, but the older books remained in circulation for decades. Webster and other authors boasted that each revision was definitive, but readers paid little mind to these claims.

From the earliest days, Webster sold his books throughout the southern states, laying the foundation for his reputation in the region. He traveled to the middle and southern states in 1785, carrying a box of his books as far south as Charleston, South Carolina, where he advertised them, gave free copies to a local school, and left several hundred behind. He lectured in Richmond and Baltimore and visited Mount Vernon seeking George Washington's endorsement for the book. (Washington declined, claiming that he was not qualified.) Part of Webster's goal in his travels was to secure state copyrights, which he did in Virginia, North Carolina, South Carolina, and Georgia before the federal copyright law was passed in 1790.[72]

Webster found a keen interest among southern readers, printers, and merchants. His books were printed in Charleston beginning at least by 1788. In 1804 an edition was printed in New Bern, North Carolina, selling for seventeen shillings and six-pence per dozen. Subsequent editions appeared in Louisville and New Orleans. An edition of 7,300 copies was produced in Lexington, Kentucky, in 1808, and although the firm that produced them failed, Webster noted that none of the books were returned to him, likely leaving them in circulation.

Webster's sales benefited from his early adoption of stereotyping, which required the creation of a single plate for each page of a book. After the page was typeset, a papier-mâché mold was made of the page and metal plates were cast from the mold. The process was first used for steady sellers—books that were reprinted in large editions such as Bibles and schoolbooks. Each book still had to be stitched and bound by hand; power presses and stereotyping simply organized the work of making books differently. By 1825 stereotyping "had been perfected to the point that casting plates from set type cost very little more than regular typesetting when spread over a large edition."[73] A stereotyped edition of Webster's *American Spelling Book* appeared in Charleston in 1815, just two years after the process was introduced in the United States; this may have been the first stereotyped edition of Webster's speller. An 1815 memo by Webster indicated that he had granted a license to Bradford & Read of Boston to print 100,000 copies in "the three Southern states." A surviving copy of the book was printed that same year in Charleston by P. W. Johnston. Another 1815 edition, now lost, was probably produced in New Orleans. Webster granted permission to produce stereotyped spellers in Savannah, Lexington, Louisville, Edenton, New Bern, Raleigh, Baltimore, Knoxville, Alexandria, and Wheeling. Although a license did not mean copies were actually printed, Webster's correspondence shows that tens of thousands of copies were printed in the southern states, including many suspected pirated copies.[74] In 1829 Webster stipulated that all licensed copies of the *Elementary Spelling Book* would be stereotyped, granting rights to the plates to his exclusive contractor who then sold licensed plates to other printers.[75]

Webster's bibliographer suggested that most of the licensed spellers produced in southern states were printed in Baltimore or in Kentucky, but it is likely that this is not a complete list. Webster's own records show that many known editions have completely disappeared. His bibliographer could not locate a single surviving copy of almost thirty editions that are recorded in Webster's accounts.[76] Copies of the *Elementary Spelling Book* known to have been printed in Mississippi and Alabama have not survived in library collections, and only a handful of those printed in Tennessee, Kentucky, and Virginia remain. An edition licensed by Sidney Babcock

(1797?–1884) of New Haven, Connecticut, son of the prominent New England printer John Babcock, was printed in Charleston in 1837, 1838, and 1839, but these are not listed by Webster's bibliographer.[77] After his death in 1843, Webster's family granted copyright to George F. Cooledge & Brother of New York. To print the book, the firm built a press, at a cost of $5,000, that turned out 525 copies per hour, or 5,250 per day. Cooledge later sold the rights, and by 1859 Appleton & Company of New York was printing 4,480 copies per day, or more than 1.5 million annually.[78]

To distribute all these books, Webster hired agents across the country, and many had contacts in the southern states. Walter Bidwell was chosen in 1830 for the midwestern region, including the Ohio River valley. He stayed briefly in Lexington, Kentucky, before moving on to Cincinnati, where he met with a Reverend Eastman, whom Webster had authorized to contract with printers in Tennessee, Mississippi, and Alabama to print his book. Webster's son, William, meanwhile, married a woman from Winchester, Virginia. His father charged him with contacting printers in the area, and to gauge his speller's influence by carefully noting the conventional spellings in the local newspaper.[79]

Academies across North Carolina adopted Webster's book.[80] Most of the books used there and in Virginia were probably printed in Philadelphia or Baltimore. Philadelphia printers had long cultivated a trade in the southern states. Most famously, the partnership of Mason Locke Weems and the printer Matthew Carey looked to the south and west for customers. In 1810 Weems ordered a hundred copies of Webster's speller from Carey for buyers in Augusta, Georgia, along with three to five hundred copies of *The Life of George Washington* and three hundred copies of Robert Russell's *Sermons on Different Important Subjects*. On a single visit to Greensboro, Georgia, Weems sold $400 worth of Carey's books in a hamlet of twenty houses; in the two years before 1810, he sold approximately $24,000 worth to buyers who were mainly from southern states.[81] Although Weems's partnership with Carey famously collapsed, there is no evidence that the market for cheap books he had cultivated in the southern states disappeared. Indeed, Henry C. Carey noted in 1854 that Philadelphia's early printers "looked chiefly to the South for a market for their books." Philadelphia firms operated branches in Baltimore, Alexandria, Fredericksburg, Richmond, Petersburg, and Norfolk in Virginia, and Charleston in South Carolina.[82] In the 1850s J. B. Lippincott & Company of Philadelphia was still an important source of schoolbooks to the region, including Webster's *Elementary Spelling Book*.[83]

By the 1840s Webster had worked for years with Cushing & Brothers of Baltimore and Kimber & Sharpless of Philadelphia. Cushing & Brothers printed ephemera, including farmer's calendars, almanacs, and comic almanacs, as well as gift books, schoolbooks, and music books. Kimber & Sharpless was a Quaker firm that printed a wide variety of schoolbooks, religious books including Bibles in English and German, a biography of George Fox, farmer's calendars, moralistic pamphlets and tracts, dictionaries, almanacs, and children's literature. Both firms produced hundreds of thousands of copies of Webster's speller in the two decades after 1820. In the 1830s alone, Cushing & Brothers printed and sold at least 112,000 copies of the *Elementary Spelling Book*.[84] The tradition of regular custom between firms in Philadelphia and the southern states extended beyond books. Gottlieb Schober purchased molds and other equipment from Kimber & Sharpless for his paper mill in Salem, North Carolina, during the 1820s.[85]

By the 1850s, in response to the popularity of Webster and others, some educators in the southern states began to argue that the region needed its own schoolbooks and should not depend on "Yankee books." Yet northeastern presses continued to produce books read across the southern states, even those penned by zealous southern enthusiasts. North Carolina's future superintendent of common schools, Calvin H. Wiley, published *The North-Carolina Reader* with Philadelphia's Lippincott, Grambo & Co. in 1851. Sales were unsatisfactory. Stereotyping cost him almost five hundred dollars up front, and he was responsible for distribution. The book's title page boasted that it would be available from agents, merchants, and booksellers in every county of North Carolina, but apparently Wiley's plans fell short. He later sold the rights for the book to a New York firm, A. S. Barnes, which published an edition in 1855 but was no more successful at selling it. Wiley tried to get state officials to purchase copies of his book for schools after he was named state superintendent, but they declined. North Carolinians, then, apparently had little interest in a brand new book, even one written by one of their own. This impulse was not peculiar to North Carolina; historians have shown that readers consistently favored older approaches and well-established schoolbook authors.[86]

The enthusiasm for southern books continued in some quarters, however. In 1863, during the Civil War, a revision of Webster's *Elementary Spelling Book* for Confederate students was produced. The editor, Reverend Robert Fleming, wrote that "for many years [Webster] has been almost the only Spelling book used in the Southern States, as well as in other sections of the old Union; and his Dictionary may be found in almost every family, occupying as it deservedly does, a pre-eminence over all others." His reverence for Webster was such that he left the text essentially unaltered, with one stark difference: every few pages, he dropped a block of biblical text into Webster's text that purportedly defended slavery. His approach was inelegant, but expedient enough in his view. He had made Webster's speller "Confederate."[87]

The modest spelling books that were the beginning of all learning were based on early modern texts that had long been considered an adequate education for common people. By the early nineteenth century, however, the meaning of reading, the purpose of education, the methods of instruction, and the meaning of liberty were all in flux, making slaveholders view literate slaves as a dire threat for the first time. Meanwhile free laborers, farmers, artisans, and free black people found that rising standards for common learning made the old standard of "spelling to ba-ker" woefully inadequate. What was needed, they decided, was the mastery of English grammar.

Grammars

Now I have a plan to cipher as far as discount and learn English Grammar
so as to teach it and to write a shining hand.
—Betsy Cooley

AMID THEIR SPINDLES, BOBBINS, AND baskets of wool, the
Cooley sisters repeatedly voiced their desire to master the rules of English
grammar. They wrote nearly as passionately about grammar as they did
about their prospects for marriage. "This is Sunday morning. . . . I intend
reading today. I can spell, read and write but I know nothing of English
Grammar," Amanda wrote in the winter of 1842. "I wish I only did understand that one important branch of learning, but I fear I never shall." A year
and a half later, she was still preoccupied with the subject. "Sunday [Au-
gust] 20th. no body has been here to day & I have been studying grammar
most all day. . . . I think if I had time I could learn grammar perfect but I
don't know when I ever can for I have now kept my journal for 18 months &
thought when I commenced it I would soon study grammar but neglected
it till now but God grant that I may perform what I have resolved this time
that is to be if possible a good grammarian in a year from now." Her sister
Betsy, too, was thinking of grammar, anxious to learn it so that she might
"write a shining hand."[1]

Learning grammar was not just a preoccupation for the Cooley sisters, it was an obsession that they shared with many others of their generation. "I can spell, read and write," Amanda declared. She had achieved a
common education, which offered the skills of basic literacy, but granted

only the ability to memorize texts and to copy them out. It was not concerned with the higher skills of comprehension, composition, or creativity. David Walker, a free black man born in North Carolina and the author of *Appeal to the Coloured Citizens of the World* (1829), scoffed that knowing how to "spell, read and write" was no learning at all. "It is lamentable, that many of our children," he wrote, "leave school knowing but a little more about the grammar of their language than a horse does about handling a musket." He ridiculed those who thought that a common education would offer a way out of the "dark and impenetrable abyss" in which African Americans lived. Walker knew that English grammar was the threshold students had to cross if they wanted to take hold of language and begin to make it their own.[2]

Many people across the southern states concurred. In Charleston, eighteen-year-old Daniel Payne forsook carpentry to begin teaching grammar and other "higher subjects" to three young students by day and three more by night. "Of geography and map-drawing, English grammar and composition I knew nothing, because they were not taught in any of the schools for colored children," the future bishop of the African Methodist Episcopal Church lamented. "I began with 'Murray's Primary Grammar,' and committed the entire book to memory, but did not understand it; so I reviewed it," he explained. In North Carolina, the free black teacher John Chavis tried to drum up students for his school by touting his knowledge of "the Theory of the English Language." "No other person in this part of the country teaches it but myself," he wrote. A few counties to the west, Brantley York, newly married and freshly licensed to preach, encountered his first English grammar only at the age of twenty-six. Inspired, York eventually began teaching the subject across western North Carolina and northern South Carolina. In 1854 he published his own grammar, "for I could find no book," he said, "that would suit my method of teaching." A few miles further west, the farmer and schoolteacher Strong Thomasson began to teach English grammar to his young wife, Mollie, two years before she began to learn how to write. "She learned and recited three lessons[s]!" he exulted. "They were of course not very long, but I am well pleased with her start. Think she'll be a grammarian some day."[3]

This is what happened when refined culture "became the property of a whole people." Those from all walks of life, many of whom were self-taught—slaves, farmers, clerks, schoolteachers, and artisans—who wanted to do more than follow a plow, throw a shuttle, or hoe a field looked to English grammar as the means by which they could make a better life. Some wanted to be schoolteachers, like the Cooley sisters and Daniel Payne. Others dreamed of writing for publication or editing a newspaper. As a young man in Illinois, Abraham Lincoln famously walked six miles for a grammar to study by firelight, "imperfectly of course," he said, but good enough to prepare him for his legendary eloquence. The power of grammar lay in its ability to enable rail-splitters, weavers, ragpickers, and former slaves everywhere from the Blue Ridge to Boston to begin to speak and write with eloquence.[4]

English grammar—"the art of speaking and writing with propriety"—allowed one to begin to submit language not only to the standards of correctness, but also to one's own intentions.[5] At a time when most people had only a common education, if that, learning grammar remained out of reach for those who could not afford to attend an academy or did not have the leisure and discipline to study it on their own. "The higher branches, such as Grammar, Geography, Philosophy, etc., were seldom or never taught in common neighborhood schools; for I never saw an English grammar in any school I attended," Brantley York (1805–1891) recalled of his early life in the Blue Ridge. John Carroll (b. 1841) had a similar experience in western Tennessee. "There was no such thing in our school as a history, geography, or English grammar in fact I never saw an English grammar until I was almost grown," he remembered, lamenting that he learned only how to spell and read and to write a "fairly legible hand."[6]

York and Carroll were compelled to explain this at the turn of the twentieth century because the position of grammar in the curriculum had changed dramatically in their lifetime. It had become compulsory for the youngest of schoolchildren. In 1904 the grammars that once marked the beginning of higher learning were "minor textbooks" used in primary schools.[7] This change can be marked in the evolving definition of "grammar school." In 1846 it was a school in which "all learned languages" (the classics) were taught, a meaning that would have been familiar to John Locke. By 1860 it was "a school in rank above a primary school and below a high school."[8] By the twentieth century, grammar school had become synonymous with elementary school in the United States; in Britain to this day it still refers to an intermediate school. The precise timing of this shift varied across the country. "Forty years ago [grammar] was taught only in Colleges, High Schools and Academies," a Methodist pastor and teacher from Arkansas observed in 1861. "It was then required of teachers to be able only to read, write and cipher. . . . It is otherwise now. . . . As a matter of course, every little boy and girl is expected to learn Grammar."[9]

Grammar, then, was critical to what was known as the diffusion of knowledge in the nineteenth century. This signaled that more and more people learned subjects that had formerly been reserved for social elites. The high-water mark of grammar's reputation in the United States fell around 1860. The custom that decreed that it be taught only to elite men disappeared; now, self-taught people of all ages, including women, free black people, and even the odd slave, were expected to learn grammar. Samuel Kirkham's popular *English Grammar in Familiar Lectures* was intended, he said, "for the use of schools and private learners," and *Godey's Lady's Book* recommended John Frost's *Practical English Grammar* (1843) as the best aid to self-study for "adults who have neglected the systematic study of grammar."[10]

The changing status of English grammar marks an important, if overlooked, step in democratizing knowledge in the early United States. The reinvention of grammar from a secondary to a primary subject shows how the stakes for learning rose sharply within a few generations. Common school students were once praised for feats of memory rather than for original thought, and none of them learned to compose their own writing.[11] But in the nineteenth century, reading "became a necessity of life," and people of all kinds were expected to be able to compose their own thoughts in writing.[12] "A knowledge [of grammar] is indispensable. . . . [It] cannot fail of being serviceable to you, even if you are destined to pass through the humblest walks of life," the grammarian Samuel Kirkham declared.[13]

The compulsory status of the higher subjects for primary students, including grammar and composition, eventually produced a new word: "literacy," or the "quality, condition, or state of being literate." The word literacy appeared in print for the first time only in 1880 in an American magazine.[14] Earlier generations knew only literate, illiterate, and illiteracy. In the premodern period, scribes performed the menial task of writing the thoughts and laws of their rulers. In 1750 an illiterate could not read Latin or Greek. In 1850 an illiterate could not read or write at all. To be literate in the eighteenth century was to be learned; even those who could read and write in the vernacular with skill could be said to be illiterate. A literate person was assumed to be virtuous because of their access to the written tradition.[15] In the nineteenth century, however, to be literate began to refer to one's ability to read and write in the vernacular. As the stakes rose for comprehension of English, illiterates became scorned figures pushed to the margins of society. These, of course, included slaves.

How to Learn Grammar

The Cooley sisters studied two of the best-known grammars in the early United States.[16] One was written by an eighteenth-century Loyalist who fled the revolution for the north of England. The other was by a Maryland teacher. Each went through scores of editions and was printed in millions of copies. Betsy was less than enthusiastic about the Loyalist Lindley Murray's famous book. "I have no Grammar book but Murrys and it is so tedious," she sighed.[17]

Nevertheless, when she took up her copy of Murray, Betsy was in good company. The list of people who knew it included Shelley, Byron, the Brontës, De Quincey, Dickens, Poe, Melville, Eliot, Frederick Douglass, the slave poet George Horton, the American Methodist Episcopal bishop Daniel Payne, and Mary Lyon, whose students (including Emily Dickinson) studied it at Mount Holyoke. The presence of Murray's book in the Blue Ridge was an eloquent testimony to his reach. It was an icon of the English-speaking world and so was its author; by the 1840s Murray had sold more schoolbooks in the United States than Noah Webster. Murray's book also taught English grammar to the British Empire and to Western

Europe; editions appeared in a number of cities in Ireland, Germany, Portugal, France, and India. His was the first English-language schoolbook to arrive in Japan. His *English Reader* (1799) and *English Grammar* (1795) sold an estimated twenty million copies by 1850, making him the largest-selling author in the world for the first half of the nineteenth century. By the time Betsy studied her copy, the book was so widely known that two British parodies had been published; one of these came out in several cheap American editions. Sales of Murray's books in the United States were four times those in Britain, and the astonishing numbers do not include pirated copies. Abridgments and compilations were thick on the shelves, and the work appeared in more than three hundred known American editions before 1850. It remained in print in the United States until the 1880s, two decades longer than in England.[18] The comparison suggested grammar's appeal to people who were bent on self-improvement in the young nation.

Murray's book was divided into the four parts of grammar first identified in the Middle Ages—orthography, "the nature and powers of letters, and the just method of spelling words"; etymology, "the different sorts of words, their various modifications, and their derivation"; syntax, "the agreement and construction of words in a sentence"; and prosody, "the true pronunciation of words, comprising accent, quantity, emphasis, pause, and tone; and . . . the laws of versification." In short, the first two parts of grammar concerned words; the second two concerned ordering them into pleasing sentences. As one mid-century grammarian explained: "Thoughts are expressed with words. Grammar teaches us how to put words together. . . . Grammar teaches us how to speak and write correctly."[19]

Murray also included an appendix that explained how "to write with perspicuity and accuracy." Essentially a brief manual of rhetoric based on the work of two eighteenth-century Scots, Hugh Blair and George Campbell, it was to be studied only after the rules of grammar had been mastered. Murray advocated a plain, native style, arguing that readers should resist the "multitude of Latin words which have of late been poured in upon our language." Low expressions such as "hurly burly," "topsy turvy," and "pellmell" were to be avoided. Readers were advised to "retrench superfluities" and "prune expression," to purify, clarify, and strengthen a sentence. Like other schoolbooks of the era, his book was a compendium of eighteenth-century culture, with plenty of quotations illustrating grammatical rules. Few of these were attributed; those that were included Dr. Johnson, *Encyclopedia Britannica,* Milton, Edward Young, and Alexander Pope.[20]

The Cooleys also studied Samuel Kirkham's *English Grammar in Familiar Lectures* (1823). It was said that Kirkham's was the book that Lincoln walked several miles to borrow. Samuel Clemens also knew the book. Kirkham was one of several authors who expanded on Murray's method to include the practice of "parsing," or analyzing sentences according to their parts. Kirkham enlarged his book and retitled it in 1825; another major revision followed in 1829. He organized it into lectures rather than sections on the elements of grammar and also included a compendium, a large folded page inserted at the front that summarized all the rules in a single table. Visual aids like Kirkham's were peddled across the country to make the Byzantine rules of grammar easier for students to grasp.

Kirkham tweaked a method from Murray, who in turn had based his ideas on the eighteenth-century Anglican bishop Robert Lowth. Like spellers and other schoolbooks, grammars eschewed novelty; nearly all of them were derived from earlier works with just enough changes that their authors could claim they had created a new method. The innovations of education reformers on questions of language, however, nearly always lost out to tradition. Noah Webster's attempts to reform American English failed utterly, as did the attempts of many other linguists to capitalize on their innovations in new books and lectures. Americans, it seemed, did not want novelty in their learning.[21]

The importance of English grammar in the early United States can be traced in the huge numbers of books compiled and printed. The number of grammars produced climbed steadily with every decade after the 1770s and peaked in the 1840s. Although perhaps not as well remembered as spellers, grammars blanketed the country. A few small printing offices continued to typeset popular schoolbooks, but they were better suited to stereotyping by large firms in New York, Baltimore, Cincinnati, Louisville, and Nashville. Of 301 English grammars written by Americans and printed in North America between 1760 and 1850, 254 were published after 1810.

During the 1820s alone, eighty-four new grammars by American authors appeared. More than four new grammar books (not new editions of older works) came out each year; between 1821 and 1830, more than seven new grammars were published every year. By 1850 approximately 1,000 American editions of English grammar books, and approximately five million copies, had been printed.[22] Lindley Murray sold an estimated 12.5 million copies of his books in 925 editions in the United States in the four decades after 1800, more than Noah Webster. Kirkham, meanwhile, estimated that, in 1837, fourteen years after it first appeared, his grammar was selling at the rate of 60,000 every year. By 1841, fifty-three editions of the work had been issued. Even the most popular novels sold quite poorly by comparison; famously, *Uncle Tom's Cabin* sold just 300,000 copies in its first year.[23]

These books were not expensive, although they usually cost a bit more than spellers. Prices for grammars generally ranged from ten to ninety cents, depending on whether they were sold bound or unbound.[24] Even so, buyers were long accustomed to driving a sharp bargain. "Here to'ther day in Fredericksbg a School Master wd not touch Murray's Grammar at 87½ cents because he said Johnson at Richmond furnishd them at 75," the itinerant bookseller Parson Weems reported early in the century.[25]

Grammar was rarely taught in common schools before the Civil War.[26] In North Carolina, common schools did not require grammar and teachers were not examined on the subject.[27] Before 1827 grammar was rarely taught outside of private academies in New York. In Pennsylvania, early common schools gave no attention to grammar. "People generally thought that if their sons acquired a knowledge of reading, writing and arithmetic, it was all sufficient," Elijah Pennybacker recalled.[28] In Massachusetts, grammar became part of the common school curriculum in 1826, while in Ohio, it became so only by the 1840s. Yet laws were often ignored. Even by the 1850s, far fewer students in Ohio common schools, for example, studied grammar than orthography and arithmetic.[29]

It may sound strange, but people avidly pursued the study of English grammar in the early nineteenth century. Because it was not offered in most primary schools, some young men became itinerant grammarians. Like tinware, needles, or books, grammar was a commodity. Along with peddlers, colporteurs, book agents, singing schoolmasters, and preachers, grammarians traveled the roads from Boston to New York, Washington, DC to Louisville, and Baltimore to Richmond, advertising their grammar classes. Many sold their own grammar books and broadsides. "The youth of this city are respectfully informed that the subscriber will commence a course of lectures on English grammar on Monday, April 28th, to continue twenty-four days," J. H. Hull announced in Alexandria, Virginia, in 1823, promising that students would be able "at the expiration of the term, to parse any common sentence accurately." He charged a fee of five dollars, which included all lectures and a copy of his book. Hull appealed to "Young Gentlemen who are engaged in the active duties of the day" to come to his evening sessions. For at least twenty-eight years, Hull lectured and printed his grammars in thirteen towns and cities from Kentucky to Virginia, New York to Boston, including Hagerstown, Maryland, and Maysville, Kentucky.[30]

Hull was one of a flock of itinerant grammarians who appeared in Alexandria that year. F. M. McCrady, T. Waugh, and James Caden all advertised their services, touting skills in bookkeeping, geography, and the use of globes.[31] As early as 1819, John Hassam arrived in Raleigh, North Carolina, from New Hampshire to teach a short course in English grammar in "twenty-four lectures of two hours each." Other itinerant grammarians advertised in Charleston, Baltimore, Augusta, Galveston, and New Orleans from the 1820s into the 1850s.[32] Some promoted books written by others, such as the prolific Vermonter Jeremiah Greenleaf, whose grammar book appeared in at least twenty editions in Vermont, Connecticut, and New York between 1819 and 1844.[33]

Itinerants and compilers alike touted visual aids for those who wanted to learn English grammar. The use of images to spur memorization goes all the way back to the classical world. Every grammarian, of course, claimed that their diagrams made the task much easier than any of their competitors' systems. Samuel Kirkham's compendium at the front of his book summarized the rules for the benefit of "self-learners."[34] Broadsides and handbills with decorative borders and large print touted original systems whereby students could learn to parse. Seth T. Hurd printed "A Grammatical Chart, or Private Instructor of the English Language, presenting at one view all the

ENGLISH GRAMMAR,

BY LECTURES:

COMPREHENDING THE

PRINCIPLES AND RULES OF SYNTACTICAL PARSING,

ON

A NEW AND HIGHLY APPROVED SYSTEM;

INTENDED AS A TEXT BOOK FOR STUDENTS;

CONTAINING

EXERCISES IN SYNTAX, RULES FOR PARSING BY TRANSPOSI-
TION, CRITICAL NOTES, AND A

LECTURE ON RHETORIC.

BY J. H. HULL.

SEVENTH EDITION.

Maysville, Kentucky:

PRINTED FOR THE AUTHOR, AT THE EAGLE OFFICE,
BY R. M. CORWINE.

::::::::::

1833.

J. H. Hull, *English Grammar by Lectures,* 7th ed. (Maysville, KY, 1833). Courtesy of American Antiquarian Society.

rudiments of English grammar" (1827). J. Knowlton printed a broadside to accompany his lectures on grammar in the 1840s. "It is particularly adapted to accompany an APPARATUS which was invented by the Author, and which is admirably calculated to elucidate the intricate study and to facilitate the acquisition of the knowledge of this important Science," he wrote. George Freidenburg's broadside "A Lecture Containing the Principles of Grammar" simply listed the main points of his lecture. Jeremiah Greenleaf produced more than one broadside to accompany his lectures and grammars. His 1841 "Grammatical Corrector" listed the rules, followed by "false grammar" and "grammar corrected." "The Self-Taught Grammarian, or Family Grammar," sold for fifty cents. "Being suspended, in the manner of a map, it will . . . be of service to the young and the old, the learned and the unlearned. The Family Grammar is what every family needs," he explained, intending his chart to be placed at the center of the house. A more novel approach appeared in J. S. Muzzy's mammoth and elaborate broadside (121 × 95 cm), "Temperance and Grammar Harmonized in This Arrangement" (1844). A temperance lecturer, Muzzy embedded his temperance message within a grammar lecture, apparently convinced that his audience would be drawn to his elaborate lithographs illustrating the follies of drink because they were compelled to learn the verb tenses that they illustrated.[35]

In North Carolina, Brantley York was among this class of itinerants. Born in Randolph County, near present-day Asheboro, York was one of nine children in what he described as a "destitute" family. His parents had only a loose affiliation with religion; his father was a Primitive Baptist with a taste for drink and no land to his name, while his mother had Methodist inclinations. Roughly educated in neighborhood schools, York worked with slaves in the fields. As a young man, he caroused with his peers — stealing watermelons, playing cards, attending dance frolics, and reading "books of vulgar and demoralizing character." In 1823, during a season of revivals, he was converted at a camp meeting and became a Methodist with a taste for temperance, settled family life, and preaching. He joined a library society organized at Ebenezer Church and began reading voraciously. Soon, he began teaching full time and was licensed as a Methodist lay preacher. York was instrumental in founding Union Institute in Rutherford County, sub-

Cabinet card of Brantley York, 1855. Courtesy of Duke
University Archives.

sequently renamed Trinity College, which is considered to be the prede-
cessor of Duke University.[36]

York traveled through North and South Carolina in the 1840s and
1850s touting his "ocular demonstration of some of the most difficult principles of the science of language" even as he himself was rapidly losing
his eyesight. He found that teaching fit quite well with his inclination to
preach. He drummed up interest in his schools at camp meetings, and met
fellow preachers from as far away as Georgia who took great interest in join-

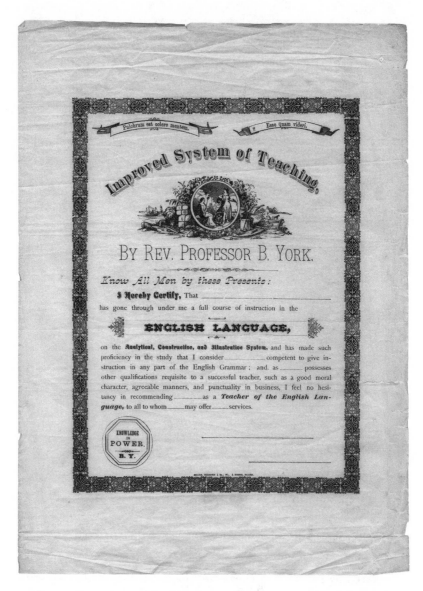

Certificate of completion, *Rev. Professor Brantley York's Improved System of Teaching*, c. 1850. Courtesy of Duke University Archives.

ing his teaching missions. He also bartered his services for goods, including three pairs of shoes at a general store.[37] At one point, he traveled a circuit of schools two hundred miles in length, teaching day and night classes on elocution and grammar along with preaching, adapting the Methodist circuit model to promote his teaching.[38] During the 1840s, he preached two or three times on Sunday in addition to his teaching. In 1846 he taught school at Providence Church in Surry County, next to the Speer farm. His eleven-day course of "scientific instruction" was composed of twenty lectures, and, it was claimed, "was equal to . . . a regular five months' session by the common mode of teaching."

York also taught Jennie Speer at the Jonesville Academy in Surry County. She called his teaching "delightful."[39] In the fall of 1846, she traveled with him to Center Church in Iredell County where she heard his students examined. Jennie approved of their "honorable examination," which she thought proved "the value of the systems invented and practiced by him."[40] York was commended in Lenoir, North Carolina, for his blackboard illustrations and the practicality of his method. A group of South Carolinians admired the proficiency with which his students were able to parse sentences.[41] Sometimes he taught with an assistant. He made as much as ten dollars a day teaching two separate classes of about twenty students each during the 1850s.[42]

York did not find any of the grammatical methods in print to his taste, so he "wrote about fifty pages of foolscap" and secured a printer for his 110-page grammar book in nearby Salisbury at the office of the local newspaper, the *Watchman*. The first edition of 2,500 copies of York's *English Grammar* appeared in 1854. Its printing required, he said, all the money he had on hand and left him a hundred dollars in debt, forcing him to leave his large family in the care of his oldest daughter and go on the road to teach, accompanied by his wife. York sought to correct what he viewed as a dismissive attitude toward learning among his forebears. The title page featured a quote from the eighteenth-century English poet Charles Churchill's "Rosciad": "Should we a parent's fault adore, / And err, because our fathers erred before?"[43]

In 1859 York began traveling and teaching to raise funds for a second,

AN

Illustrative and Constructive

GRAMMAR

OF THE

ENGLISH LANGUAGE,

ACCOMPANIED BY SEVERAL ORIGINAL DIAGRAMS, EXHIBITING AN OCULAR
ILLUSTRATION OF SOME OF THE MOST DIFFICULT PRINCIPLES OF THE
SCIENCE OF LANGUAGE ; ALSO, AN EXTENSIVE GLOSSARY
OF THE DERIVATION OF THE PRINCIPAL SCIENTIFIC
TERMS USED IN THIS WORK,
IN TWO PARTS,
FOR THE USE OF EVERY ONE WHO MAY WISH TO USE IT.

BY REV. PROF. BRANTLEY YORK.

MULTUM IN PARVO.

" That's vile ; should we a parent's fault adore,
And err, because our fathers erred before ?"

SALISBURY, N. C.

CAROLINA WATCHMAN PRESS, BY J. J. BRUNER.

1854.

Brantley York, *An Illustrative and Constructive Grammar of the English Language* (Salisbury, NC, 1854). Courtesy of The Louis Round Wilson Special Collections Library, University of North Carolina at Chapel Hill.

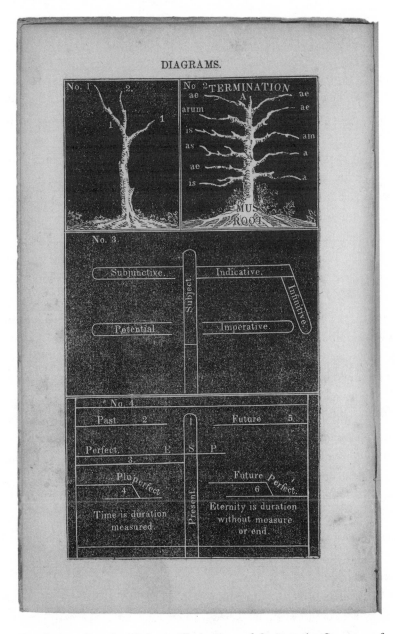

Frontispiece, Brantley York, *An Illustrative and Constructive Grammar of the English Language* (Salisbury, NC, 1854). Courtesy of The Louis Round Wilson Special Collections Library, University of North Carolina at Chapel Hill.

stereotyped edition of the grammar. One thousand copies were printed in New York. He reported that the plates were later lost, probably during the war, "which cost me several hundred dollars."[44] A Raleigh firm, the publisher of the newspaper *Spirit of the Age*, brought out his *Common School Grammar* in 1860 in an edition of five thousand copies. In the spring of 1861, York and his son Willie took the train to Morehead City, North Carolina, on the Atlantic coast so he could lecture and sell his books, but they found that "the desire for Grammar had passed away, and was supplanted by that for war." Two more editions of at least 2,500 copies were produced in Raleigh during the war, however, suggesting he underestimated his audience. The blind grammarian spent the rest of his life lecturing in meeting houses, schoolhouses, churches, and parlors from the Atlantic to the Arkansas River valley. His book continued to be printed into the 1890s on North Carolina presses. In Raleigh in 1895, four years after York's death, it was recommended for forty cents wholesale to the president of Greensboro Female College as "a N. Carolina production, of which all her true sons should be proud."[45]

The rules that students of grammar recited made the language they had learned at their mother's knee seem strange and rather mysterious. Isaac Watts observed in the eighteenth century what contemporary sociolinguists have affirmed: that children have grasped the grammar of their native tongue by age five. "All mankind are taught from their infancy to speak their mother tongue, by a natural imitation of their mothers and nurses, and those who are round about them, without any knowledge of the art of grammar." Learning grammar's art meant correcting the rough speech learned in infancy and reforming it according to the rules of those "who speak and write their own language best."[46]

Readers picked up a grammar book like York's in order to memorize it. For centuries, students had learned grammar, and everything else, by rote. They found all manner of archaic terminology in their grammars: three cases, five moods, copulatives and disjunctives, agreement and position, perfect and passive. There were directions regarding ellipses, the syntax of prepositions, parsing, and antecedents. All these rules were utterly foreign to normal conversation, but they were to be learned by heart. The pages were crammed with tiny type, and each one contained its own visual hierarchy. Students learned that type size and boldface highlighted important rules, instructing readers to attend to the boldface rules first, and only after the "general system be completed" to return to study the other sections in detail.

Grammar was prized not only for what it taught, but for how it was learned. Before about 1850, to learn grammar was to practice mental discipline, a kind of training in rigorous thought.[47] Recitation of grammatical rules fortified the memory. Rote learning—scorned in the twenty-first century in favor of critical thinking—was underwritten in the nineteenth century by the prevailing model of human psychology, known as "faculty psychology," which suggested that the brain's faculties, or powers, could be strengthened, like muscles, through exercise. John Locke named memory as the second faculty of the mind after perception.[48] The brain was believed to record physical impressions of what was remembered, and exercising it, quite apart from any comprehension of what was memorized, was a primary goal of learning.[49] Students had been drilled in Latin grammar for centuries for just this purpose. "Systematic and efficient mental training is a primary object of education, to which the acquisition of knowledge is but secondary," the state commissioner of schools in Ohio explained in 1854.[50]

Memorization began to slip from favor in the nineteenth century when a Romantic pedagogy emerged that redefined learning as creativity.[51] Students began to be perceived not only as vessels but as agents who could produce as well as receive ideas. The transition took more than a century to take hold. In some places, both approaches to learning were combined in what some have called an eclectic pedagogy.[52] In the study of grammar, parsing was the chief exercise through which students began to incorporate this new active learning, and its practice became more important over time. An exercise in Murray's book explained how to parse the sentence "Virtue ennobles us." "*Virtue* is a common substantive, of the neuter gender, the third person, the singular number, and in the nominative case. (Decline the noun.) *Ennobles* is a regular verb, active, indicative mood, present tense, and the third person singular. (Repeat the present tense, the imperfect tense, and the perfect participle.) *Us* is a personal pronoun, of the first person plural, and in the objective case. (Decline it.)" In light of exercises such as this, the Cooley sisters' worry that they might never master more than three hundred pages of Murray is entirely understandable.[53]

Memorizing grammar rules was also expected to give students access to the moral virtues of language. "To speak is a moral action," the Quaker grammarian Goold Brown, a favorite of Edgar Allan Poe, wrote, "the quality of which depends on the motive and for which we are strictly accountable." Brown quoted from the gospel of Matthew: "But I say to you, every idle word that men shall speak, they shall give an account thereof in the Day of Judgment; for by thy words thou shalt be justified, and by thy words thou shalt be condemned" (Matt. 12:36-37). In the view of Brown's generation, language was created by God, and the more refined the society or person, the more graceful and refined the language.[54]

Knowledge Is Power

Extraordinary claims were made for learning in the nineteenth century: it could push one up the social ladder, instill morality and virtue, and liberate one's body and mind. All of this was summarized in the phrase that became the watchword of the age: "knowledge is power." Its precise origin is unknown, although it was probably first used by Francis Bacon or his student Thomas Hobbes. The phrase became the standard that was hoisted over every promise of progress, a spur to even the humblest to soldier on through their books. "Knowledge is power," the impoverished Madaline Edwards copied into her diary in New Orleans in 1845. "Knowledge is power," Strong Thomasson proclaimed in his diary in 1856. The phrase was a particular favorite of African Americans during and after slavery. "Truly has it been said, 'knowledge is power.' But it is not like the withering curse of a tyrant's power; not like the degrading and brutalizing power of the slave-driver's lash, chains, and thumb-screws . . . but a power that elevates and refines the intellect," a former slave wrote.[55]

No one expected a common education to elevate or refine. Only grammar and rhetoric and other higher subjects held this power. As the nineteenth century wore on, distinctions between high and low usage of language became an ever more important mark of social status. A central motive for people to learn to speak (and to write) correctly was the growing understanding of the disadvantages of provincialisms. "Vulgar" originally described ordinary or vernacular speech, without an overtly negative connotation, but by the mid-nineteenth century, vulgar speech was considered a distinct disadvantage for people like Brantley York and his students.[56]

Considerations of grammar touched a nerve in the Cooleys' generation, as they still do in our own. The fierce debates about language in the early United States are well known, but the importance of grammar encompassed questions beyond the health of the republic.[57] The issue of proper speech in Mark Twain's generation affirms that arguments about language are deeply social.[58] In the early United States, a raw and fluid society needed to mark clear boundaries between those who were of fundamentally good intention and those who were not.[59] Speech and writing revealed one's character and position as clearly as dress, manners, and family connections; they were a valuable means to parse the hearts of strangers in a restless and growing republic.[60]

Every kind of ephemera — magazines, almanacs, newspapers, pamphlets — contained all manner of complaints, suggestions, admonitions, and rules that warned of the dire consequences of poor speech. Even as jokes and cartoons mocked grammarians as pedants, and writers such as Walt Whitman and Ralph Waldo Emerson argued that common speech was the language of democracy, the notion of correct grammar held sway. Davy Crockett boasted that he knew no grammar, yet handed the manuscript of his autobiography over to someone who could correct his syntax. If Mark Twain's Huck Finn, as one writer put it, walked naked of grammar and was unashamed, Tom Sawyer invoked the "best authorities" — Robert Lowth, Hugh Blair, Noah Webster, and Lindley Murray. "Don't you reckon that the people that made the books knows what's the correct thing to do?" he asked. Like Tom, Twain never escaped his admiration for the "best authorities."[61]

Nor did many others in his century. Adiel Sherwood was one of many who worried about the profusion of provincialisms he heard in the streets. Sherwood (1791–1879) was a native of New York who became a leading

Baptist pastor and educator in Georgia. His *Gazetteer of the State of Georgia* (1827) expressed the hope that readers would forswear vulgarisms and denied that people in Georgia were more likely to commit such offenses. "There is no section of the country," he argued, "but has more or less of them." Nevertheless, the distinctive features of what became known in Sherwood's generation as the "southern accent" can be glimpsed in his text. Among the terms he denounced were the use of "proud" for "glad," "whole heap" for "many," "disremember" for "forget," "misery" for "pain," and "done said it" for "has said it." Two editions later, Sherwood had considerably lengthened his list. "Tote," he wrote in a long passage, should not substitute for "carry or bear; this is from the Latin tollit — he carries. It became tolt in English . . . tolt is frequently found in old English books."[62]

As Sherwood's admonitions suggested, in the wake of a sea of grammars that asserted an absolute standard for correct speech and condemned vulgar dialects of all kinds, American speech remained playful and democratic, fluid, funny, profane, crude, and boisterous. Nowhere was this more apparent than in the work of antebellum humorists. The rich language of humor relied on the increasingly sophisticated ears of even the plainest of readers. Humorists' characters gleefully disregarded grammatical rules; they were funny only for readers who knew correct usage. Such stories only highlighted the connections between social influence and correct speech. As the author of *Gulliver's Travels* had explained many years earlier, "Satire is a sort of glass, wherein the beholders do generally discover everybody's face but their own; which is the chief reason for that kind reception it meets in the world, and that so very few are offended by it."[63]

In 1843 a fictional character named Jack Downing called at the Cooleys' cabin, bringing news of politics in Portland, Maine, and Washington, DC. "Sunday August 13th. 4 o'clock. . . . James is reading jack Downing's letters and they are all listening to him," Amanda wrote from across the room.[64] The *Letters of Major Jack Downing* were by the Maine writer Seba Smith (1792–1868), who introduced readers across the country, and across the Atlantic, to this rustic Yankee.[65] Downing, purportedly a major in the Downingville militia, made his way out of the Maine woods to Portland and on south to Washington, where he became a confidant of Andrew Jackson.

"I see Gineral Jackson was getting into trouble, and I footed it to Washington to give him a lift," as Downing told it.[66] The genius of Smith's comic voice was in how he took Downing's rural ways to the city. "Then I went up to the State House to see what was going on there . . . and seeing the sign of old clothes bartered, I stepped in and made a trade, and got a whole suit of superfine black broadcloth from top to toe, for a firkin of apple-sauce. . . . Accordingly, I rigged myself up in the new suit, and you'd hardly known me. I didn't like the set of the shoulders, they were so dreadful puckery; but the man said that was all right," Downing wrote.[67] The arc of the character's life story mirrored that of the author himself, a self-educated schoolteacher turned writer who moved from backwoods Maine to Portland and then on to New York City.

When James Cooley and his family listened to Smith's stories, they were engaged in what had become a national pastime. The 1840s were an auspicious moment for American humor. Comic tales appeared everywhere in print and were everywhere told aloud. Jack Downing and his peers, Sam Slick, Brother Jonathan, Mike Fink, and Davy Crockett, flourished in the three decades before the Civil War. Every serious newspaper in the country tried to hire a comic writer. Small-town papers featured humorous sketches prominently, usually on the front page unless they were displaced by a felt obligation to reprint the text of a political speech. Comic almanacs, such as the famous Crockett's, flourished for thirty years, only to disappear almost entirely by the Civil War.[68] National comic newspapers such as *Brother Jonathan* reigned. In Georgia, William Tappan Thompson found that his humorous letters, "hurriedly written to fill a corner once a week in a village newspaper," were wildly popular following their appearance in 1842. Demands from readers for back issues led to their publication as a pamphlet, which was offered free to any paid subscriber of the paper. Within two years, the letters were published by the Philadelphia firm of Carey & Hart. The book reportedly sold fifteen thousand copies in its first year and, by 1855, appeared in its seventeenth edition.[69]

Readers in the southern states were keen on self-deprecating humor, and the region produced more than its share of this genre. In 1845 Carey & Hart announced their "Library of Humorous American Works," which

THE

LIFE AND WRITINGS

OF

MAJOR JACK DOWNING,

Of Downingville,

AWAY DOWN EAST IN THE STATE OF MAINE.

WRITTEN BY HIMSELF.

(i.e, Seba Smith)

What makes all doctrines plain and clear?
About two hundred pounds a year.
And that which was proved true before,
Prove false again? Two hundred more.'
HUDIBRAS.

SECOND EDITION.

BOSTON:
LILLY, WAIT, COLMAN, & HOLDEN.
1834.

Seba Smith, *The Life and Writings of Major Jack Downing of Downingville* (Boston, 1834). Courtesy of Special Collections, University of Arkansas Libraries, Fayetteville.

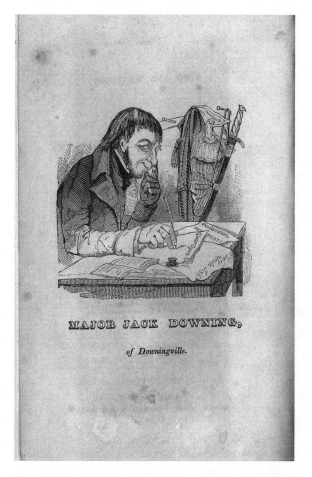

MAJOR JACK DOWNING,

of Downingville.

Frontispiece, Seba Smith, *The Life and Writings of Major Jack Downing of Downingville* (Boston, 1834). Courtesy of Special Collections, University of Arkansas Libraries, Fayetteville.

eventually, under the auspices of another publisher, included twenty-nine titles. The initial titles in the series cost fifty cents each. These included work by J. J. Hooper, Caroline Lee Hentz, and Solomon Smith. The firm expected the series to sell well in the southern states. Henry William Herbert "Frank" Forester wrote the publisher in 1845, suggesting that his story "My Shooting Box" was ready for publication and that it be sold for fifty cents with illustrations and thirty-seven and a half without them. He guaranteed that it would be promoted across the country, including the southern states, and that "there is not a doubt of its selling in all from 8 to 10-000 copies." Cary & Hart also sold five thousand copies of Sol Smith's *The Theatrical Apprenticeship and Anecdotical Recollections,* published in January 1846, in two months. Smith claimed it was selling quite well in New Orleans.[70]

James Cooley may have read Downing's letters from a newspaper. Smith first published the letters serially in the *Portland Courier* in 1830. Within three years, they had appeared in newspapers in Cincinnati, Louisville, Philadelphia, and Washington. Downing was shamelessly copied by writers across the country. One writer claimed that Smith's work was in every newspaper and on everyone's lips.[71] "As honest Jack Downing says," became a cliché. Publication of the letters in book form marked the attempt by his creator to reassert control of his creation, but Jack Downing had long since become the property of the nation. "My Ginuwine Letters," the book began. "There is a consarnt deal of letters publisht in my name that arnt ginuin; so I've resolved tu print my rale ones, and lave out the counterfeits," Downing wrote in his "Prefase."[72]

The more popular Downing became with readers, the more furiously he was denounced by critics, who bristled not only at the vulgarity of poor Jack, but of his entire genre. Downing and his ilk display questionable morals and his tales celebrate coarse language, they charged. "Throw away all those books written in low, corrupt style," advised a writer to his young women readers in 1846, "there is a class of works, most of them fictions, written in language the most vile and execrable caricature of English." This included, he said, the letters of Jack Downing.[73] Another writer, who signed himself "Simeon Smallfry" in the *Southern Literary Messenger,* denounced "improprieties of speech" in 1837 and cited Seba Smith's work as an example. "Who has not laughed over Major Jack Downing's grotesque assemblage of Yankee-isms?" he asked.[74]

The Cooleys were either unaware of such criticism or simply ignored it. Their neighborhood reveled in humorous talk, wit, jokes, and gags of all kinds. The Baptist preacher and humorist Hardin Taliaferro (1811–1875) published *Fisher's River (North Carolina): Scenes and Characters* (1859), which has been acknowledged as an important source for the tales and dialect of his native Surry County, home to the Speers and just over the state line from the Cooley farm. Taliaferro (pronounced "Tolliver"), writing as "Skitt," described the region as a place where people spoke in a richly "rustic vernacular," and for the most part "had no use for grammar nor for grammarians; they had no dictionaries." Most of the people in Taliaferro's Surry County could read and many could write.[75] But in the humorist's estimation, they did not aspire to speak and write "with propriety." In the picture he drew of his native county, the ability to read and appreciation of grammar were two entirely different things.

Taliaferro followed the same path as Mark Twain, Seba Smith, and the fictional Jack Downing: he left a rural place to make a career and gain an education in more sophisticated surroundings. By the time his account appeared in 1859, the Surry County of his childhood had changed and Taliaferro had moved southwest to become a successful pastor and writer. In his view, ranging back in his mind to his childhood took him to an "old-fashioned" place, a habit that many stories of the period encouraged. "A large portion of these early settlers," Taliaferro explained, "were wholly uneducated, and the rest of them had but a rude and imperfect rudimental education. . . . What few literary questions arose among them" were decided by Meshack Franklin, the region's only educated man, and a former member of Congress. Most of his kinfolk back in North Carolina, Taliaferro thought, were not impressed by the latest fashions or money. They judged a rifle, a fine shot-pouch, and a good knife of far more use than "larnin,' " even if they were a daring and clever folk generally.[76]

The success of Seba Smith, Hardin Taliaferro, and other humorous writers of their generation depended on readers who had either studied English grammar or had heard enough about it to know that ungrammatical English could be very funny, indeed. Readers understood that humorists exaggerated the old-fashioned habits of country people; that was part of the sleight of hand that humor required. "I study Grammar all day. . . . Oh, could I learn it with more ease without my head aching and temple throbbing and perplexed to despair," Betsy complained in late 1845.[77] Her ears were becoming attuned to differences between the formal English in her books and that which was spoken to her on the road, in church, at the courthouse, or in the kitchen. English grammar, she thought, meant something better and less banal than daily life on Coal Creek. As more people looked for their future prospects in their grammars, the differences between formal English and the unrelieved ordinariness of daily conversation were becoming clear at the very moment when southern speech was emerging as a distinctive dialect.[78]

Grammar books marked the pinnacle of the Cooleys' modest education. The sisters never went on to study rhetoric; indeed, they never even mentioned the subject. Most of what they learned about grammar they taught themselves with a little help from a local teacher. Although they tried their hand at original poetry, they never wrote the kinds of formal compositions so dreaded by students in academies and colleges. English grammar therefore stands in as an index to the linguistic sensibilities of the Cooley sisters, who wrote confidently of the prosaic but were less sure-footed when they turned to poetic sentiments. "Blessed be God we have rich possessions in the storehouse of memory, and bright figures are ever hung before us," Betsy mused at the age of eighteen, "drawn by the magic hand of hope upon the dim curtains of the future."[79]

Mastering grammar took them beyond the rudimentary skills of reading and writing toward a liberal education in the higher subjects. By midcentury, "a little reading and spelling"—a common education—was not enough to make people either educated or literate. Grammar was the first step on the path to eloquence. The ideas at the heart of William Ellery Channing's celebrated essay, "Self Culture" (1838), took hold in places beyond the reach of New England's Unitarians. The power of original thought, Channing wrote, was not limited to men of genius. "The minds of the multitude are not masses of passive matter . . . but have a native force, a spring of thought in themselves." The notion that ordinary people could write original prose became self-evident by the mid-nineteenth century. Yet it was not always so. Even a few decades earlier, the prospect that working people could aspire to eloquence and become a spring of thought in themselves was beyond imagination.[80]

Rhetorics

Would that I had the power to wield the pen of an efficient authoress.
— Jennie Speer

ALTHOUGH THEY WROTE HUNDREDS OF pages in their journals, family letters, and other papers, Jennie and Ann Speer left virtually no record of what they did every day. The contrast with the Cooley sisters' writing is striking. Amanda and Betsy described their daily lives in beautiful detail, telling the time of day and who was in the room, counting the yards of fabric they wove, and naming the many different kinds of cloth they sewed into coats. They wrote about who was fixing the fencerow, when they sheared the sheep, and how many buckets of blackberries they picked. The Speer sisters presented their world on entirely different terms. "New Years day has been ushered in most delightfully. A few gorgeous clouds float through the heavens, forming a beautiful contrast with the clear blue sky," Ann wrote on the first page of her journal. "Joy floats on every breeze, but many sad changes may come before the bell tolls or the requiem is sung for the departing year of 1853."[1] In nearly every entry that followed, she was looking up, peering into the clouds for the universal sentiments she had learned to revere in her reading. Dreams that could hardly bear the weight of language and aspiration for purity of heart were constants in the Speer sisters' writing.

The difference between the Cooley and Speer sisters' writing was to a large extent based on the level of learning they were able to achieve. While the Cooleys ended their formal education with English grammar, the Speer women went on to study rhetoric and to write compositions. They

learned to discipline their thoughts into the forms that were favored by
the eighteenth-century Scottish rhetoricians and that represented the highest expression in their own generation. Their principal instruction came
from Hugh Blair (1718–1800), whose *Lectures on Rhetoric and Belles Lettres*
(1783) was the most influential text on the subject in the Anglo-American
world. For most of the nineteenth century, nearly every secondary and university student — male or female — studied Blair.

The difference between rhetoric and grammar was clear: grammar
taught correct expression; rhetoric trained students in the art of refined
speech and writing. There were no itinerant rhetoricians trudging the roads
to recruit working people for their night classes. Rhetoric was for those who
attended academies or colleges; few people, if any, ever studied it on their
own. In Britain, rhetoric had long been the property of the gentry, who
were assumed to think in refined, abstract, and complex ways that were out
of reach for the lower classes.[2] In the United States, where a growing, yet
still small, number of people aspired to learn rhetoric's principles, the subject's reach was just beginning to broaden.

The Cooley and Speer journals affirm the difference the study of
rhetoric made in the way people recorded and perhaps even thought about
their lives. The Cooley sisters did not find appeals to eloquence or beauty in
their grammars; they found a series of rules that focused on concrete detail.
Amanda and Betsy wrote how they looked down at the work in their hands,
or across the room, or out the window; their journals richly document their
work, their reading, their visits, and their regrets. The Speers wrote from
an entirely different sensibility as they reached for words to express the sublime in nature, the beauty of God, the tragedy of unfulfilled desires, and the
inevitability of death.

The Speer sisters, practicing the values of belletristic rhetoric in their
compositions, were among the first generation of young women to study a
subject that had historically been available only to elite men. Also included
among the new students of rhetoric in the early United States were the raw
and self-educated young men who won entry into the ranks of the Methodist itinerancy. The most striking change, however, was the new conviction
that women were capable of — and entitled to — more advanced study.

Before the nineteenth century, rhetoric was the prerogative only of young men who were trained in oratory. But as rhetoric moved away from oratory toward composition in secondary school curricula, young women of Jennie's generation used their knowledge of rhetoric to speak on the page.[3] Like Charlotte Forten, who lived hundreds of miles away in Philadelphia, Jennie Speer reached for "something higher and nobler" than her quotidian life in her study of rhetoric.[4] Her enthusiasm equaled that of the Cooleys for their grammars. "I have gone through Blair's Rhetoric and commenced reviewing," she wrote. "To me there is something fascinating in his writings. I could take his Rhetoric and sit down to read it as an entertainment, I never tire in perusing his works."[5]

As taught in the pages of Hugh Blair's book, rhetoric embraced aesthetics, taste, and style. It taught students how to express their highest sensibilities in the finest language possible. The task of education was to correct tastes and fix proper habits. Rhetoric was calculated both to free the writer and to fix the writer; she could be free to express her heart only by accommodating her writing to the standards of good rhetoric. As with everything associated with refinement, propriety was all.

Jennie Speer applied herself to her studies so that she might write beautifully and teach confidently. She wrote out her brief life as the story of her connection with five schools and her commitment to reading, writing, and teaching. She never mentioned how she learned to read, but most likely she and her siblings learned at a young age in a household that revered learning and piety in equal measure. They regularly gathered in the evenings at the feet of Aquilla Speer as he read the Bible aloud. Eventually, the Speer siblings were sent to Jonesville Academy, a coeducational Methodist school across the county. Jennie then taught school for a summer and boarded with the Hauser family at Doweltown (near Yadkinville), a few miles south of the family's farm, before she began teaching at Greensboro Female College, sixty miles to the east. In 1852 she traveled seven hundred miles north to Mount Holyoke Female Seminary in South Hadley, Massachusetts, where she studied for a year before returning to teach at Greensboro Female College. Finally, she was appointed head of a seminary at Rockford, the former Surry County seat on the north bank of the Yadkin

River. She was able to teach at Rockford for only a short time before consumption forced her to resign. She died a few months later.

Jennie embodied her generation's reverence for refinement and the expanding opportunities of formal education for women. As the daughter of a tanner and farmer, she was not the social peer of many of the students at Greensboro College or Mount Holyoke Seminary. Tanning was a messy business that reeked of rotting skins, lime, and fish oil. It required scraping and soaking rotting hides in pits of chemicals, then dressing the preserved leather by shaving, splitting, oiling, and dyeing it. It was unpleasant enough that some communities banned tanyards from populated areas. Tanners had a precarious hold on respectability; the best of them usually clung to the lower margins of the middling classes and many could not reach that high. Aquilla Speer foiled such expectations by becoming a well-regarded Methodist layman and temperance advocate, whose neat white farmhouse sat at a distance from the tanyards at the creek in the hamlet of Providence, where there was a Methodist church and cemetery. Like her father, Jennie did not allow her origins to foil her ambitions. Family stories of how "those Speers girls" had some strange and grand ideas have endured. She turned down at least one offer of marriage and saw herself walking steadily ahead through the "vast field of usefulness" that was a nineteenth-century Christian woman's life, stopping to build something of lasting value on the way toward death. Her mastery of rhetoric was a crucial qualification that allowed her to teach at Greensboro Female College and to eventually become head of her own school.

The Rhetoric of Letter Writing

The advanced schooling the Speer sisters received was unusual for their generation and even more so for women in their native region, most of whom ended their learning with the spellers and "arithmeticks" that taught them to recite, copy, and figure. The Cooley sisters were able to learn English grammar, the door to higher expression, but they never had the advantage of formal training in rhetoric or composition. This was why they were intrigued when a neighbor pulled a book out of his pocket in 1843.

"N. I. King had a book here, the *Parlor Letter Writer*," Betsy Cooley wrote on a November Sabbath. Written by R. Turner, BA, the book first appeared in an American edition in 1818 from a New York firm with the full title *The Parlour Letter-writer and secretary's assistant: consisting of original letters on every occurrence in Life written in a concise and familiar style and adapted to both sexes to which are added complimentary cards, wills, bonds, etc.* Based on a work printed in eighteenth-century London, it was part of a growing genre with titles such as the *American Fashionable Letter Writer* and the *Universal Letter Writer*. Eventually, these titles numbered among the steady sellers that could be found across the country. In Milton, North Carolina, the editor of the local Whig newspaper stocked *The Complete Letter Writer* in his large bookstore, possibly a copy of the eighteenth-century author W. H. Dilworth's first American edition.[6]

By the time Betsy examined Turner's book, these manuals functioned as a kind of poor person's rhetoric. The genre was widely known among the European gentry from the early modern period. One of the most important English works was by Samuel Richardson, who gained fame on both sides of the Atlantic with his epistolary novel *Pamela*. Titles such as *The Fashionable Letter Writer or Art of Polite Correspondence* gained currency in the English colonies, and Benjamin Franklin offered his own advice on letter writing a decade after the appearance of Richardson's manual. By the early nineteenth century, every conduct and etiquette manual included a section on letter writing, and some addressed women directly. "There is one species of writing which seems to belong appropriately to the lady. I mean letter writing," one author observed. "A lady is more known and better judged by her handwriting than a man is," another explained.[7]

The number of letters written by ordinary people grew at an astonishing rate in the mid-nineteenth century as postal rates fell and families scattered across the continent. Between 1840 and 1860, the letters carried in the mails tripled in number to more than 160 million.[8] Many more letters between friends, families, and business partners circulated beyond the reach of the post office, carried by individuals. While letter writing had once been exclusively a genteel practice, by mid-century even modestly educated people wrote personal letters, as attested by the huge archives of letters written by soldiers and their families during the Civil War. When ordinary people put their thoughts and opinions into writing, they dismantled the long tradition of an "epistolary divide" between those who could compose and those who could not.[9]

Both the Cooleys and Speers wrote many letters, mainly to family members. The Cooleys corresponded regularly with their kinfolk in western Missouri, exchanging news in their letters but also in the newspapers they sent to each other. Amanda wrote regularly to her family from across the county while she was away teaching; these letters were carried by family and friends. The Speer daughters, too, wrote and received many letters. In December 1854, Ann Speer wrote out a list of the fifteen letters she had received in the previous six months, half from family members and nearly all from within her state. Jennie and Ann followed the custom of using a more familiar and lively voice in their letters than in their journals. Educated women routinely used their journals for more introspective and formal reflections, while the more conversational letters brimmed with intimacy.[10]

The number of letter-writing manuals in print grew along with the bags of letters piled up in the post offices. They gave advice not just on proper grammar, usage, and style, but also on the types of paper, the preferred colors of ink, the care of ink stands, and how to fold letters. "Plaid letters are the horror of all people who have not the eyes of a hawk," one writer warned, decrying the practice of turning letter paper ninety degrees to save paper. The large number of these that have survived in the archives suggest that this advice was often happily ignored. Manuals also stressed that handwriting should be fair and legible without ink blots or erasures, emphasizing the connections between careful writing and character. By the 1870s this conviction created a new class of handwriting analysts.[11] Hugh Blair famously observed that letter writing was "conversation carried on paper," so angry letters, like angry conversation, should be avoided.[12] Above all, they were to self-consciously model good manners.

Composing letters, like any writing, was not intuitive; it had to be learned. How, then, did people learn? The notion that letters were simply conversation obscures how complicated the work of original composition is, something that anyone who has struggled to master clear prose or has tried to see through the opacity of student writing can confirm. Even beginning letter writers quickly learned that speech and writing were entirely different, and they nervously copied phrases from manuals like Turner's or directly from other letters in the hope of getting things right.

Letter manuals taught the arts of gentility and polite address to a new audience in the nineteenth century, and the archives attest to how eagerly people learned what one scholar called the "manners of the page."[13] When Amanda Cooley opened Turner's manual, she found the world of seventeenth- and eighteenth-century belles lettres. Joseph Addison, Alexander Pope, Madame de Sevigné, and Jonathan Swift jostled for pride of place with Quintilian and Cicero as models of good letter writing. The book taught "the proper modes and forms of address" for people in "all the stations and relations of life." Gentility, Turner argued, was practical, for it improved the quality of everyday life. "We ought to write better than we speak," he urged. "The epistolary style is not the language of the vulgar; it is the style of oratory reduced to the level of common conversation."[14]

The importance of social hierarchy was evident on every page of the book. Turner assumed that his readers would write to the president, vice president, members of Congress and its officers, judges, cabinet members, governors, officers of the armed forces, justices of the peace, lawyers, bishops, clergymen, and college professors. In language that betrayed his debt to early modern authors, he stressed the social mores of a prerepublican era. Letters should attend to "the rank, fortune, and temper of persons with whom we correspond" with "a proper sense of their station and character, and of the relation in which we stand to them. . . . The least indecorum will often render a letter ridiculous or offensive." The published letters of ancient worthies such as Cicero and of European gentry—Sir William Temple, Jonathan Swift, Madame de Sevigné, and Lady Mary Wortley Montague—were invoked as suitable models for correspondence between ordinary people in the early United States. There was a style for business letters (the first and most extensive category), love letters, letters between friends and relatives, letters of advice, and travelers' letters. A letter "To a Lady" requesting her hand in marriage should begin, "My dearest Harriet, Ever since the fatal or auspicious evening that I was introduced to your endearing presence," while a letter from "a labouring man to his intended wife" should begin "when I left the country for my place in Boston, it was a heart-breaking job to part from you. However poor people must endeavor to procure an honest subsistence." Not even the most particular circumstance escaped Turner's notice. "A country woman with a large family" writing to "a respectable lady in the neighborhood, soliciting a situation for one of her daughters" should address the woman as "Respected Lady" and begin, "I trust you will excuse the liberty I take on intruding on your notice." Finally, writers should aspire to a pure language, Turner argued. They should use "nothing fetched from abroad . . . nothing, in short, but the genuine idiom of our country." Thus prohibited was the use of Latin, a danger that was happily avoided by the Cooley sisters.[15]

Rhetoric, Poetry, and the Sublime

Aside from letter-writing manuals, people found the principles of rhetoric explained at the very back of their grammar books or in magazine and newspaper articles. Those who, like the Speer siblings, attended institutions devoted to higher learning routinely learned rhetoric from Hugh Blair's eighteenth-century *Lectures on Rhetoric and Belles Lettres*. Blair was the son of an Edinburgh clerk and a moderate Presbyterian who became the most popular preacher in the city. He eventually left the pulpit to become the first Regius Professor of Rhetoric and Belles Lettres at the University of Edinburgh. His lectures were first circulated in manuscript by his students. After publication, his book was immediately adopted as the standard text at both Harvard College and Yale College in the 1780s and it gained currency throughout Europe as it was translated into French, Spanish, Italian, Russian, and German. It was the standard text studied in the Anglo-American world.[16]

Blair emphasized taste, style, and elegance of expression. Drawing on the unpublished lectures of Adam Smith, he argued for a belletristic style that underscored the connections between taste and social status, sharply contrasting the expression of the upper and lower classes. Letter-writing manuals and rhetorics assured people in the early United States that such skills were available not just by virtue of blood or inheritance — they could be learned. Taste, Blair explained, was the ability to receive beauty from nature and art. Although his book offered a model for male discourse in "the polished nations of Europe," it was duly studied by women in towns like Jonesville, where they learned from Blair to form their own thoughts on paper in the universal and abstract categories associated with refined sensibilities. The Speer sisters solemnly invoked solitude and silence as they contemplated the beauties of nature or the horrors of death. "I leave the busy world and seek the shade of the glen, and behold nature as she breathes her evening devotions," nineteen-year-old Ann Speer wrote in a composition. "But look! A blast and the trees wave apart! Through this transient window the sunbeams glance and illuminate the forest ere his disk sinks in the west."[17]

Blair's *Lectures* introduced the sublime, a theme at the heart of Romantic poetry, to students across the Anglo-American world, many of whom would try to evoke it in their own poems and compositions. Blair equated the sublime with grandeur, although others said it called forth a sense of danger, awe, and astonishment, even terror or horror. The best source of the sublime was nature, and its contemplation led poets and writers to consider "mighty power and strength," Blair wrote. "A stream that runs within its banks is a beautiful object, but when it rushes down with the impetuosity and noise of a torrent, it presently becomes a sublime one." The sublime did not consider, Blair explained, the "gay landscape, the flowering field, or the flourishing city," only the dark mountain or the rushing torrent.[18] Blair wrote before the poetry of William Wordsworth took hold, but in "Lines Composed a Few Miles above Tintern Abbey" (1798) the poet offered a view of the sublime in lines that would be memorized by generations of students.

> For I have learned
> To look on nature, not as in the hour
> Of thoughtless youth; but hearing oftentimes
> The still sad music of humanity,
> Nor harsh nor grating, though of ample power
> To chasten and subdue. And I have felt

A presence that disturbs me with the joy
Of elevated thoughts; a sense sublime
Of something far more deeply interfused,
Whose dwelling is the light of setting suns,
And the round ocean and the living air,
And the blue sky, and in the mind of man.[19]

By the time Jennie and Ann Speer began their studies, no one in the United States could escape poetry—by Wordsworth or other now long-forgotten writers. People of all stations in life, the educated and uneducated, were mad about it. "Poetry constitutes much of my reading," Ann Speer wrote at eighteen, praising the eighteenth-century poet Edward Young for his "sublime" imagination and "glowing" descriptions.[20] Poetry could be found almost everywhere. Books filled with poems could be had, of course, but these were relatively expensive. Most people learned poems in the pages of magazines, newspapers, or almanacs. Broadsides were printed in every small printing office at the expense of local poets. People who could not read heard poems recited on the street, often as song. Many sacred songs were well-known poems and people routinely read hymnbooks aloud as "sacred poetry." Like Bible verses, poems were on the lips of tradesmen and schoolgirls, copied into commonplace books, printed in small-town newspapers and on the well-thumbed pages of almanacs. People bought volumes of verse by Edward Young and John Milton from circuit riders and read columns of verse in every kind of magazine.

Moreover, aspiring poets were everywhere, especially among the young, and many aspired to be published. One editor warned would-be poets that there was "postage to pay, paper to waste, and patience to weary" with the piles of submissions he received. Poetry inspired a new and wildly popular genre known as the gift-book or annual. Lavishly produced, usually with gilded stamped cloth bindings in richly colored cotton or silk, these volumes were filled with fine engravings and the work of some of the best-known authors in the Anglo-American tradition. They were attractively priced so they could be offered as a token of tasteful affection to friends and relatives at Christmas, New Year's, and birthdays. Jennie Speer gave her father such a gilded gift-book compiled by the Sons of Temperance, *The National Temperance Offering, and Sons and Daughters of Temperance Gift* (1850).[21]

A maxim of the era was that good poetry, like the study of rhetoric, taught people to think and feel in refined ways. According to nineteenth-century psychology, known as philosophy of mind, language exercised a tangible power over the mind. The doctrines of Scottish moral philosophy espoused by Adam Smith, Hugh Blair, and Francis Hutcheson held that the mind was composed of various faculties, including a moral faculty known as taste. Because the beautiful was true, it naturally refined the mind. But things were complicated, for not all people could recognize beauty and some were more sensitive to it than others. Like any faculty, taste could be improved. Like the human body, it could be strengthened through exercise. Listening to music, gazing at works of art, and reading poems and literary works of genius refined intellectual and moral sensibilities—a conviction that lives on in our own museum galleries and opera houses. "Aliment taken into the mind operates like aliment taken into the body, by assimilation. It is converted, as it were, into the very substance of the soul, and imparts to it its own character," an editor explained.[22]

Poetry cultivated a taste for beauty and truth that was believed to perfect the human soul. The most popular poets of the period, particularly Lydia Sigourney and Felicia Hemans, regularly took up Christian themes. The connections between religious emotion and poetic enthusiasm were believed to be very strong, and poetry was at least as important as fiction in lodging sentimental imagery and Romantic strains of thought in Christian minds.[23] Ann Speer's journal offered evidence of this synthesis. Writing on Good Friday, she noted, "how sublime to think that Christ should give his life as a ransom for our sin polluted souls!"[24] Taste, the sublime, and morality merged in the conviction that refined language, particularly that of fine poetry, refined the taste, quickened the imagination, purified the feelings, and fostered moral virtue. "Poetry comes to us clothed in robes of purity, and bearing sentiments of a lofty and truthful character," the writer of a conduct manual explained, suggesting how perfectly Hugh Blair's rhetorical aesthetics spread Romantic sentiments in his generation.[25]

Rhetoric in Jonesville

The Speer sisters began writing compositions in earnest while they were students at the Jonesville Academy, about eight miles east of the Speer farm. Jonesville was a small but lively place. By the late 1850s, the hamlet had several doctors, an itinerant dentist, an attorney, a newspaper, and a dry goods store.[26] The academy, founded by Methodist circuit rider James Parks in the 1790s, was granted a state charter in 1818. Joshua Speer, an uncle to Jennie and Ann, was an early trustee.

The school's mission to the Methodists of the western North Carolina Piedmont gave it a utilitarian character that was shared by many academies across the southern states. It educated circuit riders' children without charge for more than four decades, serving as an outpost of aspiration in a small village located in a county without a printer, local newspaper, or bookseller.[27] When William L. Van Eaton became head of the academy, he not only sold books to his own students, but also offered them to neighboring teachers at a discount. Piano was offered on a pianoforte that had likely been shipped down from Baltimore.[28] The subjects introduced to students in their books and invited lectures ranged broadly from the classical world to modern Europe to the Arctic and India. In short, Jonesville Academy was part of what has been called the "village enlightenment" in the early United States.[29]

The acceptance of the daughters and sons of ministers with less money than ambition marked the school as the kind of place that aspired to push its students up the social ladder rather than fit them for a station they had inherited. Some Jonesville women went on to study at Greensboro Female College, while some male graduates went to the North Carolina Normal College or to Emory & Henry College in Virginia. By the time Jennie arrived, the school had separate male and female departments housed in separate buildings. This, too, suggested that the school was not the equal of more exclusive institutions, which were single sex. "Seclusion from the danger of associations which are frequently sources of regret to parents," including boys, was a prerogative of wealth.[30]

Jennie arrived at Jonesville sometime around December of 1845 in the wake of her older brother Asbury. She was seventeen years old. Along with the other women students, she roomed in the house of the academy's head and boarded at a local hotel. Eight years later, when Ann Speer was a teacher at the school, the catalogue showed sixty men and fifty-one women enrolled for the 1853–1854 session. There were probably fewer students when Jennie arrived, but the school was entering a period of energy and prosperity that would end only during the Civil War, when it was looted by Union troops. The staff included at least two women instructors in the female department.[31] All the male students were from nearby counties except for one from Lynchburg, Virginia. All the female students hailed from North Carolina, except for four young women from Grayson County, Virginia, who may have been known to Amanda Cooley.[32] Tuition and board for a twenty-one-week session varied from $31 to $38, excepting "extras" in the female department. Vocal music was taught free of charge, while piano students paid a fee. The Speer family apparently could not afford the fees for piano, as Jennie despaired over not knowing how to play. By the time of her death, however, she owned a piano that she acquired when she was given full charge of the school at Rockford in 1854.[33]

Formal study of English began with Webster's dictionary and Peter Bullion's grammar, "with Pope's Essay on Man for a parsing book." Students at Jonesville also studied Richard Green Parker's *Aid to Composition* (1844). The book was intended for college-level students; it remained in print for more than thirty years and saw at least twenty-one printings.[34] Its use at Jonesville indicated some pedagogical innovation on the part of the teachers. It also suggested their aspirations for their students. Composition was a new subject, created out of the same rising expectations for learning that encouraged people to study grammar. Parker, a Boston schoolmaster, wrote texts on composition based on Hugh Blair's lectures, bringing his rhetorical theories to a more practical level. Engaging in one of the great debates on the subject, Parker argued that rhetoric was an art rather than a science. His book dominated composition instruction, although he frankly admitted that he included little that was new, and that some passages were drawn almost verbatim from other works.[35] Parker borrowed not only from Hugh Blair, but also from the Scottish rhetoricians Richard Whately and

Alexander Jamieson, Isaac Watts, John Locke, Lindley Murray, and other authors well known to Jennie's generation. Jennie and Ann had to wait until they arrived at Greensboro Female College before they could study Blair's book itself.

Jennie was taught mainly by women, but she usually remarked on the men in her diary. "I am engaged in the delightful task of improving my mind under the instructions of Rev. Brantly York," she wrote on her arrival in Jonesville. York and William L. Van Eaton were Jennie's first mentors. Both were Methodists who used teaching to enhance their professional fortunes. Van Eaton had arrived in Jonesville in 1843. A native of Davie County, just to the south, he attended Emory & Henry, the new Methodist college in southwest Virginia. After his studies, he returned to Surry County and married a local woman. He had the old school in Jonesville torn down and raised funds to build a new chapel and schoolhouse, followed by a separate building to house female students. He owned at least five slaves in the early 1850s. After the war, he sold the school and, for a time, was a traveling agent for a tobacco company.[36] Brantley York was gone from Jonesville by 1848, perhaps because his own ambition clashed with Van Eaton's.[37] Born in 1805 to a tenant farmer, York worked alongside slaves in the fields as a youth, but he was ambitious for something better. His autobiography includes several revealing anecdotes of his employers telling him he was destined for better things. York was a peripatetic figure. He taught English grammar in various parts of North and South Carolina, eventually with his own book, and continued to travel and teach even after he went blind.[38]

In June 1848, Jennie wrote a composition that she probably recited at Jonesville Academy's final public examination. This festive occasion was enjoyed by the entire town, who listened to examinations, recitations of poetry, addresses, and musical performances, including duets. Students processed into the chapel, where the walls were decorated with students' paintings and needlework, and the school's extensive "apparatus," including maps, charts, and diagrams "and other mediums through which knowledge may be obtained." Women recited dialogues and played the piano, performances that were "highly creditable and loudly cheered by the audience." By the time the candles were lit in the evening, the medals for best female and male student had been awarded, "with shouts of approbation, long and loud from the assembled hundreds in attendance."[39]

The composition shows Jennie to be an accomplished writer who, if her expression was a bit stilted, had thoroughly imbibed the principles of rhetoric. "Harmony of Nature" described the harmony present in the landscape and in animal and plant life. Reading had fired her imagination to wander far from her native landscape, as she included references to the "proudly waving cedars of Lebanon" and the "ostrich which roams thoughtless over the wilds of Africa." She referred to the "particles of matter" that always "address to this general law" of harmony, moving from earth to the "entire solar system," where "for six thousand years the planets have performed their revolutions in perfect order." She concluded by assuring her audience to have no fear, for "the whole economy of nature will continue to move on in one harmonious progression" at the bid of the Almighty Power who created it.[40] Jennie's triumphant recitation in a far corner of North Carolina showed her to be an able student of the subject that she needed to master if her ambitions to teach were to be realized. It also suggested the riches she had gleaned from the modest array of reading materials she had at hand.

Composition Day

Greensboro Female College, sixty miles east of the Speer farm, was not a lively place, according at least to the written rules. Discipline was strict, silence was upheld, and students wore the plainest of uniforms "to prevent unnecessary expense, and loss of time in devotion to dress." Mazarine blue worsted was worn in winter and plain white jackonet in summer. "Silks, swiss, gay patterns, flounces, and jewelry will be useless and should be left at home," the college catalogue sternly instructed.[41] Greensboro was the first female college chartered in North Carolina and one of the first chartered south of the Potomac. The $20,000 building opened its doors in 1846 on forty acres just west of downtown Greensboro. More than a hundred students gathered on the campus to begin studies on the last Wednesday in July. The strict rules could not squelch all the fun, however. "I have just

come from one of the girls rooms where we have all been playing I had a
very pleasant time in there," a student wrote to her brother in 1849.[42]

Jennie arrived the same year to teach in the preparatory department
before moving into college-level instruction the following year. The three-
year college curriculum was similar to that of other rigorous women's
schools — it offered all the subjects customarily taught to male students. The
English curriculum included grammar in the preparatory year and rhetoric
for the first half of the second year. Composition was taught throughout the
second and third years from texts by G. P. Quackenbos and Richard Parker;
rhetoric from Hugh Blair and Richard Whately. The school had two literary
societies in which compositions were read aloud.

Jennie, who was known in Greensboro as Jane, was hired to teach by
college president Reverend Charles Deems. She excelled at teaching even
as she continually questioned her own abilities. She also continued her own
studies, taking advantage of the school's growing library to read widely in
history. "I rose this morning at four and have had a long while to read and
study," she wrote one December; she was always pressing ahead to make
the most of her time.[43]

Like all women's schools, Greensboro Female College was infused
with religious purpose that made piety as important as academic work. Students attended worship every week and Jennie led regular prayer meetings.
Her task as a teacher went far beyond the formal curriculum; she excelled
as a pastor to her students and, on at least two occasions, sat vigil at their
deathbeds. In the spring of 1851, a revival in Greensboro spread to the
school and Jennie became a preacher to her students, soberly determining
to call for their conversion even though she felt unequal to the task.[44]

Jennie seemed to easily gain the confidence of those whom she met at
the college, and this was particularly important for her ambition to write for
publication. She viewed her journal and her composition writing as practice for this, because it gave her "increasing command over language."[45]
She had expressed interest in publishing in her journal as early as 1848,
variously saying that she wished to write a book or articles for the rest of her
life. Reverend Sidney Bumpass and his wife Frances, who lived across the
street from the college, encouraged Jennie to contribute to their newspaper,

the *Weekly Message,* which she eventually did. She also found a patron in Reverend Deems, who determined to send her to Mount Holyoke Seminary in Massachusetts for a year of study in order for her to observe the famous school and report back to him.[46] Deems openly admired the methods used by the school's founder, Mary Lyon. Jennie accordingly made the long journey and arrived, a year later than initially planned, in the fall of 1852.

The surviving account of her year at Mount Holyoke begins abruptly with her decision to leave. She wrote from Sunderland, about twenty-three miles north of the seminary in the Connecticut River valley, mortified over her "disappointment in examination." She had apparently failed to pass the rigorous entrance examination on first try, which required "a good knowledge of English Grammar, and of Modern Geography, and a readiness in Mental Arithmetic . . . a good knowledge of Michell's Ancient Geography, of Andrews' and Stoddard's Latin Grammar, Andrews' Latin Reader, and Cornelius Nepos, of the History of the United States, and of Watts on the Mind, is also required." The oral examination was performed in front of ten or fifteen other students and several teachers. Those who failed the first time could try again, but if they failed the second time, they were sent home. The poet Emily Dickinson, two years older than Jennie, attended Mt. Holyoke in 1847–1848. "I never would endure the suspense which I endured during those three days again for all the treasures of the world," Dickinson recalled of the exam. Whether she failed her initial exam from nerves or from a lack of preparation, Jennie was never quite sure she was academically prepared for Mount Holyoke. She also felt she was beneath the status of her peers, even though the school cultivated a reputation for educating the daughters of poor farmers and artisans. "While I was busy helping my father in the field, or my mother in the house, they were enjoying all the advantages of refined society; books, and schools," she wrote of her peers. A few days later, she resolved to care less for what others thought of her, as "neither am I gifted or rich."[47]

Jennie did prevail on her second entrance examination. She arrived in South Hadley, Massachusetts, when she was twenty-three years old, the only student from North Carolina to attend the seminary before the Civil War. She admired New England immensely and was rapt with what she called "the Institution's" mission and practices. "I could live here for life," she had gushed not long after her arrival.[48] Her junior (first-year) class was full of women six and seven years younger than she was. The school seemed to take life even more seriously than she did herself. Mary Lyon, who died several years before Jennie's arrival, had founded her school on two principles — intellectual rigor and Christian piety — both of which were to serve the end of Christian benevolence. In the view of Lyon and her teachers, middle-class women were literally called to transform the world as Christian missionaries and teachers.[49] Jennie's own sense of calling to be a teacher fit perfectly with what she found at Mount Holyoke. She also found an enthusiasm for foreign missions much like that at Greensboro Female College. Ellen Morphis Wood (1837–1864), a student at Greensboro just after Jennie left, was the first woman missionary from North Carolina. She died in China in 1864.

The curriculum at Mount Holyoke was uncompromising. First-year students like Jennie took English grammar, composition, remedial Latin, Bible, ancient and modern history, algebra, geometry, physiology, and calisthenics in addition to extra subjects like drawing, music, French, and botany. The academic work was circumscribed by a rigid schedule of domestic work. Everything depended on this system. Indeed, the manual labors performed by students were one of the most controversial things about the school; they did their own laundry and kitchen work. Bells rang every half hour from 5:00 a.m. until 10:00 p.m. Students had to copy seventy rules from dictation into their notebooks. There were rules about attendance, punctuality, keeping quiet and speaking in whispers, limiting visiting, and taking care of the property, among others. Students were strictly required to report any violations of the rules, and these were read out weekly before the whole school. "During meals scarcely a word was spoken, & many there are who cannot eat because of deep feeling," one student wrote. "The whole house is as still as on the Sabbath. Every footstep is light, & every voice hushed."[50]

Composition writing, accomplished on "composition days," universally dreaded by students, was at the heart of the curriculum. Four hours each Saturday, and some evenings, were given over to writing; each com-

position was to be worked on for a minimum of eight hours. On "composition evenings," "curtains were drawn, lamps lighted, and paper, pen and
ink brought from their places to the table."[51] Each student copied her best
work from the year to be archived in a closet across from the school's reading room, folded and piled on floor-to-ceiling shelves; the best of these
would be read at the annual anniversary celebration. Students wrote on
large sheets of lined paper folded in half to create a four-page booklet. Students first read their compositions to their "sections," then folded the booklet into thirds, wrote the title, date, and their name across the top, and
handed them to their teachers for marking.[52] The pressures surrounding
this task were such that despairing students were often tempted to cheat.
Mollie Harper, a student at Greensboro Female College in 1850, wrote her
brother that she was willing "to try to write one," but she wanted him to
send her a composition so that she could compare them and read the best
one. "Now do please don't disappoint me by not writing me one," she said.
"One of the girls says she [also] wants you to write a composition."[53]

In an untitled piece, Jennie described her frustration. On a cold foggy
Saturday in early February that was too wet for her to "go out to take a bit
of fresh air and quicken my sluggish thoughts," she wrote about the silence
in the building, the striking bell, and her roommates who "were in about
the same sad case as myself." One sat on a low stool at her feet, another
sat with her foot on the stove-hearth, trying to "fix in her mind some Geological facts. Now she presses the text book to her head, and the long sigh,
and contracted brow say how fruitless is the attempt." Jennie's intelligence
and earnest ambition showed in her desire "to write something that has not
been written a thousand times already." But concluding that this was not
possible, she determined that "this then shall be the last time I will throw
my time away in needless repining. Hence forth I will try to write something
that will be of some profit to me."[54]

In schools across the country, composition subjects ranged from the
tedious to the eccentric. Students wrote about composition writing itself,
the history of the Bible, astronomy, and female education. But they also
wrote humorous fictional stories with a heavy-handed moral tinge. Jennie's
surviving compositions range from "Babylon," to "The Time to Die," to

"The Beautiful Lies in the Depths of the Soul." "There sat the youth absorbed, lost in admiration," she wrote. As he watched the sunset, "some majestic elms" were reflected in the river, and clouds of "snowy whiteness [were] tipped with the deep gold of eventide." Those who passed him "knew not that the beauteous scene had so bound him to the spot. They saw nothing uncommon, they felt no delight. The beautiful lies in the depths of the soul," the piece ended.[55] The scene that Jennie imagined drew on the language of taste, beauty, and the sublime that she had learned in her rhetoric and books of poetry.

Like her older sister, Ann Speer spent a good part of her time in school writing compositions. Particularly good examples survive from her work at Jonesville Academy and Greensboro Female College in 1854. As Allen Speer noted, she was temperamentally different from her more sober sister.[56] Her themes centered on family, nature, God, and death; her voice was more exuberant than her sister's yet still disciplined by the models offered in her studies. "In my hand I held a flaming meteor that dazzled mine eyes," one began.[57] She even practiced this formal style in her journal and family letters. "What shall I write?" she wrote to her mother from Jonesville. "If I were to send memory flower gatherings through the beauties of the past, and collect all the rare and beautiful things that once gave charm to life, it would only be a repetition of scenes and things that once passed before your eyes."[58]

Modern readers find it hard to take such language seriously. Sentimental style has been alternately criticized and praised by scholars, and has been associated with a lack of authenticity.[59] Ann, for example, regularly confessed that she loved to dwell on her melancholy feelings. Yet the writing of women like Ann and Jennie shows how they apprenticed themselves to their reading as they copied (sometimes poorly) the sentimental style of their era. Its language and imagery were available to readers at all levels in the ephemera, including newspapers and almanacs, dispersed across the southern states. This style seemed to matter less to readers like the Cooley sisters, although their poetry and prose strained toward some of its conventions. For women like the Speer sisters, however, skill in sentimental rhetoric was highly valued as a sign of refinement and taste.

The Rhetoric of Consumption

Jennie and Ann Speer and Amanda Cooley were all dead of consumption by the spring of 1858, a disease that was difficult to diagnose and impossible to cure. It literally consumed the bodies of its victims, beginning with a persistent cough, pain in the chest, accelerated pulse, and difficulty breathing. Coughing became severe and frequent and the person expectorated thick mucus and pus. Fevers could spike twice daily, and ulcers in the throat made speaking difficult. The final stage was marked by severe emaciation, constant joint pain, swelling of the legs, excessive sweating, and colic pain accompanied by diarrhea. Patients routinely experienced a choking and suffocating sensation from lungs full of liquid. Hemorrhaging resulted in bloody phlegm that poured from the mouth and nostrils and could be measured by the pint. The horror of all this was magnified as the patient usually remained lucid until the moment of death.[60]

The epidemiology of tuberculosis was vague enough that few physicians were willing to offer a firm diagnosis of consumption until it had entered its final, and always fatal, stage. The disease was distressingly inconstant; victims sometimes "recovered" to feel almost normal for months before symptoms reappeared worse than before. Treatments varied, suggesting a desperate struggle that could not be won. Therapies were based on either the ancient view of humoral medicine, which sought to balance the elements in the body, or the view that the disease was caused by a vague irritation arising from climate, lack of exercise, or diet.[61] Folk cures were legion. Patients were sometimes bled two to three ounces every day and given syrup made from honey, comfrey root, sarsaparilla, wine, horseradish, licorice, or sugar. Trees were tapped to make spruce beer, turpentine, pitch, and rosin. Inhalants were also used. "Take a piece of rosin and turpentine, and place them on the chafing dish, cause the patient to inhale the smoke," read one 1815 recipe from South Carolina. Amanda Cooley reported regular doctor's visits as her condition worsened. She took cod liver oil, various pills, and hoarhound syrup and drank cherry bark tea. Jennie also reported taking pills. Ann thought that her condition had become fatal because she had initially ignored the physician's advice.[62]

Aquilla and Elizabeth Speer lost three children to consumption between 1856 and 1858, two in 1856 alone. Jennie's brother Aaron returned to
the farm at Providence from Missouri six months before he died in January 1856 at twenty-five; Jennie died at twenty-eight in late December of that
year, six months after giving up her academy in Rockford; and Ann died
in April 1858 just before her twenty-fourth birthday.[63] The Cooleys, meanwhile, lost Amanda Jane to consumption just short of her thirty-fourth
birthday in the spring of 1854. Her nephew Stephen Isaac "Ika" Smith,
who had lived with the family from infancy, died of it three years later, at
the age of twenty. Their experience was devastating, but it was not extraordinary. Consumption was the number one cause of death in the United
States. At its peak at mid-century, it was responsible for one in five American deaths, killing more women than men. Virtually all people knew the
disease firsthand in their own family or among their friends.[64]

The debate about consumption inclined toward middle-class con-
cerns. Some argued that its cause was environmental; cold and windy cli-
mates were considered harmful. Others maintained that it was caused by
lax parental discipline and pernicious habits, particularly indolence and
"self-pollution." Victims were counseled to eat only mild and unstimulating
food, such as milk and bread; follow a regime of gentle exercise, preferably
in sunlight; and travel to a place with a mild climate.[65] Some blame for the
illness fell on the newly popular sedentary and bookish occupations—law,
the ministry, and teaching. With anxieties rooted in the shift from an agricultural to a manufacturing economy, people seized upon civilization itself
as a primary cause of consumption, which raised troubling questions about
whether the very process of education and refinement condemned people
to poor health and whether middle-class habits were deadly. From the moment that man "seeks to live by his wits rather than by the sweat of his
brow," one physician observed in 1850, "from that moment his intellectual
and physical energies are at perpetual war with each other." It was a vicious
circle. "As he advances in refinement and knowledge, he retrogrades in
physical strength."[66] Intellectual labor needed to be balanced with rigorous
physical exercise, a view that persists in our own era.

Women teachers were thought to be at particular risk. They invited neuralgia, hysteria, and even infertility when they devoted too much energy to reading and thought.[67] Some of Jennie Speer's neighbors may have blamed her bookishness and ambition for her disease; others probably blamed her time in the cold Massachusetts winter. The hazards of teaching were legion. Confinement in schoolrooms and lack of activity invited curvature of the spine and sapped women of their "natural energy and sprightliness," a doctor wrote in the *Southern Literary Messenger* in 1839. "The chief source of all the ills that affect teachers is derangement of the digestive organs," a writer declared in 1852. Many were the devoted teachers who found that their health had failed because of the "vitiated atmosphere of the schoolroom," and noise and disorder therein. A regimen of open-air exercise would allow teachers to rest their exhausted mental powers and forget the schoolroom.[68]

Whatever the cause, consumption was more than a disease in the nineteenth century; it was also a middle-class aesthetic. Considered a sign of genius among men, "consumptive" defined the ideal of physical beauty for women, for whom robust health was considered vulgar and unrefined. Wan heroines crowded the pages of novels and books of poetry. In her response to Harriet Beecher Stowe's *Uncle Tom's Cabin*, Caroline Lee Hentz's popular novel offered a typical vision of a consumptive. "The faint blue meandering of her temple veins was visible through her alabaster skin. Then her eyes of such velvet softness, such languishing brightness—had they not the fatal beauty which marks the victims of consumption? Those long, pensive, dark lashes—did they not seem to weep over the radiance doomed to an early fading?"[69]

For the Speer and Cooley women, the consequences of illness extended beyond the daily humiliations of irregular bowels, paralyzing fatigue, and pounding headaches. Consumption changed the way they wrote. After the signs of the disease were undeniable, all three women adopted a rhetoric of illness and death, developing a style that moved away from the conventions they had learned in their schoolbooks. Amanda Cooley began uncharacteristically to comment on her bodily symptoms, and reflect more openly on her emotional state and the religious meaning of her life. The change in the Speer sisters' writing was even more pronounced. Both of them used the language of Christian piety. In the case of Ann more than Jennie, her writing was still heavily colored by the aesthetics valued by rhetoricians and poets.

Amanda Cooley's habit of recording details about her daily life never completely left her, but she began to interleave these with frank descriptions of how consumption afflicted her body and spirits. During the fall of 1852, Amanda was teaching a three-month school session at Colonel Hale's in Grayson County. One night, she was awakened by a noise outside her window. Frightened, she cried out for the family to come. Hale ran after the man, who was thought to be his slave Ike, with his gun. "How I feel I cannot tell," Amanda wrote the next day, explaining that the incident sparked "a coughing fit" in which she "spit up about half a pint of bloody froth. I slept none all night and to day I am so sore and weak I scarce can walk alone." A few days later, she shut down her school and returned home, never to teach again.[70]

Two years before her death, Amanda used a phrase that would appear in many later entries. "I do not think I shall ever be well any more," she wrote, seeming to find the description helped to convince her of the prognosis. The cherry pectoral, hoarhound, and cod liver oil she took hardly seemed to relieve her headache, cough, and swollen face. The plasters she used on her chest never seemed to give her relief. Her diary betrayed her low spirits, which were compounded by the family's realization that her seventeen-year-old nephew Ika also suffered from the disease. The inconstancy of the symptoms confused her. "I sometimes think I shall die soon & sometimes think I shall partially recover my health," she confided.[71]

She also became uncharacteristically reflective, especially about God — something she rarely wrote about before she was ill. Neither Amanda nor the other Cooleys exhibited a profound Christian piety, but they clearly had a solid faith, expressed mainly in their routine trips to church, camp meetings, and neighborhood singings. "The Lord knows best what to do for me," she wrote, "and if it were his will I should like to get well again." After a stretch of particularly bad health in the spring of 1853, Amanda wrote with unusual emotion and eloquence, the final time she mentioned God before she died a year later. "I have no fear of Death and yet it is a dark valley to pass through from which we all shrink back and linger on the brink of the grave dreading to pass through the dark and narrow channel which separates us from our departed friends," she wrote. "I would gladly linger here awhile longer if it be the will of God to let me do so. It is true a great many of my earthly ties are broken, but I yet have some ties to earth which it is hard for me to burst and give up."[72]

Among Amanda's "ties to earth" was her fiancé Logan Roberts. She had had few if any suitors, and by her early thirties, she was a confirmed spinster by community standards. With the marriage of her older brother James, she and her mother had become tenants in their own house, subject to the authority of his new wife. In the fall of 1852, on a September Thursday, Amanda's prospects suddenly changed. "I have been all day with a tooth ache and just came from school to find a letter filling three sheets from L. D. Roberts and I have just read it and am bewildered in my fancies," Amanda wrote. The letter requested permission to formally court her, which she apparently granted. Roberts made an appearance at the cabin a few times over the next months. By May she wrote about him as Logan, and by July a single cryptic sentence marked their engagement: "I expect to marry about November." November came and went, however, with no wedding. Roberts never appeared; instead, he had "gone to the south," presumably on business. Finally, during his visit to the family the following April, the couple set their wedding date for May 2. Curiously, Amanda never mentioned her poor health during that final month. Perhaps she enjoyed a respite from her symptoms or perhaps the wedding was a welcome distraction. "I have so many things to think of I do not know what to do," she wrote two days before the wedding. "Wednesday we scoured & washed and Thursday ironed, Friday sewed my bonnet, red calico dress." The family also fed and housed several guests in addition to making trips to town. Amanda recorded a financial settlement with James that showed how she kept a measure of financial independence even while living with the family. She accepted his note for $220 while offering him an unspecified allowance for his contribution to the marriage preparations. This was her final entry in the journal. Whatever respite she had enjoyed cruelly ended just days after her wedding. She died at eight o'clock in the morning on May 20, 1854, at the age of thirty-three.[73]

In contrast to Amanda's resigned piety, Jennie and Ann Speer framed nearly every recorded thought about their sickness with Christian hope. Consumption's victims usually realized their grim prognosis years before their death, and they lived in a society that was exquisitely aware of mortality. The first composition Jennie wrote at Mount Holyoke was titled "A Time to Die." Conceding that most people dreaded death as a "grim monster," she maintained that while spiritual death was horrible to think of, temporal death was "a faithful friend and messenger sent by a kind Father." Jennie framed the essay with excerpts from "The Hour of Death," a poem by the British writer Felicia Hemans. She offered several examples of holy deaths to support her view; one was the death of a student at Greensboro Female College where she and others had sat vigil by her bedside. Characteristically, she emphasized her teaching. "Could I choose for myself, I would do my work quickly and go home," she wrote. "The only monument I would ask, the simple white rose planted by affectionate pupils. My only requiem, the song of summer birds."[74]

After mentioning a cough, headaches, and fatigue frequently in the spring of 1853, Jennie finally admitted her fear that "a fatal disease is secretly wasting away my life" for the first time as she prepared to leave Mount Holyoke to return to Greensboro. She shrank from naming both the disease itself and nearly all its symptoms. By the following spring, her condition was impossible to deny, either to herself or to her family. "To night a burden of sadness is upon my heart," she wrote. "I long to be at rest. . . . And yet I would contend right womanly with life's bitterest trials."[75]

Jennie unburdened herself in her journal. Her faith was never in question, but she grieved for the work she would leave unfinished. She determined, as ever, to make the most of her days, copied out poems that held special meaning for her, and poignantly cried out to God. "Father, save me, save me," she wrote. She prayed for strength to continue her work, suspecting that her devotion to it was shortening her life. Occasionally, she gathered some energy and determined to live a more vigorous life. But the disease was relentless. By the time she left Greensboro to take charge of the academy at Rockford in the spring of 1856, she was often too ill to travel the seven miles to her parents' farm. Her writing became less frequent as her health worsened. By the fall of 1856, she was at home "confined to a sick room" and heartbroken that she had been forced to stop teaching and close her school. "I am worn out, completely broken down. . . . My physician gives me but little hope," she wrote in the last entry of her diary. Then, so characteristically, she ended with, "But may be I can turn my life to account some other way." She died three and a half months later at the age of twenty-eight.[76]

Ann, meanwhile, understood the seriousness of her illness at least eight months before her death. "This weakness and pressure in my lungs speak too plainly of the future for me to misunderstand," she wrote in late summer of 1857. "Sometimes I almost long to go to my brother & sisters and be free from sin & free from earth. . . . I would love to live for my parents & brother's sake, but if my Father says come, Oh let me fly away to Him." Where Jennie grieved the loss of her vocation, Ann invoked the sacredness of family, particularly those who had died. "Our family circle is broken here, and the remaining members are sorrow hearted and weary," she wrote. "Oh my Father, I pray for thy holy spirit to hush this anguish in my heart . . . but I will strive to give up my earthly loves." Even as Ann lay ill, her writing stayed impressively close to the rhetorical models held up to students in her generation. "Oh shall that blessed home be reached that the weary heart has pined for. . . . Oh let us not sorrow tho' life's heart strings wear asunder and the soul's casket crumble to dust, life, eternal life is just ahead — oh blessed Father support me in thy everlasting arms of love."[77]

Jennie and Ann Speer were among a tiny number of North Carolina women who had the advantages of a good English education all the way through to rhetoric and composition writing. This, more than any other skill, made them attractive candidates to teach in academies and colleges in their generation. Those who did not have these advantages learned the principles of rhetoric and refined writing in other ways, through letter-writing manuals or magazine articles. Like English grammar, composition would become part of the primary curriculum before the end of the century as expectations continued to be raised for what it meant to be literate.

PART TWO

A Musical, Literary, and Christian Miscellany

This, then, is the end of his striving: to be a co-worker in the kingdom of culture.
—W. E. B. Du Bois, *The Souls of Black Folk*

It is not ultimately the printed page that is important in the singing. Many of the singers, steeped in these melodies from childhood, sit with their books on their laps but with their eyes gazing elsewhere.
—Buell E. Cobb, Jr., *The Sacred Harp: A Tradition and Its Music*

The ancient argument over whether the letters on the page are inferior to living speech sets up a false contrast, for both writing and speech transmit cultural memory. This was especially true in the early United States. A distinguished folklorist observed many years ago that American folklore was indebted to "a grid of mechanical as well as human circuits."[1] Print inscribed a new set of American stories and songs but it also rehearsed many others that were decades or even centuries old for readers who incorporated these into an already rich oral tradition.

In part 2, I explore how print inspired rural people—even those who could not read—to create new songs, poems, and stories, and embrace new religious doctrines. Because we know little about the print that circulated in the nineteenth-century South, this section focuses on documenting the presence of a variety of printed texts, some of which were composed and printed in the region, others which were published elsewhere only to become familiar in everyday life.

In chapter 4, I examine hymnbooks, songbooks, and shape-note tunebooks to show how people created an oral tradition of sacred song with print. Chapter 5 demonstrates how print underwrote the stories that circulated in the South. Chapter 6 describes how the spread of print encouraged new converts and promoted new doctrines and religious practices across a region known for its furious sectarian arguments.

FOUR

Songs

There is none here but Elizabeth, Juliann, Ika & Jinsy and
while I am writing the rest are all singing.
—Amanda Cooley

THE EARLY SOUTH WAS FULL OF SONG. Roads and path-
ways, hills, creeks, fields, and hollows resounded with humming, whis-
tling, and singing of all kinds. When Cecil Sharp traveled the Blue Ridge to
search for English folk songs in 1917, he encountered entire communities
in which singing was nearly as common as speaking. People sang at home,
at revival meetings and singings, at dances, weddings, wakes, and funerals.
They pulled out their accordions, banjos, and fiddles from their cupboards
and gathered in crowds at camp meetings where the power of singing was
considered to be equal to that of prayer. They sang on lonely walks, while
they were grieving, and when they were afraid. One night the Cooley sisters sang "good songs very loud to put off the time" as they waited for their
brother James to appear on the path out of the darkness. "I do long to sing
good," Betsy wrote.[1]

The full richness of early American song converged on the Blue
Ridge. The region's reputation for fine music only grew as time passed. The
rutted roads were thick with settlers, slaves, and travelers moving south
and west who left songs behind them. Emigrants trundled along the Great
Wagon Road, hauling songs along with their household goods. Singing
masters crisscrossed the mountains peddling their skills and their tunebooks. Itinerant preachers and peddlers carried song along with religious

doctrines, hymnbooks and songsters, clocks, and tinware. Slaves carried spirituals and banjos from the Atlantic coast through the Blue Ridge to the Mississippi River.[2]

In late 1851, three runaway slaves sang loudly even as they were about to be hanged before a huge crowd at the Grayson County, Virginia, courthouse in Independence. Four men—Simon, Lewis, Jack, and Henry—had been encouraged by antislavery preachers to flee north to Ohio. Taking a canoe along the New River, they traveled by night and lay by during the day. They were soon overtaken by a group of armed men. Henry fled into the river before surrendering, but Simon, Lewis, and Jack put up a fight, killing one white man and wounding three others before their capture.[3]

At the time of their two-month imprisonment, Amanda Cooley was teaching school in Independence. Her sleeping quarters were close enough to the jail that she could hear the "awful" sound of the men wailing and praying in their cells. By mid-October, the trial was over. The day before the hanging, Amanda's older brother, sister, and nephew, along with hundreds of other people, came "crowding and pushing" into the village to watch the spectacle. "They all seemed so penitent and submissive," Amanda wrote. "Poor creatures they all bad farewell as they left the jail and went off . . . singing 'you may take me to the east you may take me to the west so I hear the trumpet sounding in that morning' and on the gallows they sang prayed and exhorted till they were launched into eternity."[4]

The spiritual Amanda heard is one of the most famous of all American spirituals. "When I Hear That Trumpet Sound" was known to W. E. B. Du Bois as one of the "sorrow songs," and it was part of the repertoire of the famous Fisk Jubilee Singers as early as 1872. Its exact origins are unknown, but it came to Grayson County from points east, possibly from the Sea Islands. It calls to mind the Book of Revelation and the return of Christ at the end of the age, signaled with a trumpet. Amanda's view that the singers were penitential was probably shared by other witnesses that day. But apocalyptic themes have been subversive since the earliest days of Christianity. The key is the word "but" at the beginning of the second line, which posits a gulf between the one doing the burying and the one being buried. It points to another world where power relations would be upended and justice would be meted out. The men who were hanged in Independence voiced their fear, hope, and defiance in a song that they and Amanda Cooley knew by heart, probably from childhood.[5]

> You may bury me in the east, You may bury me in the west
> But I'll hear that trumpet sound in the morning
> In that morning, my Lord, how I long to go
> For to hear that trumpet sound in the morning.

The prominence of the oral tradition in transmitting spirituals like the one Amanda recorded has veiled the rich history of printed song in the South. The region's indigenous song included not only slave spirituals but also a rich repertoire of sacred song, which began circulating in print at the end of the eighteenth century. By the 1840s, song texts circulated across the southern states in hymnbooks, broadsides, pamphlets, almanacs, magazines, and newspapers. Hymnbooks printed in Baltimore, Philadelphia, or Cincinnati appeared in "staggering" numbers of editions and copies.[6] Tens of thousands (by some estimates, hundreds of thousands) of songsters, or small pamphlets, were printed to be distributed one saddlebag or box at a time. With the advent of new printing technology, musical notation became common in a wide range of publications, including almanacs, dancing manuals, guides to the meaning of dreams, joke books, fortune-telling manuals, and even guides to Freemasonry.

Both tunes and texts of songs moved into the oral tradition from print.[7] Slave and master, pietist and Methodist, weaver and miner all learned songs by ear even if they had no books, read poorly, or not at all. Slaves memorized eighteenth-century English hymns in worship services, adapting them to their own tunes and uses, while spiritual songs composed in the midst of camp meeting fervor circulated freely by ear and in print to be learned by both those who could read and those who could not. Spirituals were sung into being by slaves who combined African traditions with imagery, stories, and language from the King James Bible.

Musicologists have painstakingly recovered the history of white and black spirituals to revise older assumptions that Yankee singing masters taught people in the southern states to sing from shape-note tunebooks. George Pullen Jackson (1874–1953), the influential scholar of what he called "white spirituals," declared the southern states to be "culturally virgin" territory that needed the inspiration of New England traditions. His theories served—intentionally or not—the politics of the Cold War era, when musicologists were looking for a pure American song emanating from the home of the Pilgrims. Other musicologists built on Jackson's work to highlight the importance of Pennsylvania compilers in creating tunebooks used in the southern states.[8]

Yet the South's indigenous tradition of printed song predated the singing school tradition documented by Jackson and his students.[9] Scores of hymnbooks, songbooks, and songsters were printed in the southern states before northeastern singing masters arrived, while others printed on presses in Philadelphia and points north were compiled from songs that were first sung in the South. The full recovery of indigenous sacred song is not feasible, as much of it appeared in broadsides or pamphlets that were never intended to survive. As a result, single copies of some songbooks survive, while others that initially appeared in thousands of copies have vanished altogether. As one musicologist asked, "How do we write a history of artifacts [that] were loved and used until they literally fell apart?"[10]

The history of printed sacred song, like that of print and reading more generally, tends to blur geographical boundaries. Confident assertions that a particular song or collection is northern or southern are often impossible in light of the way song was learned and disseminated across the early United States. Songbook compilers were often natives of the southern states whose work was printed on northeastern presses. They would customarily engage a local printer to produce a first edition, often as a pamphlet, at their own expense, and were left to distribute and sell the books themselves. If the demand proved great enough, the compiler turned to a publisher in a large city like Cincinnati or Philadelphia to produce and distribute bound volumes to a wider audience. Because of this, our sources for what has become known as southern song were products of northern presses. The most influential shape-note tunebook among southern singers before the Civil War, William Walker's *Southern Harmony* (1835), was first printed in New Haven, Connecticut, with later editions produced in Philadelphia. The landmark *Sacred Harp* (1844), compiled by Georgian Elisha J. King and South Carolinian Benjamin Franklin White, was also published in Philadelphia.

Printed sacred song had a complex taxonomy that included thousands of separate works in many forms. Three of the most popular in the early nineteenth century are examined here—hymnbooks, camp meeting songbooks, and shape-note tunebooks. Each had a different purpose. Hymnbooks were used exclusively in praise and worship at Sunday services and did not customarily include musical notation until later in the century. Songs were annotated with the meter and author of the text. Southern pastors compiled hymnbooks featuring a mix of Anglo-American hymnody by eighteenth-century authors such as Isaac Watts, Charles and John Wesley, John Rippon, and John Newton, along with newer camp meeting songs. Depending on the binding, hymnbooks commonly cost less than fifty cents per copy. In 1827 Methodists sold Sunday school hymnbooks at $1.50 per dozen or $12.00 per hundred. They were so common that they were not routinely referred to by name; agents and merchants ordered hymnbooks without regard to the particular editions the printer had on hand.[11]

A second category, called camp meeting songs, sometimes appeared in hymnbooks, but initially circulated as single sheets. These were composed spontaneously at camp meetings, usually when older hymn texts were sung to popular tunes. Some originated in eighteenth-century revivals. If they proved popular enough, they were gathered and printed in small pamphlets, and the most beloved eventually made their way into hymnbooks. As with hymns, printed camp meeting songs did not include musical notation. These were considered by many as too unseemly for worship services; they were generally sung at baptisms, revivals, ordinations, and social singings—neighborhood gatherings at private homes that were social, not religious, occasions.

A third type of printed sacred song was the shape-note tunebooks. What is now known as Sacred Harp singing—which uses printed musical notation with a four-note or seven-note shape system—took hold of singers in the 1830s and has never let go. The shape-note system was invented by a

Philadelphian in 1798, but it stormed the southern and western states; enthusiasts continue to gather regularly from Tokyo to Hamburg. Shape-note tunebooks were not intended for use in worship, but for singing schools led by teachers who sometimes compiled the books they taught. These featured few original tunes; like the camp meeting songs, they drew on popular fuging tunes, revival shouts, reform tunes, and hymns. Unlike hymns and spiritual songs, shape-note singing owed its very existence to print.[12]

African American Spirituals and English Hymns

Print was critical to both the creation and dissemination of African American spirituals.[13] Composers drew on imagery and stories from the King James Bible that enslaved people memorized in revivals, in worship services, and at their mother's knee. Observers often marveled at slaves' ability to memorize long passages, even entire chapters. The heroes of the scriptures became intimates of the slaves; they spoke of Brother Moses and Sister Mary. As one South Carolina slave explained, "an' den I went to hebben, and dere I see de Lord Jesus a sittin' behind de door an' a reading his Bible."[14]

Yet print's importance to slave spirituals extended beyond its biblical roots. Musicologist Eileen Southern has disproved the view that spirituals were born in the fields of southern plantations. Instead, she argues, they originated in the worship of independent black congregations in the Philadelphia area.[15] The crucial source is an early hymnbook compiled by Richard Allen, a former slave who became the first bishop of the African Methodist Episcopal Church. Printed in 1801 in Philadelphia, Allen's *A Collection of Hymns and Spiritual Songs from Various Authors* took its title from a phrase in Psalm 150, "hymns and spiritual songs," perhaps following on the standard collection by that name by the eighteenth-century English hymnist Isaac Watts. It was the first collection of sacred song that was highly regarded by black Christians and the first to include the "wandering choruses"—short refrains attached randomly to standard hymn stanzas—that were characteristic of black song. Critically, Southern has traced texts in the landmark collection *Slave Songs of the United States* (1867) back to Allen's hymnbook.[16]

A

COLLECTION

OF

HYMNS & SPIRITUAL SONGS,

FROM VARIOUS AUTHORS.

BY THE REV. RICHARD ALLEN,
MINISTER OF THE AFRICAN METHODIST
EPISCOPAL CHURCH.

Philadelphia:
PRINTED BY T. L. PLOWMAN,
CARTER'S-ALLEY.
1801.
Sold at No. 150, Spruce-street.

Richard Allen, *A Collection of Hymns & Spiritual Songs from Various Authors* (Philadelphia, 1801). Courtesy of American Antiquarian Society.

An expanded second edition of Allen's collection appeared later the same year, suggesting the popularity of the work. No copies of the first edition, and only one copy of the second, survive. Of the sixty-four songs in the second edition, almost half are from the Anglo-American tradition. There are thirteen by Isaac Watts, five by the Wesleys, three by the English Anglican John Newton (author of "Amazing Grace"), and ten others that were written by English and Scottish authors, including the poet Alexander Pope. The rest of the songs in Allen's collection are camp meeting songs by American-born authors including Henry Alline, Caleb Taylor, Sarah Jones, and possibly the Methodist William Colbert. Some of the songs, particularly "See How the Nations Rage Together," were probably written by Allen himself.[17] Typically for his time, Allen included no musical notation or names of the authors of the texts.

Allen's hymnbook profoundly influenced black sacred song because his Philadelphia congregation—Bethel Church, known as Mother Bethel—was the most important independent black congregation in the nation. Black and white visitors flocked to its services to hear the singing, and when the African Methodist Episcopal Church spread as far south as Charleston, South Carolina, Allen's hymnbook did, too. Texts chosen by Allen in the two decades after the book was published appeared in at least ten other popular sacred songbook compilations.[18] There was a particularly close relationship between Allen's book and later editions of *Hymns and Spiritual Songs for the Use of Christians,* known as the Baltimore Collection for its place of publication. An anonymous compilation that first appeared in 1801, it became a crucial source for both black and white spirituals.

Allen was steeped in the rich singing tradition of Methodism, a new denomination that quickly became the largest in the United States. Singing at early biracial Methodist meetings was notorious. A congregation in Richmond was denied use of the Henrico County courthouse because their singing and shouting apparently disturbed the neighborhood peace. When the newly formed Methodist Episcopal Church South printed its first hymnbook in Richmond in 1847, one reviewer praised it in excruciating detail for sixty-one pages, concluding that the book was second in importance only to the Bible itself. "It brings down the doctrines of Christianity to the popular mind and insinuates them into the soul," he wrote. The first Methodist hymnbook had been brought over from England in 1784 in unbound sheets by Thomas Coke. By the nineteenth century, hymnbooks were a staple of Methodist printing, beginning in 1802 with the publication of *The Methodist Pocket Hymn Book*. The importance of these books to the tradition is clear, as this was the first work to be stereotyped by Methodists, in 1821.[19]

Many of the texts in Allen's collection were sung to popular tunes that one white critic denigrated as "merry airs." Black sacred song was less likely to improvise on the texts than the tunes; it often combined older texts with newer tunes, a tradition taken from African song.[20] African Americans were accustomed to "lining out" hymns. This was a holdover from an older tradition of singing the psalms; it relied on a leader who sang a line to be echoed by the congregation. This was to convey the text rather than the tune because singers usually knew the tunes by heart.[21]

The popularity of English hymn texts among slaves is well documented. Anglican hymnody by Isaac Watts, John and Charles Wesley, John Newton, John Rippon, and John Cennick was introduced into the southeastern colonies by Anglican missionaries and became popular during the eighteenth-century revivals. Enslaved singers were particularly fond of Watts's hymns. Samuel Davies, the Presbyterian revival leader in Hanover, Virginia, wrote to a New England bookseller in 1751: "The books I principally want for [the slaves] are, Watts's Psalms and Hymns, and Bibles. . . . There are no books that they learn so soon, or take so much Pleasure in." Remarkably, Davies's account shows that some slaves read hymnbooks, as there were "so many of them with their Psalm or Hymn Books, assisting their fellows, who are beginners, to find the place; and then all breaking out in a torrent of sacred harmony."[22]

When independent black churches were established, English hymns became the core of congregational song. Members of the First African Baptist Church of Savannah, organized in 1788, sang Watts's hymns while they processed to the river to perform baptisms and lined them out in their worship services.[23] The two-hundred-member black Methodist Protestant congregation in Augusta almost certainly relied on hymns in the *Methodist Protestant Hymn-Book* (Baltimore, 1837), which combined the Wesleys' and Watts's hymns with Moravian songs and John Harrod's popular *Social and Camp Meeting Hymns for the Pious* (Baltimore, 1817).[24] George Moses Horton, the published slave poet of North Carolina, attributed much of his vocabulary and sense of rhyme and meter to his mother's Methodist hymnbook and the New Testament, along with other books of poetry.[25] The renowned singer Rev. C. J. Johnson recalled how his grandmother in Georgia "walked through the house singing a hymn" as he held on to her long apron. "I would listen to her, then I would get the little children . . . up under the house and teach them how to sing like Grandmaw. We would sing hymns. That is the way it started."[26]

Betsy Cooley wrote about the importance of English hymns to slaves in her account of her three-month journey to Missouri. In April 1846 she left her family and friends behind to move west. Married for less than a month, she and James McClure intended to begin a new life in Texas. After a sad farewell, the young couple began the long trip over the Virginia Blue Ridge and west across Tennessee. As they turned south toward New Orleans, the news of Texas became ominous. In Mississippi, seventy-five volunteer soldiers for Texas came on board their boat, "the ladies standing on the banks and such cheering and clapping of hands, waving hats and handkerchiefs I never did see." Fearing the looming Mexican American War, the couple made the long trip back to New Orleans and north to St. Louis, where they took a boat on the Missouri River. They finally reached Independence, Missouri, on June 24.[27]

On their three-month trip, they met many people on the roads and rivers, including "Carolinians" and "negro drivers," a "nasty strumpet," a simple-hearted Italian girl, "rowdies," and fine St. Louis women who made Betsy feel "as mute as a mouse." Their fellow travelers' hearts were filled with song and the air resounded day and night with fiddlers and accordions. While still in eastern Tennessee, the couple fell in with some slave traders, one of whom sang "Glorious Light of Zion." Known as "Zion's Light," this was a common meter hymn that was widely printed in Baptist, Primitive Baptist, and Disciples of Christ hymnbooks. It appeared in the South Carolinian William Dossey's popular collection *The Choice* (1820) and William Walker's shape-note tunebook *Southern Harmony* (1835). "Now down into the water, / Will we young converts go, / There went our Lord and master, / When he was here below," the slave traders sang. One night, the McClures camped in the Holston River valley, south of Cumberland Gap. "The stars are sparkling brightly, new moon; Cook gone to the house, Thomas gone to bed, Mc. [her husband] sick a little and lying with his head in my lap and asleep," Betsy wrote by the campfire. "Part of the blacks asleep and part of them singing 'Hark from the Tomb' slow and melancholy."[28]

"Hark! from the Tombs a Doleful Sound" was written by the eighteenth-century English nonconformist Isaac Watts, whose hymns dominated sacred song in Betsy's generation and are still widely sung. Described as a funeral hymn, it appeared in many eighteenth- and early nineteenth-century hymnbooks and shape-note tunebooks, along with other works by Watts. As sung by the slaves, it was akin to a "sorrow song," yet the final verse introduced a note of hope: "when we drop this dying flesh, we'll rise above the sky." Like "When I Hear That Trumpet Sound," Watts's hymn urged singers to raise their eyes above the horizon and to envision a new life.

> Hark! from the tombs a doleful sound;
> My ears, attend the cry;
> "Ye living men, come view the ground
> Where you must shortly lie. . . ."

Print carried the text of Watts's hymn across an ocean and through the years to these slaves who were trudging, likely to an early death, toward the Mississippi Delta. Betsy Cooley and these enslaved singers remembered Watts's poetry together that clear night in a Tennessee glen. Both knew the hymn by heart.

As with many other things in the life of a slave, hymns could become a weapon. Masters often forced slaves to sing. They favored proper hymns that could be sung on the auction block or in the fields, because, in their view, when slaves were singing they could not be scheming a rebellion. "'Make a noise, make a noise' and 'bear a hand,' are the words usually addressed to the slaves when there is silence amongst them," Frederick

Douglass wrote.[29] Reverend Charles Colcock Jones, the Georgia Presbyterian who founded the mission to the slaves, encouraged them to learn
Watts's hymns so that they might "lay aside the extravagant and nonsensical chants, and catches and hallelujah songs of their own composing."[30]
Yet slaves revised English hymns to suit their own needs and tastes, using
African song structure to convert English texts into pleas for deliverance
from their earthly masters. They attached, for example, black folk-hymn
couplets such as "My work on earth will soon be done; / And then I'm going
home" or "I'm not too mean to serve the Lord; / He's done so much for
me" to Anglo-American hymn texts.[31] They also created a tradition called
"Dr. Watts Hymn Singing," a distinctive practice that elaborated on (but in
some cases departed completely from) the hymns of Watts and the Wesleys.
It survives to this day.

Isaac Watts towered above the rest of the English composers. His
was the most popular compilation in Anglo-America, and copies printed
in North America and imported from Britain showered the country. His
Psalms, Hymns and Spiritual Songs appeared in 177 editions in eighteenth-
century America alone, and it continued to be reprinted in large numbers
in the nineteenth century. Copies were available for five shillings each in
backcountry North Carolina even before the American Revolution. Watts's
bibliographer found 487 editions of his hymns printed in the United States
and Britain between 1792 and 1860, including editions by printers in Maryland, North Carolina, and Kentucky. Philadelphia was the primary source
of Watts's hymns for singers in the southern states. W. W. Woodward, who
had deputized scores of pastors across the South as his agents, printed nine
editions in the city between 1805 and 1819 with others appearing almost annually until 1830. McCarty and Davis of Philadelphia printed four editions
between 1818 and 1830. Clark and Lippincott, also of Philadelphia, printed
several editions of Watts's hymnbook in the 1830s, continuing production
into the 1840s. The firm collaborated on an edition of Watts's hymns with
John L. Dagg, a Georgia Baptist who headed the Alabama Female Athe-
neum before becoming president of Mercer University in the 1840s. Clark
and Lippincott reputedly conducted a majority of its business in the southern states.[32]

Watts's hymns also circulated in other compilations. They made up the majority of the songs in William Walker's *Southern Harmony* (1835), the most popular shape-note tunebook in the South, and filled the pages of hymnbooks compiled by pastors such as Jesse Mercer (Georgia), Silas Noel (Kentucky), William Dossey (South Carolina), John Purify (North Carolina), Staunton Burdett (South Carolina), and William Buck (Kentucky). Disseminated in many printed forms and sung in Sunday services and at baptisms, revivals and camp meetings, social singings, and brush arbor meetings, Watts's hymns gave voice to the religious experiences of free and enslaved people across the southern states.

Camp Meeting Spiritual Songs

Camp meetings were also a rich source for printed song. Camp meeting songs were composed as spontaneous acts of penitence or worship, and became part of an oral tradition that was codified in print. Singers sometimes created new texts for the large repertoire of tunes they carried in their heads.[33] Those who attended camp meetings testified that God spoke to them directly through song and accorded spiritual power to those who sang. At the famous Cane Ridge, Kentucky, revival in 1801, which was attended by ten to twenty-five thousand people and continued for a week, people were said to have "collected in numberless small circles of twelve or twenty singing hymns; all serious; many walking to and fro, with anxiety pictured on their countenances."[34] The best of these spontaneous songs gained a following and were disseminated in manuscript before they were printed as sheets. Those that proved popular were then compiled into songsters, and the most popular of these eventually made their way into printed books.[35]

Like the camp meetings themselves, this genre was shared by black and white singers. The campgrounds were largely segregated—African Americans either gathered behind the preacher's stand or to one side, and they also slept in separate areas. Yet singing could bridge this divide briefly, if never completely. While the preaching underscored the authority of white men, singing stressed that the spirit of God was available to all. Racial barriers could be put aside momentarily, particularly in the "singing ecstasy" that closed the meetings. Camp meeting songs were derided by some white critics who associated them with African American singers and called those who sang them illiterate.[36] The brief habits of mutuality in interracial singing and worship at camp meetings began to deteriorate after the 1830s, but by that time a rich shared body of songs and singing styles, black and white together, had already been set in print and ingrained in memory.

The first major collection of camp meeting songs, known as the Baltimore Collection, appeared in 1801, the same year as the Cane Ridge Revival and the publication of Richard Allen's hymnbook. A second edition borrowed heavily from Allen's collection, and copies were later printed in Philadelphia; Lexington, Kentucky; Salisbury, North Carolina; and Wilmington, North Carolina. It spread Allen's favorites to free and enslaved singers across the region. Musicologist Richard Hulan has noted that Allen "stands at the head not only of the [black spiritual tradition] but also of the camp meeting spiritual tradition."[37]

The speed with which these songbooks spread across the country testifies not only to their popularity, but also to their profitability. Thousands of copies were snapped up. Even the most modest of pamphlets could appear in initial print runs of a thousand copies. Pamphlets and books of songs were taken from state to state by ministers who crisscrossed the Southeast to attend revival meetings. The camp meeting songs, then, spread north and east out of the southern states. Lemuel Birkitt, an early leader of the Kehukee Baptists of eastern North Carolina, enlisted a local printer to produce several pamphlets "which contained a small collection of spiritual songs, some of which he had brought from the western countries. They were in great demand. As many as about 6,000 books were disposed of in two years."[38]

The earliest collections of camp meeting songs were printed on presses scattered across the southern states, particularly in the Upper South—Kentucky, Virginia, North Carolina—where the camp meeting tradition was the strongest. Of at least fifty-two early collections of camp meeting songs that appeared before 1812, a third were printed in the southern states and the others found a large audience there. Thomas S. Hinde, the compiler of the influential *The Pilgrim's Songster* (Cincinnati, 1810), highlighted the work of two Methodists in early Kentucky, John Adam Granade and Caleb Jarvis Taylor, both of whom compiled pamphlets of songs in Lexington in 1804. No copy of Granade's *The Pilgrim's Songster* (Lexington, 1804) survives, but Hinde's book included more than thirty of his songs. Caleb Taylor's *Spiritual Songs* (Lexington, 1804) was a small pamphlet of thirty pages. A single known copy survives in the Cincinnati Public Library, without covers, each page torn in half and hand-stitched back together. "These two poets composed their songs during the great revivals of religion in the states of Kentucky and Tennessee about the years 1802, 3 and 4. . . . Their hymns and spiritual songs breathe the spirit of the times," Hinde wrote in his introduction. "These excellent songs were written in the midst of the holy flame, in the height of the revival. . . . It was not only at the meetings that they were sung; but making so deep an impression upon the minds of the people at this period, they were soon learned by thousands; who made the shops, the fields, the woods, the hills and the vales to echo with the melody of their voices."[39]

Camp meeting songs were spread from Kentucky and Tennessee to the East Coast by men like the well-known revivalist Lorenzo Dow. He almost certainly carried copies of songbooks from Lexington, Kentucky, to North Carolina in 1804, where the songs were reprinted in other collections. Dow also published a collection of Granade's work on his second trip to England and Ireland, in 1805, where the camp songs became important to the hymnody of the English Primitive Methodist Church. Reverend Stith Mead, a Georgia Baptist who later moved to Virginia, also carried songs from the Kentucky camp meetings into eastern North Carolina; his *Hymns and Spiritual Songs* was printed in Richmond in 1807.[40] Kentucky and North Carolina printers brought out several early collections of camp meeting songs. The Kentucky collections included Starke DuPuy's *A Selection of Hymns and Sacred Songs* (Frankfort, 1811), and Silas Mercer Noel's *A Hymn Book* (Frankfort, 1814). The twenty-second edition of DuPuy's book appeared in 1841, and according to family historians, the book sold more than 100,000 copies.[41] Compilations known to have been printed in North Carolina included Elisha Battle, *A Collection of Hymns & Spiritual*

Songs, for Public and Family Worship (Raleigh, 1814); *A Choice Collection of Hymns and Spiritual Songs, Designed for the Use of the Pious in All Denominations* (New Bern, 1807); Salmon Hall, *A New Collection of the Most Approved Hymns and Spiritual Songs* (New Bern, 1804); David B. Mintz, *Collection of Hymns and Spiritual Songs, Mostly New* (New Bern, 1806) and *The Spiritual Song Book, Designed as an Assistant for the Pious of All Denominations* (Halifax, 1805). The Baptist preacher John Purify brought out *A Selection of Hymns and Spiritual Songs, in Two Parts* from Bell & Lawrence in Raleigh in 1823.

The popularity of these songs continued in later decades. Hinde's *Pilgrim's Songster* (1810) was issued in three editions of at least ten thousand copies by 1828; several editions were printed in Philadelphia and Baltimore. An early Methodist historian claimed that, although none of the songs in the book were "acceptable for worship" by mid-century, the book was treasured. Absalom Graves (1768–1836) published *Hymns, Psalms, and Spiritual Songs,* a collection of more than 250 songs "including some never before in print" in 1825 with a Frankfort, Kentucky, printer; he brought out a second edition four years later in Cincinnati. Matthew Gardner, a one-time Baptist who became a minister of the Christian Church in southern Ohio and northern Kentucky, also compiled a popular hymnbook. In 1821, he printed a thousand copies; three years later, he produced another three thousand copies, which sold for fifty cents each. He distributed them to what he called "book stores," likely small printing offices and general stores. "Where book stores would not buy, I left the books, with instructions to send them out by their agents, for country customers," he wrote, adding that he was always paid by the storekeepers, but that he lost some money from the preachers who never paid him. In 1826 he printed a third edition that was bound in Cincinnati. "It was not stereotyped, but each edition had to be reset, and the proofs read, and corrections made," he admitted. Three years later, there was a fourth edition of three thousand copies, adding up to more than ten thousand copies in print altogether. Surviving copies suggest that he worked with at least three different printers. The Presbyterian Thomas Cleland printed a collection called simply *Evangelical Hymns,* intended for "private, family, social, and public worship" from the Lexing-

A SELECTION

Elizabeth OF *Alston*

HYMNS

AND

SPIRITUAL SONGS,

IN TWO PARTS,

PART I. CONTAINING THE SONGS,
PART II. CONTAINING THE HYMNS,

DESIGNED FOR THE USE OF CONGREGATIONS.

BY JOHN PURIFY,

PASTOR OF THE BAPTIST CHURCH, AT THE CROSS ROADS
MEETING HOUSE, WAKE COUNTY, N. C.

" My inquiry has not been, whose songs and hymns
I shall choose ; but what songs and hymns ; and hence
it will be seen that Christians, of all denominations, may
sing side by side, and very often join in the same tri-
umph, using the same words ; and, when Christ has
been the subject of the song, we may say,
" *Let Europe and Asia resound*
With Africa, His fame ;
And thou, America, in songs,
Redeeming love proclaim."

Raleigh:

Printed by J. Gales & Son,
1831.

John Purify, *A Selection of Hymns and Spiritual Songs* (Raleigh, NC, 1831).
Courtesy of The Louis Round Wilson Special Collections Library, University of North Carolina at Chapel Hill.

ton press of T. T. Skillman in 1825. It included hymns by Watts, Newton, Cowper, Doddridge, and "several original" songs, selling for a dollar a copy. A third edition appeared in 1829.[42]

If thousands of printed pamphlets and books spread camp meeting songs from west to east, they also transmitted songs from the southern to the northern states. The Baptist John Leland, for example, who preached in Virginia from 1776 to 1791 before returning to New England, was a prolific songwriter whose work was well known to singers in the South. Five of his songs were included in Richard and Andrew Broaddus's early and influential *Collection of Sacred Ballads* (Richmond, 1790) and later circulated in New England. Collections produced in New Hampshire and Boston by Joshua Smith, Elias Smith, and Abner Jones in the two decades after 1790 brought many southern camp meeting songs north. Camp meeting songs spread to points north, east, and west, because of the explosive growth of Methodism, which began in the Upper South, and as itinerants spread, so did their camp meetings and songs. By 1810 camp meetings numbered in the hundreds, with one for virtually every Methodist circuit. By 1820 this number had grown to one thousand and, by 1843, there were at least seventeen Methodist camp meeting songbooks in print.[43]

Hymnbooks and Tunebooks

Protestants were just as likely to argue about singing as they were about religious doctrine in the early nineteenth century. Camp meeting songs sparked intense controversies, and like the songs, these controversies were set in type.[44] Those who were loyal to Anglo-American hymns argued that they were the only appropriate songs for worship, while others favored the popular tunes and informal texts of camp meeting songs. Some purists even maintained that the early modern practice of psalm singing, called "the Old Way," was the only song appropriate for worship services. "The divisions about Psalmody seem rather to increase, many have entirely quit coming to meeting," a weary Kentucky Presbyterian reported after years of debate.[45]

As the decades passed and congregations in towns and cities began to build splendid churches with velvet pew cushions, pianos, and choirs, camp meeting songs were regarded as too rough and undignified for solemn worship. "I love to hear the thrilling melodies of our churches well sung. They create within us feelings of love," Ann Speer wrote, suggesting that poor singing would do otherwise.[46] One writer lamented the "barbarous" language and "defective" rhymes that caused pain to discerning ears. A Methodist explained these were inappropriate for worship because they contained "the personal religious experience of the writer."[47] Yet, even as European music and choirs became popular, compilers continued to include at least a few songs that originated in the camp meeting tradition. They apologized for doing so, which suggests that those who profited from the lively hymnbook trade played to all sides.[48]

Hymnbooks also reflected doctrinal schisms. When a split occurred, such as between Methodists and Methodist Protestants, or between Primitive and Missionary Baptists, a new hymnbook nearly always marked the occasion. Primitive Baptists rejected polyphonic hymn singing accompanied by instruments, just as they scorned the mission societies and the Sunday schools held dear by Missionary Baptists. Their singing continued to rest on eighteenth-century Anglo-American hymnody. They revered Isaac Watts as one of the best of the "modern" hymn writers.[49] Benjamin Lloyd (1804–1860) of Alabama brought out a Primitive Baptist hymnbook in 1841 that remains in print and is still used by Black Primitive Baptists. Lloyd was a Georgia native, son of a farmer and slaveholder. After his conversion, he moved in 1834 with several other Primitive Baptists to Alabama. A man of energy and means, he became a merchant in LaFayette and a leader of the local Primitive Baptist congregation, later serving as a local official in Greenville, Alabama. He marketed his hymnbook in religious periodicals, including the *Primitive Baptist, Signs of the Times,* and the *Southern Baptist Messenger.* At his death, he directed his executors to continue publication of the hymnbook, which they did, from Texas and later from California.[50]

The first print run of Lloyd's hymnbook appeared in Wetumpka, Alabama, in 1841. The 1,500 copies included those in plain binding for $1 each, while morocco leather with gilt sold for $1.50. The book included 700 hymns, fifty-eight of which also appeared in Georgia Baptist Jesse

Mercer's *Cluster of Hymns and Spiritual Songs* (1810). Other sources included eighteenth-century British authors Watts, the Wesleys, Newton, Doddridge, and Cowper. A second edition, also about 1,500 copies printed in Wetumpka, appeared in 1843. In 1845 Lloyd brought out a revised third edition with a New York firm. He enlisted agents in Eastern Seaboard states and into the Trans-Mississippi to sell his books. Several competitors subsequently appeared as some claimed that Lloyd's selection slighted the doctrines of John Calvin.[51]

Those who compiled hymnbooks for the so-called Christian movement, known later as the Disciples of Christ, were also keen on policing doctrinal boundaries in their song. The earliest compilations in this tradition were camp meeting songbooks. Barton Stone, who preached at Cane Ridge and was recognized as a founder of the tradition, compiled *The Christian's Hymn Book* (Lexington, Kentucky, 1805), probably as a pamphlet. This was later enlarged as Stone's *Christian Hymn Book* (Dayton, Ohio, 1810). No copies of the first or second edition have survived, but the third edition included three hundred hymns, most of which were by Isaac Watts. When, in the 1830s, several groups came together to form the Disciples of Christ, their leaders immediately determined to produce a hymnbook that would "consolidate the union happily begun among us." The result, *Psalms, Hymns and Spiritual Songs* (Carthage, Ohio, 1835) became the core of song in that denomination for the rest of the century.[52]

Baptist and Methodist pastors from the southern states compiled scores of hymnbooks. At least thirty-six Baptist hymnbooks were produced in the South between 1790 and 1860; this figure does not include those that were printed in northern cities. Many went through several editions; some remained in print until the late nineteenth century. Some contained more than a thousand songs, and others numbered just a few hundred. Still others were printed initially as pamphlets, such as the work of Baptist Andrew Broaddus of Virginia, the *Collection of Sacred Ballads* (1790). Broaddus explained that his pamphlet was needed because many of the songs he included were circulating in manuscript copies. "Many persons who are desirous of having them; and have not time and opportunity to write them, are necessitated to go without. Also, the many errors common in most of the written ballads have been cause of grief to divers well wishers to religion," he wrote. In 1844 fifteen-year-old Jennie Speer copied lines from Broaddus's "O for Sanctifying Grace" in her journal. The theme of this piece—"For love's refining fire, / Lord, we beg for Jesus' sake, / A sweet refreshing shower"—resonated with the doctrines of Holiness Methodism she would later embrace.[53]

One especially influential Baptist compilation was the quaintly named *Cluster of Spiritual Songs, Divine Hymns and Social Poems*. Compiled by Georgian Jesse Mercer, it first appeared as a small pamphlet from an Augusta printer in 1817. Mercer enlisted William W. Woodward of Philadelphia to print a second edition. Woodward recruited at least forty-seven ministers—Presbyterians, Congregationalists, Baptists, and Methodists—to sell his books between 1800 and 1825; many of these were in rural Virginia, Kentucky, Alabama, and Tennessee. "I received a letter from Mr. Jesse Mercer a few days past informing me that he had left in your hands a number of his hymnbooks & that by writing to you, I might procure as many as I could dispose of in our parts," a Baptist wrote to Woodward from Virginia in 1817. "I can probably dispose of 100 copies & should be glad if you would pack up in a box about that number. . . . Mr. Mercer has said nothing about the place or mode of payment. He has probably informed you. If I am to send you the money you will signify it by letter & the mode. If I hear nothing from you I shall send the money to Georgia."[54]

Mercer worked closely with Woodward through the 1820s, advising him in much the same way as Mason Locke Weems worked with Philadelphia printer Matthew Carey. Heavy and expensive books would not sell well, Mercer warned Woodward, although he was able to collect some subscriptions for more elaborate productions. "I find the book business to be *slow* in this state, except small pieces and periodic works, or *song books*," he emphasized from Powelton, Georgia, in 1823. "The *Cluster* has a rapid sale, and the demand is increasing. I am told in S.C., N.C. and even in Va and Alabama, and Mississippi it is frequently inquired after. What will you give for copy-Right? or [for] what will you publish another edition of 10,000? or what share will you allow me of that number?"[55]

The *Cluster* was offered in several bindings, ranging from plain cloth to gilt to calf leather. In the early 1820s, prices went from seventy-five cents for plain cloth to $2.25 for the morocco leather binding.[56] About 2,500 copies were printed in the first Augusta edition, while later that year 2,500 copies of a revised edition were printed in Philadelphia (likely by Woodward), where Mercer traveled to attend the Baptist General Convention. Later editions appeared in 1820, 1826, and 1835. The 1835 "corrected and enlarged" edition was the last one produced during Mercer's lifetime. An 1835 Philadelphia imprint of Charles de Silver & Sons lists eleven firms in ten states that sold the *Cluster*. These wholesale booksellers distributed copies from Boston to Savannah, and west to Cincinnati, Ohio. In 1829 one publisher claimed that there were more than 33,000 copies of the *Cluster* in print.[57]

The *Cluster* included hymns from several sources; at least seventeen had appeared in Richard Allen's *Collection of Spiritual Songs and Hymns*. Mercer included works by Isaac Watts, John and Charles Wesley, Joseph Hart, Selina Shirley, John Newton, and the English Baptist John Rippon. His 1823 edition contained twenty-three hymns written by women and one by the Native American Samson Occom. Mercer wrote five of the hymns himself.[58] The *Cluster* was credited as an important source for three shape-note tunebooks — William Walker's *Southern Harmony* (New Haven, Connecticut, 1835), the *Sacred Harp* (Philadelphia, 1844), and the *Social Harp* (Philadelphia, 1855). The collection's popularity began to wane at mid-century, although it remained in print until 1875. As late as 1885, black Georgia Baptists sang "an old familiar hymn" from the book at a church gathering.[59]

Shape-note tunebooks began to be printed in the 1830s. The origins of shape-note singing, sometimes known as "Sacred Harp singing," lay in tunebooks. These were differentiated from songbooks and hymnbooks, which could be tucked into a pocket; they were large oblong books that featured a single tune and text on each page. Invented by a Philadelphian in 1798, the shape-note system featured notes as separate shapes — triangles and squares, for example — and singers learned to associate a tone with each one. The books were used in "singing schools" taught by itinerant singing masters, who earned fees for several sessions of instruction and a copy of the book. Ananias Davisson, a Shenandoah Valley printer, saw his *Kentucky Harmony* (Harrisonburg, Virginia, 1816) and *Supplement to the Kentucky Harmony* (Harrisonburg, Virginia, 1820) gain wide influence among later compilers. Davisson's work opened the "Southern age" of composer-compilers, which lasted until mid-century, when four-note tunebooks began to be replaced by a seven-note system.[60]

Itinerant singing masters dispersed across the country on roads that were already crowded with revivalists and preachers, book agents, and peddlers of all kinds. Like itinerant grammarians, these men sold their skills along with their books. "Hundreds of the country idlers, too lazy or too stupid for farmer or mechanics, 'go to singing school for a spell,' get diplomas from others scarcely better qualified than themselves," a writer complained in 1848, "and then with their brethren, the far famed 'Yankee Peddlars,' itinerate to all parts of the land, to corrupt the taste and pervert the judgement of the unfortunate people who, for want of a better, have to put up with them." The compiler of the *Sacred Harp*, South Carolinian Benjamin Franklin White, was one of those singing masters. His tunebook, and many others, helped make what was known as "social singing," in the words of one historian, "a fever" before the Civil War.[61]

Shape-note tunebooks trained amateur singers to read musical notation. Before the early eighteenth century, this was rare even for instrumentalists; tunes were simply memorized. Singers were instructed to sing texts "to the tune of . . ." by congregational leaders. Innovations in printing made systems of musical notation easier to reproduce, and by the mid-1840s, printed sheet music, pianos, organs, and choirs began to appear even in rural congregations. Printed notation encouraged the standardization of tunes and texts by mid-century.[62] Most of those compiled by southerners were printed on presses in the Upper South, the Ohio Valley, or Philadelphia. Of forty-one tunebooks compiled by twenty-five men in the southern states between 1816 and 1860, twenty-six were produced on presses in Virginia, Tennessee, Maryland, and Kentucky. The remaining fifteen titles were printed in Cincinnati and Philadelphia. Remarkably, tunebooks continue to be discovered and so it is not possible to say that any such list is definitive.[63]

William Walker (1809–1875), who worked for many years as a book-

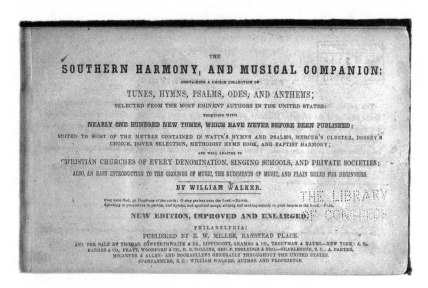

William Walker, *Southern Harmony and Musical Companion,* rev. ed. (Philadelphia, 1847). Courtesy of Library of Congress.

seller in Spartanburg, South Carolina, compiled three separate tunebooks, including his *Southern Harmony,* which became the most popular of all tunebooks among southern singers before the Civil War. Although no exact figures survive, it appeared in at least five editions between 1835 and 1854. One of his publishers claimed to have sold 600,000 copies. He produced the first edition in Connecticut, but quickly moved to a Philadelphia firm. His book's long title was typical of the era, as he tried to lure buyers by showing the familiarity of his songs: "The Southern Harmony, and musical companion : containing a choice collection of tunes, hymns, psalms, odes, and anthems : selected from the most eminent authors in the United States : together with nearly one hundred new tunes, which have never before been published ; suited to most of the metres contained in Watts's hymns and psalms, Mercer's cluster, Dossey's choice, Dover selection, Methodist hymn book, and Baptist harmony ; and well adapted to Christian churches of every denomination, singing schools, and private societies : also, an easy introduction to the grounds of music, the rudiments of music, and plain rules for beginners by William Walker." Walker also included some original songs. He was a legendary figure by his death in 1875; stories attested that his last words were a hymn by Watts and that a white dove flew into his coffin.[64]

Print was crucial to the creation and transmission of the traditional repertory of black and white sacred music in the South. The sale of tens of thousands, and even hundreds of thousands, of pamphlets and books in the southern states shows that an indigenous tradition of sacred song flourished long before the arrival of Yankee singing masters, and it offers a tantalizing glimpse of how enthusiastically compilers, authors, and printers responded to the demands of their customers. This repertory bore the creative imprint of black and white, literate and illiterate singers, along with the great hymn writers of the Anglo-American tradition. Much of this music circulated in print before it entered the oral tradition.

Black Primitive Baptists, who still use Benjamin Lloyd's 1841 hymnal, *The Primitive Hymns,* continue to sing scores of sacred songs like those first printed in Jesse Mercer's *Cluster of Spiritual Songs*—a mix of African American spirituals and favorites from Anglo-American hymnody by composers such as Isaac Watts, the Wesleys, and John Newton. For singers in the southern states, then, print was what it has been for people ever since the fifteenth century, a vessel of cultural memory and a source of remarkable creativity.

FIVE

Stories

April the 17th — half after five in the evening — it has been a steady wet day.
I have been reading Eugene Aram all day long.
— Betsy Cooley

IN THE SPRING AND FALL OF 1842, Amanda and Betsy Cooley read a spate of English novels. Amanda was twenty-two and Betsy was seventeen. Betsy mentioned two authors by name, Edward Bulwer-Lytton and Frederick Marryat. She seems to have loved them, as she read three of Bulwer-Lytton's novels — *Eugene Aram* (1832), *The Pilgrims of the Rhine* (1834), and *Rienzi* (1835) — in rapid succession. "I have employed myself reading the pilgrim of the Rhine it has some very interesting pieces in it," she wrote.[1]

Edward Bulwer-Lytton (1803–1873) was one of the most popular writers of the Victorian era. Multiple editions of his work were published in New York, Philadelphia, Paris, Brussels, Frankfurt, and Stuttgart. His sales rivaled those of Dickens. Revered as one of the most distinguished men of the time, he lies buried in Poet's Corner in Westminster Abbey. His books made him rich; he was known as a ruthless negotiator with publishers and editors.[2] Yet even such a man might have had difficulty envisioning his book in the hands of a young weaver in the Blue Ridge. Betsy's prosaic days were lived, as she herself said, estranged from the "poetical sentiments" his novels inspired in her. Born and raised on Coal Creek, she had never traveled farther than the next county, yet her reading seemed to spark something new in her. "I feel as I have read today that I have many Poetical sentiments but have not language to express them," she wrote. "I have ever desired to see Towns & Rivers and people."[3] She, like other provincial readers, felt the gap between her life and what she read yawn ever wider.

This distance could be measured not only across space, but also across time. Page after page declared that rural readers were somehow living behind the times, cut off from the places where history was being made and progress was being accomplished. The year before Betsy read Bulwer-Lytton, a Methodist editor looked out of his office at the corner of Eighth and Main Streets in Cincinnati and made readers like her disappear. The Reverend Leonidas Hamline was writing an essay for the first issue of his new magazine, the *Ladies Repository and Gatherings of the West,* which was intended primarily as a Protestant alternative to *Godey's Lady's Book.* Readers of the first issue learned the fate of Portuguese emperors and teetered on the brink of new scientific discoveries; they considered solemn poems about graveyards and how old letters spoke of a "world of sweet remembrance."[4] People subscribed in droves, up to forty thousand of them by the end of the journal's first decade alone, and the *Repository* became one of the most enduring and popular magazines of the period.

Hamline was enthusiastic about how his magazine would fill the needs of a new generation of women. "Time breeds revolutions," he wrote. "It has wonderfully changed the domestic habits of females, making some of their ancient and honorable callings obsolete," including spinning and weaving. The "labor of the wheel and loom suddenly changed hands," Hamline explained, "leaving nothing for the domestic needle except the light affair of caps and collars." Hamline had in mind, of course, the red brick mills being raised in the north of England and across the United States, floor after floor roaring with clattering power looms. Freed from the demand of making homespun to clothe their families, Hamline thought, women could toil for "ornaments of mind." And with that, he dispatched the daily labor of artisan readers like Betsy Cooley with a few strokes of his pen.[5]

Hamline's perspective was typical of writers at the time, whose ideology of progress nearly always outran the actual pace of change. The times were more complicated than he imagined. Amanda and Betsy routinely purchased machine-made cloth, lace, and ribbons for their dresses and handmade bonnets at the local mercantile even as they plied their shuttles to weave linsey-woolsey and jean, and sewed their counterpanes. Power looms did not yet rule the day nor did all women enjoy the leisure of the "light affair of caps and collars." Hamline was among the legion of writers and editors who overestimated the pace of change in part because of the story of their own lives. Hamline had trained himself up and out of the fields by his reading, first for the Presbyterian ministry, then for the bar, and finally for the Methodists, who eventually made him a bishop. He had no reason to be reticent about the power of the printed page to change the world.[6]

Nor did Sarah Josepha Hale, who edited *Godey's Lady's Book* from Philadelphia. The Cooleys subscribed to *Godey's*, carefully stitching the issues together for safekeeping. Like rural readers across the country, through the pages of Hale's magazine they became familiar with the manners, values, neighborhoods, merchants, and even street addresses in cities they would never see. By the 1840s, they regularly read about a world very different from the one they woke up to every morning. Images of world capitals, the South Seas, and exotic lands of all kinds were woven into their imaginations to reframe their sense of what their own lives meant. In early 1852, Amanda Cooley paid four dollars to renew her subscription to *Godey's Lady's Book* and to subscribe to *Graham's Magazine*. She opened the July issue of *Graham's* to find a review of Nathaniel Hawthorne's new novel, *Blithedale Romance,* a poem about Cleopatra, and stories about the Aztecs, Greeks, and Israelites. On page 7, she found an illustrated account of steam presses at R. Hoe & Company of New York City. The writer marveled again and again at the brilliance of the "splendid machines," which he measured mainly by their speed and size. "The great and fast printing eight-cylinder machine" was "33 feet long, 14 feet 8 inches high and 6 feet wide." No fewer than eight people were required to feed 2,400 sheets of paper into each of its eight cylinders to produce 20,000 impressions per hour.[7]

Printing presses kept time in the nineteenth century. Print reshaped readers' sensibilities of past, present, and future, plotting them on the landscape of a nation divided between plodding countryside and galloping cities. It compelled rural readers to marvel at the pace of change and progress in other places. In a century that seemed to be overrun with revolutions of all kinds — communications, politics, industry, and transport — readers in the Blue Ridge were told to anticipate change, to embrace it, to herald it. Yet Betsy Cooley did not wake up one morning to find a revolution on her doorstep. Change proceeded more slowly than it was portrayed in print, particularly outside the cities. Change was not always welcome — it could come in the form of financial misfortune, disfiguring illness, or death. The life of an unmarried woman was completely changed by the death of her father; the life of a slave was upended by the death of a master.

People in rural communities did not so much resist change as embrace it warily. Most were fascinated, if unsettled, by the progress described in their magazines and newspapers. Writers and editors conjured up a glorious past and hailed the future, sometimes in the same paragraph, in places miles or oceans away from where readers like the Cooleys lived. Print encouraged readers to look back — to Milton and Shakespeare, to Rome and Egypt, to Michelangelo and Alexander Pope — to find brilliance in what people had made and thought. Steam presses churned out thousands of impressions an hour, reproducing poetry and prose written hundreds of years earlier. The books printed in the nineteenth century, like those first printed by Gutenberg, made old stories accessible to a far greater number of people, introducing new generations of American readers to tales beyond memory and classic texts written in first-century Rome or seventeenth-century England.[8]

Chapbooks and Almanacs

Bulwer-Lytton's sentimental stories arrived in a mountain region that was already rich in stories. Native American tales mingled with those brought by slaves and settlers with roots in the British Isles or the Continent. By the nineteenth century, these stories could travel equally well by spoken word and through print; many circulated in print even before entering the oral tradition.

In North America, almanacs, pamphlets, and newspapers generally took the place of the chapbooks that circulated stories in Britain and

Europe, but the chapbook form was well-known to American readers.[9] In the colonial period, imported chapbooks were so cheap and plentiful that few local printers bothered to produce them. Daniel Drake's family took a copy of *The Famous History of Montelion, Knight of the Oracle,* a chapbook of a seventeenth-century romance, when they left New Jersey for Kentucky in 1788. Joseph Doddridge reported that, in western Virginia in the late eighteenth century, young people told one another "dramatic narrations" that were "chiefly concerning Jack and the giant. Many of these stories were tales of knight errantry, in which some captive virgin was released from captivity and restored to her lover." Stories of Robin Hood and English ballads that told tragic tales of love and murder circulated widely in the mountains. These were committed to memory and handed down from generation to generation.[10] Readers in Orange County, North Carolina, bought scores of these "small histories," imported from Glasgow before the revolution.[11] These recounted tales of Robinson Crusoe, Valentine and Orson, Reynard the Fox, and Don Quixote, and drew from *Aesop's Fables,* the *Arabian Nights,* and the *Lilliputian Magazine.* Crusoe was particularly well known. William H. Robinson, a slave born in 1848, took the name of Robinson after his father, who knew the tale well.[12]

Chapbooks continued to circulate into the nineteenth century. Readers in Wythe County, Virginia, could choose from dozens on sale at Trigg's store in the early nineteenth century.[13] The works of Mason Locke Weems, the famous itinerant parson-bookseller who wrote the legend of Washington and the cherry tree, were issued as chapbooks. At least two Philadelphia printers with regular custom in the southern states produced chapbooks—Benjamin Warner and Matthew Carey.[14] The genre survived primarily in the United States as children's literature, which included the publications of the American Sunday School Union.

Readers like the Cooleys also reveled in a rich oral tradition. Tall tales, fables, and jokes circulated freely. Travelers brought stories of places and people from the road, and some tales had been handed down for so long that their origins were unknown. Old Scratch, the devil, was a favorite character, as were witches and thieves. Jennie and Ann Speer grew up relishing the stories of the revolution told by their grandmother, who was twelve years old when the war began. The family routinely gathered by the fireside to hear her "old legends of other days or the daring of some gallant patriot." Their aunt Nancy Speer, who lost her eyesight in her twenties and who lived with them, was known for her stories of early explorers and settlers in the mountains.[15]

Stories that circulated in print entered the oral tradition and were repeated even by those who could not read. This generation learned Captain Frederick Marryat's tales of mutinies and maritime battles and Lydia Sigourney's rendering of Pocahontas as a "Forest-child, amid flowers at play!"[16] Stories from *Tom Jones, The Vicar of Wakefield, Don Quixote, Robinson Crusoe,* the *Arabian Nights,* and others had a long history of circulation. In the early 1830s, copies of *Robinson Crusoe* and *Don Quixote* were available in western Missouri. Readers in northern Alabama in the early 1810s owned copies of British gothic novels by Jane Porter, Elizabeth Hamilton, Sarah Green, and Regina Maria Roche. In the 1820s, readers in Florida could purchase or borrow fiction including *Mysteries of Udolpho* by Ann Radcliffe, *Thaddeus of Warsaw* by Jane Porter, *Robinson Crusoe, Arabian Nights,* and *Kelroy,* a gothic novel by Rebecca Rush. Other popular stories included *Aesop's Fables* and works by Tobias Smollett, Samuel Richardson, Henry Fielding, Maria Edgeworth, and the ubiquitous Walter Scott. Such books were things of wonder to illiterate people, who would thumb through them for the illustrations.[17]

If books were out of reach for many people, almanacs were the "most despised, most prolific, most indispensable of books which every man uses and no man praises" in the nineteenth century.[18] Almanacs were the single most common reading material in many households other than the Bible. Those who read nothing else, or even could not read at all, learned to decipher the phases of the moon, and the times for sunrise and sunset. Usually costing between five and ten cents, almanacs were rough pamphlets that were handled by all sorts of people. They used them to set the time according to the sun, as every town set its own time in the nineteenth century. They were also used as daybooks or diaries. A Georgia farmer recorded the weather and his planting schedule in pencil on pages he inserted into the almanac. "Rained all night . . . Began to plant corn . . . Peach trees in full bloom," he wrote in March of 1848.[19] William Ellery Channing's poem "The Wanderer" (1871) included a stanza that described the lowly almanac and its readers.

> Books to them
> Are the faint dreams of students, save that one—
> The battered Almanac,—split to the core,
> Fly-blown, and tattered, that above the fire
> Devoted smokes, and furnishes the fates,
> And perigees and apogees of moons.

Almanacs were an ancient form; the origin of the name is obscure, although it is rumored to have been derived from a Spanish-Arabic term meaning "to reckon." Usually ranging from twenty-four to forty-eight pages, stitched into a standard pamphlet form, they included a calendar with the times of sunrise and sunset as well as phases of the moon, tide tables, weather forecasts, planting dates, and facts, proverbs, and home remedies. Large printing offices that established regular publication of a newspaper began issuing almanacs soon afterwards, suggesting their profitability.[20] They were published with specific calculations for particular cities. People known as philomaths, who often worked as teachers or surveyors, made the necessary calculations based on the stars. The calendar for the *Kentucky Farmer's Almanac for 1846* was calculated by Samuel D. M'Cullough, A.M.[21] *The Christian Farmer's Almanack for 1829* was typical in its expansive claim to be "calculated for the meridian of Cincinnati, and will serve, with very little variation, for all the Western States."[22] In addition to those printed by commercial firms, a profusion of specialized almanacs were printed on behalf of state agricultural societies, political parties, Protestant reform organizations, and Catholic laypeople. There were almanacs devoted to temperance, humor, Whig and Democratic politics, phrenology, anti-Masonic polemics, music, fishing, and mechanics.

Almanacs also served as rough schoolbooks and even miniature encyclopedias. They offered essays, fables, poetry, anecdotes, important news, random statistics, medical advice, and jokes, riddles, proverbs, and para-

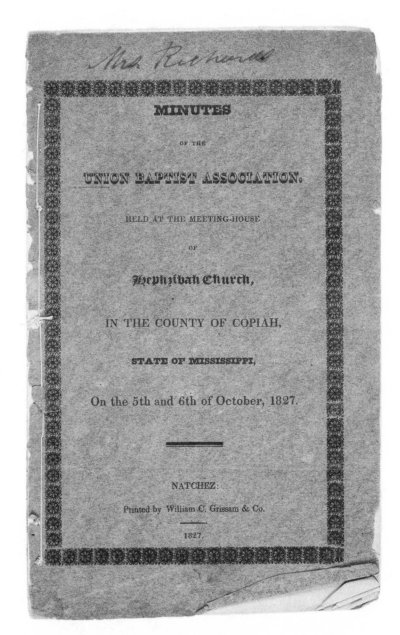

MINUTES

OF THE

UNION BAPTIST ASSOCIATION,

HELD AT THE MEETING-HOUSE

OF

Hephzibah Church,

IN THE COUNTY OF COPIAH,

STATE OF MISSISSIPPI,

On the 5th and 6th of October, 1827.

NATCHEZ:

Printed by William C. Grissam & Co.

1827.

Union Baptist Association *Minutes,* Copiah County, Mississippi (Natchez, MS, 1827). Courtesy of American Antiquarian Society.

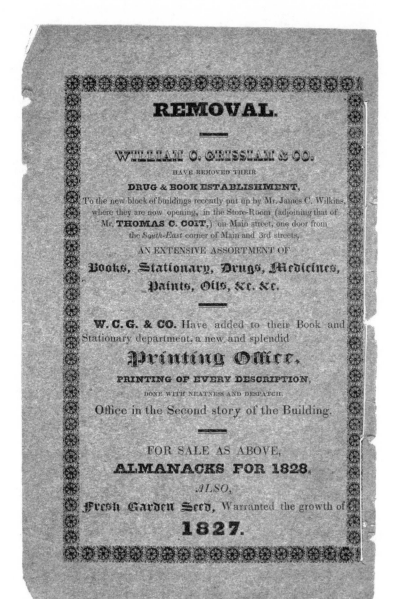

REMOVAL.

WILLIAM C. GRISSAM & CO.

HAVE REMOVED THEIR

DRUG & BOOK ESTABLISHMENT,

To the new block of buildings recently put up by Mr. James C. Wilkins,
where they are now opening, in the Store-Room (adjoining that of
Mr. **THOMAS C. COIT,**) on Main street, one door from
the *South-East* corner of Main and 3rd streets,

AN EXTENSIVE ASSORTMENT OF

Books, Stationary, Drugs, Medicines,

Paints, Oils, &c. &c.

W. C. G. & CO. Have added to their Book and
Stationary department, a new and splendid

Printing Office,

PRINTING OF EVERY DESCRIPTION,

DONE WITH NEATNESS AND DESPATCH.

Office in the Second story of the Building.

FOR SALE AS ABOVE,

ALMANACKS FOR 1828.

ALSO,

Fresh Garden Seed, Warranted the growth of

1827.

Back cover, Union Baptist Association *Minutes,* Copiah County, Mississippi
(Natchez, MS, 1827), with advertisement for almanacs. Courtesy of American Antiquarian Society.

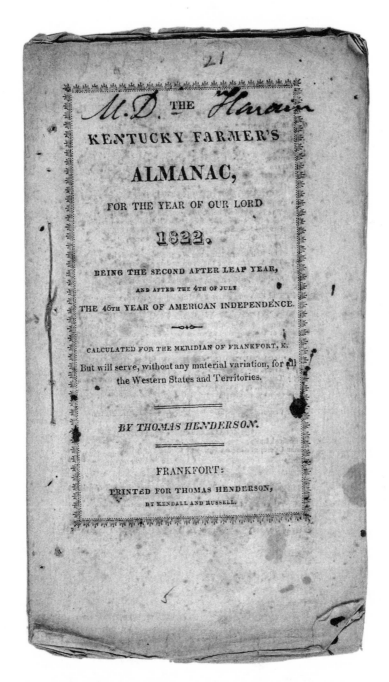

The Kentucky Farmer's Almanac (Frankfort, KY, 1822). Courtesy of American Antiquarian Society.

Back cover, *The Kentucky Farmer's Almanac* (Frankfort, KY, 1822), with advertisement for books on sale at the printer's office. Courtesy of American Antiquarian Society.

doxes, reprinted from elsewhere. Readers of *The Franklin Almanac for 1821*, printed in Richmond, Virginia, found an entire page devoted to enigmas, rebuses, and charades, some of which were attributed to writers in England. "Question by Mr. O'Conner, New-York. A heavy ball dropping into a hyperboloidal cup, filled with water, discharged the greatest possible quantity; the transverse axis of the cup's generating curve was eight inches, and the distance between its focus and centre, which was equal to the cup's perpendicular altitude, was five inches; required, the ball's diameter?"[23] In another almanac, readers found proverbs such as "rebel not against the dictates of reason" and "meditation is the fountain of discourse" printed in the margins. S. S. Steele's *Louisiana Almanac for 1845* included a "Calendar of Useful Knowledge" on topics ranging from American history to agriculture to the arts and sciences. Steele lured buyers in a crowded field by offering "an immense amount" of information that he claimed was "valuable to every citizen of North America."[24]

Almanacs were also sources of popular poetry, including ditties, simple quatrains describing the changing seasons, and more elaborate productions. Many poems, like those printed in newspapers, appeared without attribution. Named authors included Shakespeare, Wordsworth, and Milton, along with many lesser-known writers. Advertisers competed for coveted space in these modest books; back covers often featured full-page ads for books. The *Kentucky Farmers' Almanac for 1846*, published by Charles Marshall of Lexington, Kentucky, included a particularly elaborate advertisement featuring a fourteen-page list of books, periodicals, Bibles, musical instruments, paper, quills, pocket and blank account books, and wallpaper for sale at his Main Street store. The back cover of the *Western and Southern Almanac of 1847*, published by G. H. Monsarrat of Louisville at the Baptist Publication Depot, featured advertisements for nine Baptist newspapers and bookstores in Mobile, Alabama, and Richmond, Virginia. The Baptists were apparently happy to return such favors. The Union Baptist Association of Copiah County, Mississippi, advertised the local Natchez printer's almanac on the back cover of their association minutes for 1827.[25]

English Novels in the Blue Ridge

With the exception of the phrase "It was a dark and stormy night," little of Edward Bulwer-Lytton's oeuvre outlived him. During his lifetime, Bulwer-Lytton was loathed by two different types of critics. Writers like Edgar Allan Poe found his work to be woefully lacking in artistic merit.[26] A second group was quite certain that he and his ilk would destroy the morals of the nation. Daniel Webster famously blamed Bulwer-Lytton for endowing "vice with attraction."[27]

Webster was probably thinking of the novel that Betsy read in the spring of 1842, *Eugene Aram.* One of the novels in the Newgate school—named after the notorious eighteenth-century London prison—it told the story of a man who was hanged for the murder of his best friend. Bulwer-Lytton was one of a host of nineteenth-century writers who made readers spectators to horrific crimes. He argued that his plots were on the side of bourgeois morality because they demonstrated that crime destroyed the finest minds and characters, but his critics were not persuaded, possibly because of what the author himself said. "The element of the highest genius is not among the village gossips of Miss Austen," he scoffed, "it is in crime and passion, for the two are linked together."[28]

In the age of the steam press, fears about the propriety of reading were voiced across the country. Some bewailed their own habits, like the young Alabama Baptist who thought of his novel reading as a kind of lust, and agonized in his diary over his sinfulness and shame.[29] Young women were thought to be particularly subject to overwrought emotional reactions to fiction. Teachers and parents alike took up the cry. "Novel Reading a Cause of Female Depravity," warned one editor.[30] Humor was also dangerous. "Throw away all those books written in a low and corrupt style," one professor commanded. "The letters of Sam Slick and Jack Downing are specimens of this style."[31]

Jennie Speer was a vigilant reader, patrolling her emotions and actions, always fixing the boundaries of propriety. One afternoon, she sank into a doorframe, absorbed in a well-known literary magazine. But some unnamed temptation troubled her enough that she rose in disgust and cast it aside, taking the time to record the incident and vowing never to read such trifles again. The first essay she submitted for publication in a Methodist newspaper condemned such reading.

Jennie found models for such vigilance in her reading. In the spring of 1844, she read the life story of a "great and good woman," the Baptist missionary Harriet Newell. "I have found great encouragement from her writings, and my [prayer] is that I may imitate her in virtue and usefulness."[32] Newell died at the age of nineteen in November 1812, a few months after sailing for India with her new husband and the well-known missionary couple Adoniram and Ann Hasseltine Judson. Like the Judsons, she was celebrated by several generations, who even named their children after early missionaries. Newell's fame rested on printed copies of the sermon preached in her memory by the Rev. Leonard Woods in Haverhill, Massachusetts, and on her memoir, which appeared in multiple editions on both sides of the Atlantic—in London, New York, Cincinnati, Dublin, Edinburgh, and Derby. A French translation appeared in 1835. Newell's story was first printed by the American Tract Society in 1813 and, by the 1830s, an edition was available from the American Sunday School Union, with a frontispiece showing a slight and sober young woman. Her story was also recounted in countless magazine and newspaper articles.

Born in Haverhill, Massachusetts, in 1793, Newell experienced a conversion at the age of thirteen, and spent much of her life worrying that she was not sufficiently "improving the time," a phrase known to all the faithful. One of the best ways to do this, she explained, was through reading, which she mentioned on nearly every page. After her conversion, she was sent to school. There, her religious enthusiasm waned, a development mirrored in her reading habits, she said. "My Bible, once so lovely, was entirely neglected. Novels and romances engaged my thoughts, and hour after hour was foolishly and sinfully spent in perusal of them."[33]

Many deemed the hysterical tone taken by critics of gothic novels to be disproportionate to the threat.[34] The Cooley sisters seemed unconcerned with the dangers of fiction. They appeared to revel in Bulwer-Lytton's ghastly adventures. *Eugene Aram* was one of Lytton's most consistently popular books during his lifetime. The novel was based on the life of a Yorkshire philologist (1704–1759), a self-taught scholar. In 1758, while working on an Anglo-Celtic lexicon, Eugene Aram was arrested and hanged for the murder, fourteen years previous, of a friend named Daniel Clark. The episode became infamous in the early nineteenth century through a poem by Thomas Hood, "The Dream of Eugene Aram," and later through Bulwer-Lytton's novel. Aram confesses to the murder in the book's penultimate chapter, although his great love Madeleine, the embodiment of a pure Victorian heroine, dies still believing in Aram's innocence.[35]

Among southern readers, a consensus never emerged against the dangers of fiction. Instead, many applauded the potential of fiction to promote taste, piety, and morals. Readers in Richmond borrowed Walter Scott's Waverley novels from one another and from private libraries and apparently devoured them enthusiastically; it is well known that Scott's reputation in the southern states was unsurpassed by that of any other author.[36] Sunday school tracts and religious magazines freely used fiction to promote Christian piety. Explicitly Christian novels began to appear by mid-century, many of them written by women. George Boardman Taylor, a Virginia Baptist pastor, wrote several novels in the 1860s that were published in New York, Boston, and Philadelphia, by the American Baptist Publication Society (ABPS) and other firms. By the final decades of the century, the ABPS had produced scores of fictional titles. The Southern Baptist Publication Society, too, produced fiction, such as Virginian Sallie Hughes's moralistic second novel *Lucy Hall; or, Responsibility Realized* (1860), which relates how Lucy was convicted of her sins and baptized, then evangelized her friend Janie.[37]

Fiction in Periodicals

How did readers like Betsy Cooley decide which novels to read? Where did they find them?[38] Advertisements from publishing firms listed many titles in the magazines and newspapers the Cooleys read from Philadelphia and New York. Betsy may have ordered those she fancied through the mail. In the late 1850s the Speers' neighbor Strong Thomasson read no fewer than twenty different periodicals (some of which he subscribed to). After reading a review of Washington Irving's three-volume *Life of Washington,* he determined to acquire it, although it is not clear whether he ever did.[39] Notices of new books also regularly appeared in other books. Betsy may have found an appealing novel in her local mercantile, although such establishments primarily stocked steady sellers such as schoolbooks and religious works. She may have bought books from one of the book peddlers who frequented the Cooley farm or borrowed them from a friend.

It is impossible to identify precisely which editions the Cooley sisters read. Multiple editions of Bulwer-Lytton and Frederick Marryat, many of them pirated, appeared on both sides of the Atlantic. Elizabeth breezed through three titles by Bulwer-Lytton that were originally published in the 1830s. She may have read them in a two-volume set from a Boston publisher, which appeared in 1837.[40] It is more likely that she read inexpensive books produced from stereotype plates owned by Harper & Brothers of New York. Harper's signed a formal agreement with Bulwer-Lytton in 1835 to stereotype all his works, telling him that "in this country your name is a tower of strength."[41] This was unusual. International copyright did not exist until 1891, and nearly all foreign works published before that time ignored the authors' rights to profit from the sale of their work. Pirating was standard practice among American publishing firms, especially because it made it more attractive to take financial risks on foreign authors, rather than on domestic writers, who had to be paid.

The Cooleys read Bulwer-Lytton at a propitious moment for fiction in the Anglo-American world. The depression of 1837–1843 was a watershed for the American book trade. In the estimation of one scholar, no other event in the nineteenth century was so influential.[42] Technological change, economic depression, and reader demand converged to produce a riotous spirit of competition among New York publishers in the early 1840s. This rivalry made fiction available more cheaply and in greater quantity than ever before, at the very moment that Betsy was enjoying Bulwer-Lytton's novels.

One Sunday morning, Betsy stayed home from church meeting. "Jan 29 1843. This day James went to meeting. I could have went if I had wished it—but it was cold and I had some newspapers I wished to peruse—the *Western Missouri* and *Brother Jonathan.*"[43] The Cooleys regularly read

Missouri newspapers sent by their relatives through the mail. *Brother Jonathan*, the other paper that engaged Betsy, was for a brief time one of the best-known productions of the American press. Along with its chief rival the *New World*, *Brother Jonathan* was known as a "story paper" because it published entire novels in double columns, and it could be bought for pennies. Such a format would "carry them farther than any old-fashioned bookselling machinery possibly could," the editor of the *New World* declared.[44] The name "Brother Jonathan" was taken from a widely known revolutionary folk hero; this first "Yankee" was "an out-at-elbows New England country boy" who eventually adopted the costume that became known as Uncle Sam.[45]

Weeklies such as *Brother Jonathan* and the *New World* competed fiercely for fiction readers with books published by Harper & Brothers of New York, which was emerging as the premier publishing house in the country. A writer at the *New York Herald* darkly predicted in March 1843 that this "terrible contest" would lead to three results: "First, the ruin of all publishers; second, the fortunes of all vendors in the large cities; and third, the spread of literary taste among the people."[46] The previous November, the editors of *Brother Jonathan* had placed an announcement in the pages of what may have been the very issue that kept Betsy home from church. "Dickens's *American Notes* came on the Great Western on Sunday Evening, according to promise and the announcement of the work for republication naturally excited great curiosity. During Monday thousands of copies were printed in Extra Brother Jonathans and circulated throughout the city."[47] Steamships were crucial to the piracy of British texts like Dickens's. The trick worked like this: an agent in London procured a book immediately on publication and rushed it to Liverpool, where it was put on board the Great Western steamship. The new regular steamship service from Liverpool to New York cut the travel time across the Atlantic from one or two months to only two weeks.[48] In New York, even before it was tied up at the docks, the ship was boarded by agents who rushed the books to typesetters. With the typesetters working day and night, pirated novels could begin printing within twenty-four hours of their arrival in port.

Brother Jonathan appeared in a variety of formats as part of a complex scheme to catch the attention of American readers by the late 1840s, includ-

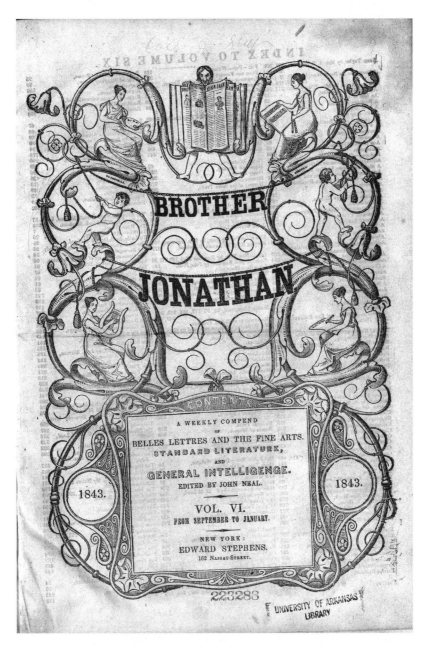

Brother Jonathan, A Weekly Compendium of Belles Lettres and the Fine Arts, Standard Literature, and General Intelligence (New York, 1843). Courtesy of Special Collections, University of Arkansas Libraries, Fayetteville.

ing a weekly and semiannual illustrated special numbers for Christmas and the Fourth of July. In addition, the "Brother Jonathan Monthly Library" produced novels in pamphlet format, printed in double columns. These unbound "extras" could be sent through the mail at the cheap newspaper rate. In 1841 the *New World* brought out its first extra edition of Charles Lever's *Charles O'Malley*, which sold for fifty cents. *Brother Jonathan* answered by bringing out the same novel for twenty-five cents. Harper's and other publishers had long printed novels bound in cloth for a dollar, but these were still too dear for many readers. As the story papers undersold these books, they drove down the cost of novels to as little as six cents each. The success of pamphlet novels forced Harper & Brothers to slash the price of some titles in their "Library of Select Fiction" to twelve and a half cents each, while volumes in "The Harper's Family Library" in brown paper covers sold for twenty-five cents each.[49] Betsy Cooley generally sold her white linsey for between twenty-five and thirty-five cents per yard, which took much of a day's work to weave.

By the time *Brother Jonathan* and the *New World* produced their extras, periodical fiction was already commonplace. Adam Waldie advertised his "NEW, CHEAP, AND POPULAR PERIODICAL, entitled the SELECT CIRCULATING LIBRARY" in newspapers across the country in the early 1830s. His ad in a Hillsborough, North Carolina, paper described his plan. "Take the Waverley novels, for example; the Chronicles of Canongate occupy two volumes, which are sold at $1.25 to $1.50. The whole number would be readily contained in three numbers of this periodical at an expense of thirty-seven cents, postage included!" The annual subscription was five dollars. "The whole fifty-two numbers will form a volume, well worth preservation, of 832 pages, equal in quantity to 1200 pages [in a book]."[50]

Story papers were cheap, plentiful, and crammed with a variety of subjects and genres. For a brief time, they were also literally huge. In November 1839 the *New World* published the first of its "Leviathan" editions for six cents apiece. These "mammoth weeklies" or "monster folios" continued to grow in size. In less than two years, they reached five feet eight inches long and four feet four inches wide, culminating in the famous Christmas Leviathan of 1841, which measured more than four feet long and six feet wide and offered its stupefied readers, who were forced to sprawl on the floor to read, 3,500 square inches of type. Sales strategies included bribing city newsboys with hot coffee, trips to the theater, and warm gloves. Copies were sent to postmasters across the country, and agents plied the streets far from New York City. The *New World* was read as far south as Charleston, South Carolina, where one agent was detained for distributing an edition that included a speech on emancipation in the British West Indies.[51]

For a brief time, these weeklies were the most notorious papers in the country. They were easy targets for critics of the "cheap press."[52] Yet they offered some of the best literature of the day. American authors featured in them included James Aldrich, Cornelius Mathews, John Pierpont, Washington Allston, Epes Sargent, John Neal, Seba Smith, Henry Longfellow, William Gilmore Simms, Washington Irving, William Cullen Bryant, and Nathaniel Willis, as well as Walt Whitman, whose poems and stories were also published in the *New World*. The weeklies pirated the works of as many British writers as they could, including Charles Lamb, Sheridan Knowles, Percy Bysshe Shelley, Frederick Marryat, William Ainsworth, Charles Dickens, Benjamin Disraeli, and Mary Russell Mitford. Sections included "Spirit of the English Press," "Original Papers," "Principal Editorial Articles," "News of the Week," and finally, "Miscellaneous." There were short stories and poems, "Our Weekly Gossip," literary notices, and the latest foreign news. In short, there was more than enough to keep Betsy's attention on a Sunday morning.

Her copy of *Brother Jonathan* probably arrived in the pocket or saddlebag of her brother James, who went to town for the mail at least once a week. "Town" in January of 1843 was Hillsville, the new county seat of Carroll County, established just the previous year. The mails were critical to the success of periodicals such as *Brother Jonathan*. Aside from paid agents—*Brother Jonathan* had fifty-seven scattered across North America in 1841—the post offered the best opportunity to develop a national market. Editors, publishers, and readers—whether they lived in Vermont or Virginia—all benefited from cheap postal rates and a staggering increase in the number of post offices throughout the country in the early nineteenth century. The Windsor District of Vermont saw a nearly fourfold expansion between 1800 and 1825. Alabama had ninety-four post offices in 1825; by 1839 the number had multiplied fivefold to 438, and by 1859 had almost doubled again to 810 offices. Rural Virginia saw a similar increase. In 1800 the Shenandoah Valley counted sixteen post offices; by 1840 that number had grown to fifty.[53]

Periodicals such as *Brother Jonathan* benefited from particularly attractive postal rates.[54] After 1792 postal rates privileged newspapers and magazines. The rates were intended to distinguish between merchandise and "vehicles for the dissemination of intelligence and culture"; the postmaster general did not look kindly on sending books through the mails. Unlike periodicals and newspapers, the logic went, books were not time bound, they burdened the mails, they damaged letters and newspapers, and they could be carried by private freight. Thus, postal regulations enticed publishers to issue book material in a newspaper format. All postage was paid by the recipients; newspapers were most favored at one and a half cents, letters cost six to twenty-five cents per sheet, pamphlets and magazines fell somewhere in between. In the southern states, hundreds of periodicals took advantage of these rates. Jonathan Wells has shown that the number of periodicals printed in the region increased tenfold between the first decade of the nineteenth century and the 1850s, from about twenty-two to 214. These periodicals, along with the story papers and their extras, were read and reread, recited aloud, and passed around until their stories became canonical.[55]

History and Biography

Histories, especially historical biographies, were an early staple of the popular press. Even as people in the Blue Ridge began to turn west toward Missouri and Texas, they were busy recording the history of the places they left behind, especially stories about the Revolutionary War. When the Cooley and Speer daughters were born in the 1820s, the history of the trans-Appalachia region was already being written by those who feared that the old ways could be lost forever if they were not set in type.

The Blue Ridge was full of people who were not inclined to stay. The 1840s and 1850s saw countless sons and daughters flee the hollows and hilltops settled by their fathers and grandfathers for opportunities further west. The New River plateau and Yadkin valley began emptying within decades of their first settlement in the 1780s. By 1850 more than 388,000 native Virginians were living in other states. In the decade after 1830 alone, the state lost about 375,000 voluntary migrants, not counting slaves, initially to Tennessee, Ohio, Kentucky, Indiana, Missouri, and Illinois, and later to Alabama, Mississippi, and Louisiana. Virginians had moved across the Mississippi even before the Louisiana Purchase, but after 1803, they were drawn in ever larger numbers to the bottomlands along the Missouri and Mississippi Rivers. The highest numbers went either due west, to Tennessee and on to Missouri, or southwest to Alabama and Mississippi. The ties between the New River plateau and the region around Independence, Missouri, were particularly strong. One popular guidebook showed Independence teetering on the edge of a landscape void of political boundaries and covered with the names of Indian tribes: Wyandot, Sac, Fox, and Kickapoo.[56] When Grayson County was subdivided in 1842, the new county seat in Grayson was named after Independence, the town at the head of the Santa Fe Trail where many of the county's sons and daughters had settled.

The Cooley children, whose birthdates spanned a quarter of a century, were especially restless. Martin, the eldest son, was sixteen by the time Amanda was born. He died in South Carolina before he was able to fulfill his plan to go to western Missouri, but his widow took their children on to Oregon. His younger brother William traveled to Independence with his wife Parthena, his sister Nancy, and brother-in-law Hezekiah Smith about 1840. "A Man that will try can get along in this country," he reported back to Virginia. "I can tell you that I have had my hands full ever since [I wrote you] I have had as much as I could do every day." William's fortunes soon fell; his wife died before he returned for a long visit to Coal Creek in late 1846, and he himself died shortly after he arrived back in Missouri. Both Amanda and Betsy expected to go west after they married. Long before she left, Betsy wrote of going west with her brothers. She wished, she wrote, "I was there, or had the chance to go to see some of the wide and broad world more than I ever have seen for I live in seclusion and I reckon a moderate portion of happiness."[57]

The Speers, too, looked west. A cousin of Jennie and Ann's grandfather, Henry Speer, who had been a captain in the American Revolution, crossed the Appalachians into Kentucky sometime after 1800, and was never heard from again. Their uncle Joshua moved to Tennessee, where he became a Campbellite preacher. Their brother Aaron, a teacher, moved to Tennessee and then on to Missouri. So many left that those who stayed behind had something to answer for. Until a few months before she died, Jennie was haunted by a sense that she could accomplish God's mission for her only in a new place, and she variously thought that place was Oregon, Texas, or California.

In the midst of all of this upheaval, people became aware that the "old days" in the Blue Ridge could be forgotten. Some of the earliest works printed in southern Appalachia were histories of the early settlement. Joseph Doddridge's *Notes on the Settlement and Indian Wars of the Western Parts of Virginia & Pennsylvania,* printed in the western Virginia town of Wellsburgh in 1824, was known to Theodore Roosevelt as a particularly rich account of everyday life in the eighteenth century. Doddridge (1769–1826) was born in western Pennsylvania but moved with his family to western Virginia when he was four years old. He later became an Episcopal priest. He persevered in his writing and printing, even being forced to apologize to his subscribers in 1823 because one book's announced publication "was rendered impracticable for some time past, by the want of water in the stream on which the [paper]mill is situated."[58]

Unlike many of the chroniclers of early Kentucky, Doddridge recorded not only stories of Indian warfare, but also the "society and manners of the first settlers of the Western Country." The first two-thirds of his book offers a long description of the clothing, houses, work, sports, weddings, and other customs. He had little to say about printing, but did note that his father, who never spent more than six weeks in school, was fine at penmanship and arithmetic and wrote letters, bonds, and deeds for his neighbors.[59] In 1823 Doddridge appended a curious dialogue to a "dramatic piece" printed in a nearby town. Dating from 1821, when it was apparently performed at Alexander Campbell's seminary in Buffaloe, Virginia, it was called "A Dialogue Between a Dandy and a Back-Woods-Man." The point, Doddridge said, was to offer a "portrait of the manners of former times" in order to favor the present day.[60] Yet the work seemed somehow to suggest the opposite: his Back-Woods-Man was noble and heroic, while the Dandy was clueless and patronizing about the old ways. The Dandy charged Back-Woods-Man with being "a semi-barbarian," but his foe retorted that the Dandy resembled the image of a fool his daughter had shown him in the local newspaper.

While European Romantics were rediscovering the "folk"—the term "folk-lore" was coined in 1846—Americans like Doddridge were busy introducing the Blue Ridge into the parlors of New York and London.[61] As Doddridge's dialogue suggested, the most famous of the new American characters was the backwoodsman, and some of the most memorable specimens of the type hailed from the Blue Ridge. "Half horse, half alligator . . . the most cunning of creatures of the backwoods, a raccoon, a 'ring-tailed roarer,'" Constance Rourke described this new hero in her classic study on American humor. "Heels cracking, he leapt into the air to proclaim his attributes" including astounding physical strength combined with 'a certain jollity of mind, pickled in the scorn of fortune.'"[62] Daniel Boone (1734-1820) settled on the Yadkin River in North Carolina in 1751, calling the region home for the next two decades before moving on to Kentucky. Stephen F. Austin (1793-1836), born in Wythe County, Virginia, was known as the "Father of Texas" and became a fixture in schoolbook histories by the 1850s. The east Tennessean David Crockett (1786-1836) drove cattle to market across the Blue Ridge as a young man before becoming an outspoken politician; he died at the Battle of the Alamo. Crockett's biography was issued by a New York publisher two years before his death, in a decade that saw his reputation as a folk hero blossom in a variety of printed apocryphal accounts.

Daniel Boone, of course, was the most famous of all. The Speer daughters were distantly related to him by marriage and heard stories about him as children; they lived just down the road from Boonville, a town named after his family. The Yadkin River valley was filled with tales of Boone, and with people who were eager to claim a connection with the hero. Yet the legend of Boone was ultimately preserved for posterity in print. An account of his life, *The Adventures of Daniel Boone,* first appeared in 1784 and soon became famous. Boone also wrote his own story, which appeared posthumously in 1823. By mid-century, more than sixty accounts of his life had been published in books and compilations, in addition to scores of references in early schoolbooks (including the popular Peter Parley series), magazine articles, and poems.[63] He inspired writers as diverse as James Fenimore Cooper, Lord Byron, and John James Audubon, and his biographers were not always careful with the truth.[64] By 1847 Boone's story had been featured in a volume of Jared Sparks's *The Library of American Biography.*[65]

The Cooley and Speer families both enjoyed reading biographies, although for different reasons. While the Speer daughters focused on those in the vein of Christian hagiography, the Cooleys generally read biography and history for entertainment. They read *The Life and Adventures of Black Hawk With Sketches of Keokuk, the Sac and Fox Indians, and the Black Hawk War* (Cincinnati, 1839) and a life of Francis Marion, along with an early account of the war with Mexico. They did not seem to share the taste of their generation for evangelical reform.

Jennie Speer read a number of biographies during her brief life, having picked up this practice early on from Sunday school tracts and schoolbooks. The Speers knew Jacob Abbott's popular series of the lives of kings and queens. Born in Maine, Abbott graduated from Bowdoin College in 1820 and later taught there, counting Henry Longfellow as a student.[66] Like his brother, John S. C. Abbott, he was a prolific author and popular on both sides of the Atlantic, eventually producing more than two hundred books. Among them were the "Rollo" books, a series claimed by some to be the most popular children's books of the day. Abraham Lincoln credited Abbott's histories with giving him "just that knowledge of past men and events which I need. . . . To them I am indebted for about all the historical knowledge I have."[67]

Readers' expectations for biography were shaped by the classics, particularly Plutarch's Lives, which appeared in a wide array of editions.[68]

Readers found their familiarity with Plutarch reinforced in both fiction and nonfiction, as he was mentioned in novels as different as Mary Shelley's *Frankenstein* and Dickens's *Our Mutual Friend,* and in the essays of Jean-Jacques Rousseau and Thomas Carlyle. James Boswell, another biographer who was important for nineteenth-century readers, also alluded to Plutarch in his life of Samuel Johnson. A eulogist of Henry Clay recalled how he found Clay with a copy of Plutarch in his hands when he encountered him in Germany. Clay, like many others, read biography to become "deeply versed in all the springs of human action."[69]

Many nineteenth-century readers chose works on politicians. Favorites included George Washington, Benjamin Franklin, and John Adams. Mason Locke Weems is credited with imagining the nation into being through his apocryphal accounts of George Washington and Francis Marion, the Swamp Fox. Other popular figures included Aaron Burr, Patrick Henry, Andrew Jackson, Daniel Webster, John Calhoun, Henry Clay, and Gilbert du Motier, the Marquis de Lafayette. Fiction writers also produced biographies, among them Washington Irving (Columbus, Goldsmith, and Washington) and William Gilmore Simms (Marion, Captain John Smith, Chevalier Bayard, and Nathaniel Greene) and there was a high demand for the lives of poets and novelists, particularly if they had died young.

The writing and reading practices of nineteenth-century Americans had deeply Christian roots, and evangelicals shaped the ancient tradition of hagiography to their own purposes. The lives of clerics were featured in many of the didactic works published by the American Sunday School Union and the American Tract Society.[70] Women were particularly committed to biography, as their habit of journal writing encouraged self-examination and reflection. Most women recorded their thoughts expecting that they would be read by family members. Both the Speer and Cooley families read family members' journals after their deaths. They were particularly interested in lives that became "living sermons" as they mirrored the greatest of biographies, that of the life of Christ.[71] Christian biography found a worthy subject in the life of early missionaries.[72] Adoniram Judson and his wife, Ann Hasseltine, were known to several generations of Protestant evangelicals as the founders of the American Board of Commissioners for Foreign Missions. The Judsons sailed for Calcutta in 1812, but were refused sanctuary by the British. Judson made his way in, only to endure the death of two wives and several children, among other hardships. He returned to the United States in 1845 to find himself a household name. The Baptists promptly sent him on a national tour. Thousands of Americans named their children after members of the Judson family, and their fame was prolonged by the numerous biographies that appeared after Judson's death in 1850. The story of Ann Hasseltine Judson, who died in India, appeared in numerous compilations, including Sarah Josepha Hale's *Woman's Record* (1855) and Lydia Maria Child's *Good Wives* (1833), as well as in materials published by the American Sunday School Union. The family's story also inspired poets such as Lydia Huntley Sigourney, "the American Mrs. Hemans," who wrote about Ann Judson after reading her memoir.

Rural readers revered stories that evoked not only their own era, but also the past. American heroes and English paupers, medieval queens and imaginary Indians combined to become their canon, inspiring a sense of possibility that was nurtured by knowledge of things beyond their experience. People who had never ventured beyond their own county learned stories that created a new context for their own thoughts and actions. Nearly all of them divided the world into metropole and province, city and country, and explained—explicitly or implicitly—that the arc of human progress bent in only one direction. As they read and retold stories of missionaries, Rhine fairies, and folk heroes, rural readers reckoned with their place in the world, which nearly always seemed on the periphery of what was most important in their books.

SIX

Doctrines

July 28th James went to Joshua Hankses to repair his clock
and got a newspaper, a pamphlet about universalism.
— Betsy Cooley

THE UNIVERSALIST TRACT THAT ARRIVED at Coal Creek in
James Cooley's pocket was a speck of sand in the mountain of controversial
religious literature that made its way into the Blue Ridge. Like other Protestant sects, the Universalists put their convictions into print: there was a Universalist almanac as well as Sunday school papers, hymnbooks, tracts, pamphlets, periodicals, and books. Universalist newspapers appeared across
the country, ten in the southern states alone between 1826 and 1861.[1] The
doctrine sparked fierce debate in the Upper South, not least because the
Universalists' conviction that the wicked did not go to hell was considered
to be particularly dangerous in a slave society. Charges and countercharges
were made in papers from Maryland to South Carolina, Georgia to Alabama. Universalist editors were generally a peripatetic group with unsettled
convictions, joining one sect only to leave it for another, and penning furious tracts and founding newspapers only to watch them fail, then moving
on, usually to a different state.

The Cooleys' Quaker lineage probably predisposed them to Universalism, as the group attracted many Quakers, Baptists, and German pietists.
In western Virginia, it was associated with Germans in the Shenandoah
Valley. Universalists preached in Lynchburg in the 1830s before organizing
there in 1841, and this group may have been the source of James Cooley's

tract. The Cooleys' interest in the doctrine appeared to be an abiding one. Three years after the tract appeared, Julia Ann Cooley was still reading Universalist newspapers. "She finds treasures she never thought of before," Amanda wrote.[2]

Religious disputes in the Blue Ridge, as elsewhere in the country, were given a long life by print. Even in a famously partisan era, political differences paled in comparison to the varieties of Christian doctrine and the controversy they inspired. Upon meeting a stranger, the first question asked was nearly always where they stood with regard to religion. "The particular denomination that you belong to seems the most essential point," a visitor to the southern states remarked in 1854.[3] Doctrinal debates comprised some of the most rigorous intellectual work done by rural people. Men and women argued with Bibles and well-thumbed Testaments in hand, carefully parsing individual verses to refute their opponents. Vicious controversies raged between those within the same denominations, printed sermons denounced religious leaders, and public debates between pastors drew thousands, with the proceedings then printed and widely circulated. Preaching and ritual remained central to religious practice, of course. Sunday meetings, camp meetings and revivals, baptisms and funerals showed a people in thrall to oratory. Yet even these were publicized in print and reported on after the fact. Printed sermons were legion.

Julia Ann or James Cooley may never have met a Universalist; they certainly did not have a congregation in their county. Their interest in the doctrine was sparked by their reading, making them an ideal audience for the armies of men (and the occasional woman) who wrote and printed religious polemic. New sects quickly printed up their founding documents, statements of faith, sermons, and minutes of assemblies. Hundreds, and in some cases thousands, of copies of polemic pamphlets found an audience far beyond the range of the spoken word. Letters to the editor, newspapers, and tracts called for others to join the cause. Religious newspapers sailed through the mails into rural neighborhoods across the southern states.[4] In the thirty years after 1790, 172 religious newspapers were founded in the United States; 360 more appeared in the following decade. Three-fourths of these only survived for a few years, but new titles appeared in sufficient numbers to make up for the attrition. By 1829 two New York City religious newspapers claimed the highest circulation in the world, with many others counting circulation rates far in excess of the most popular political journals. Religious print happily ignored regional bounds, and flourished across the southern states from the earliest days of settlement; Baptist association minutes rivaled government documents as the earliest imprints from territorial presses.[5] Sectarians loudly asserted their right to their own views while only grudgingly granting their opponents the right to be wrong.

The relatively small confines of Surry and Grayson Counties in the Blue Ridge were blessed with all manner of Protestant sects and their printed debates. Moravian and Mormon missionaries, revivalists of all stripes, and the occasional Roman Catholic priest drummed up converts.[6] Barton Stone, later a founder of the Christian Church, visited the area in the 1790s, and renowned revivalist Lorenzo Dow did so in 1804. By the 1840s, Baptists and Methodists outnumbered all the others and both denominations divided several times over, their bitter fights proving that the worst arguments happen within families. Among the Baptists, the bitterest split was between the Primitives and the Missionaries, who quarreled so fiercely that hard feelings lasted for generations after their formal separation in the 1830s. Methodists divided at least four ways; their Wesleyan roots and a shared disdain for Baptists of any kind could not make up for their internal differences. A small group of the fiercely antislavery Wesleyan Methodists in the Blue Ridge was bolstered by the arrival of several missionaries from Ohio in the late 1840s. Methodist Protestants marched off to form their own conference in 1828, unable to fathom that their episcopacy would not grant them their "religious and civil rights."[7] They continued to circulate pamphlets and tracts denouncing the polity of the Methodist Episcopal Church more than a decade after the formal disunion. By the 1840s, the Methodist Protestants were prominent in Surry County and counted more than three thousand members across North Carolina.[8] In 1844 their opponents, the national Methodist Episcopal Church, divided over slavery into northern and southern branches. Durwood Dunn has documented how these bitter controversies changed congregations in the Holston Conference, which extended from southwestern Virginia into eastern Tennessee. The main debates pitted itinerant preachers against those who "located"—sometimes called "local preachers"—creating such deep divisions that they influenced political loyalties during the Civil War. Most Methodist itinerants sympathized with the Confederacy, while most of the located preachers became Unionists.[9] Mormon missionaries arrived in the late 1830s to claim scores of converts in the area, some of whom eventually emigrated to Utah. The Disciples of Christ, called Christians, quarreled most loudly with Baptists but seldom missed an opportunity to argue with anyone. One of their strongholds in North Carolina centered on Surry County.[10] Quakers established a foothold on the New River plateau when they migrated from North Carolina after the American Revolution. By 1803 at least three Quaker meetings convened in Grayson County—Mount Pleasant, Chestnut Creek, and Fruit Hill. Meanwhile, agents from various state and national Bible societies—the American Tract Society, the American Sunday School Union, temperance societies, and others—moved determinedly over the roads that crisscrossed the mountains.

The Cooleys were of Quaker lineage, although as slaveholders by the 1840s, they held this tradition at arm's length. Benjamin's father Abraham had sailed with his family from England to New York, where Benjamin was born in 1774, before the family moved south. They went first to Surry County, and then a few years later northwest up onto the New River plateau. There, they attended Methodist, Quaker, and Baptist services in neighbors' homes and schoolhouses, along with Methodist quarterly meetings, Baptist association meetings, temperance meetings, camp meetings, and neighborhood hymn sings. Several of the preachers they heard were Methodists of the Holston Conference.[11] "Tuesday evening Sept. 7," Amanda wrote in 1852. "Just from camp meeting and such a time as we have had . . . to day got four Greensborough papers but no letters many persons were shouting singing &c. but I did not get happy."[12]

The fortunes of the Quakers in the Blue Ridge followed those of the Cooley family. A perfect storm of antislavery sentiment and a lack of arable land in the mountains scattered people across the continent from Oregon to Missouri to South Carolina. Many of the Quakers left for Ohio. The number of Quakers in Grayson County peaked about 1800 only to wane thirty years later because of outmigration; their meetings endured for a single generation and were "put down" in 1830. In North Carolina, the New Garden yearly meeting, where antislavery sentiment flourished, lost 162 families and eighty-three individuals to Ohio by 1866.[13]

Wesleyan Methodists

A small band of antislavery Wesleyan Methodists in the Blue Ridge endured beatings, imprisonment, and hangings in the years after 1845. Their zeal for distributing literature only aggravated their persecution. Rev. Jarvis C. Bacon of Ohio, along with a handful of other young men, answered a call from a small group of North Carolina Wesleyans. "There are many Methodists with whom I am practically acquainted, who, together with myself, feel so conscientiously scrupulous on the subject of slavery, that we cannot hold fellowship with the M.E. Church, South," a resident of Jamestown, near Greensboro, North Carolina, wrote, asking for missionaries to be sent. Among other problems, his group of about fifty people, including the printer John Sherwood, refused to cede their church property to a group of proslavery Methodists, who had formally organized the previous year "without our consent." "We wish therefore to obtain a copy of your *Discipline,* and should it be such that we can conscientiously subscribe, we wish to connect ourselves with you."[14] Two years later, the first of several missionaries arrived from Ohio to preach and distribute antislavery literature. By 1848 eight Wesleyan churches, or chapels, had been established in North Carolina and, within two years, twenty congregations were meeting in Grayson and Marshall Counties in Virginia, and in Guilford, Forsyth, Chatham, Randolph, and Montgomery Counties in North Carolina. By the time the Wesleyans were violently expelled from the region in 1860, five hundred members and an unknown number of adherents were meeting across the region.[15]

Print was crucial to the Wesleyans' mission. Five months after Bacon arrived in Grayson County in October 1848, he was arrested for circulating copies of an antislavery sermon. He was found not guilty and continued proselytizing. His successes led him to ask for more help from Ohio, and

Jesse McBride and Adam Crooks soon arrived. Both were also agents of the American Foreign and Anti-Slavery Society, lecturing and distributing literature. They were seized by mobs and forcibly removed from pulpits, and they apparently inspired several runaway slaves, who were later caught and hanged. Bacon was twice indicted, for preaching and for circulating the *Narrative of Frederick Douglass*. On the latter charge he was convicted, but the Virginia Supreme Court reversed the conviction on appeal. Bacon was driven from the area by incensed locals anyway. His colleague McBride had the worst of it, however. He was convicted of distributing an antislavery pamphlet based on the Ten Commandments and sentenced to be pilloried, to receive twenty lashes on his bare back, and to spend a year in prison.[16]

Wesleyan zeal in the region was not easily vanquished. In the late 1850s, sixty-two-year-old Daniel Worth left Ohio to go preach in his native North Carolina. He arrived with books and other antislavery literature, including fifty copies of North Carolinian Hinton Rowan Helper's notorious book *The Impending Crisis of the South*. He reportedly sold all of these and seventy more, along with subscriptions to Horace Greeley's *New-York Daily Tribune*. In December 1859, he was arrested for distributing incendiary literature. At the trial, he defended himself by reading for an hour from Helper's book. He was convicted and jailed for one year. While he was behind bars, Helper brought out a new edition of his book that included Worth's endorsement. After his release, Worth worked for the American Anti-Slavery Society in Ohio, where he died in 1863.[17]

Mormons

Print was also central to the success of Mormons in the South, where some 230 Mormon missionaries made an estimated 1,300 converts before the Civil War. Of twenty-three men who were appointed first apostles of the Mormon church, eleven spent time as missionaries in the southern states before 1860. Wilford Woodruff, who became the fourth president of the LDS Church, traveled through Arkansas, Tennessee, and Kentucky in 1835–1836, baptizing scores of people, including several Disciples of Christ preachers.[18] Jedediah Grant, later a Mormon apostle, made two trips to the Blue Ridge in the late 1830s and early 1840s. The first lasted for several months in the fall of 1837 and centered on Stokes and Surry Counties in North Carolina, where he baptized converts and debated with Methodist and Baptist "priests," "all of which resulted in faver of the truth," and "persecution." Grant was attacked not only in person, but also in print. He did battle, he said, with the "deceptive" editors of religious newspapers "who are duly blackening their columns with the most unhallowed falsehoods that have ever disgraced civilized society." These included false stories that Joseph Smith had been jailed for murder. Grant reported that many people talked with him about slavery, prompting him to ask a Missouri elder in May 1838 to send "some of the papers containing the letters of br. Joseph [Smith] on slavery" to the post office in Stokes County, North Carolina. Grant returned in the spring of 1839 to preach in Wythe and Patrick Counties in Virginia and Surry and Stokes Counties in North Carolina for three more years, sometimes traveling with his brother.

Grant's trip became legendary when the Mormon newspaper *Times and Seasons* published his letter in late 1840. It recounted his journey through four North Carolina counties, including Surry, and five in Virginia. He lamented the "scurrilous reports, and base epithets" that were circulated in print by "some of the upper Missouri land vermins" who spread "slander and abuse with a lavish hand." Grant was renowned for his spontaneous preaching. He regaled a large crowd, including lawyers and ministers, in the Tazewell, Virginia, courthouse after being handed a piece of paper with a Bible verse. The admiring crowd's generous collection enabled him to buy a "fine suit of clothes, a horse, saddle, and bridle." Grant also debated a "very eminent" Baptist, possibly Rev. Noah Carlton Baldwin, in a packed meetinghouse. Forty years later, Surry County was still considered by Mormon missionaries to be a secure place for their message, and memory of Grant survived well into the next century.[19]

Primitive Baptists

Some of the most bitter of all the sectarian arguments in the Blue Ridge were between the Missionary Baptists and the antimission, or "Primitive," Baptists. "We have had great confusion," the weary missionary Baptist preacher Noah Carlton Baldwin (1817–1903) wrote from Kingsport, Tennessee, in 1858. "But the Lord has kept my indignation from rising in the midst, even of threats of tarring and feathering me, and riding me on a rail."[20] Born to Methodists Enoch and Esther Baker Baldwin in Ashe County in far northwest North Carolina, Baldwin became a Methodist exhorter before being ordained as a Baptist in 1840. After marrying Nancy McMillen, he began a long career in pulpits in southwestern Virginia and eastern Tennessee.

Baldwin did well enough to buy his first slave and property near Abingdon, Virginia, in the early 1850s, where he built a brick home. There his wife died, and he married a local woman, Lavinia M., a few years later. "I think she is amiable and pious," he wrote. "I love her ardently and I trust she has a high regard for me." He was known for his debating skills, his opposition to medical doctors, and his support of temperance. Yet he was no teetotaler. He enjoyed his toddies and eggnogs, played the fiddle, and loved to dance. Baldwin was dogged alternately by Presbyterians and Methodists (whom he called "paedos," for "paedobaptist" or one who baptizes infants) on one side and antimission Baptists on the other. A thoughtful, self-educated man, he was a careful reader who regularly lamented his sins. "This evening half past 8 o'clock while the little tree frogs are singing their mournful songs all around my humble dwelling I am impressed with the thought of death and the silence of the tomb," he wrote in his diary. For urging his churches to take benevolent action, "I was much persecuted as a 'money-hunter' and 'divider of churches,'" he wrote, describing antimission opposition. When he publicly debated a professor at Emory & Henry College, the Methodist school in southwestern Virginia, he marveled that such an intelligent man could hold to such grievous doctrinal error. He was ridiculed by Methodists and Presbyterians for his stance against infant baptism and was "turned out" of more than one of his congregations. By 1862 he had moved to Blountville, Tennessee, where his house burned down during the war.[21]

Baldwin and his peers fought an uphill battle in the Blue Ridge, where most Baptists stood in opposition to missions, Sunday schools, temperance, and paid preachers who took notes into the pulpit. These Primitive

Baptists also refused to "fellowship" with members of fraternal organizations such as the Masons and Odd Fellows and temperance societies. They were not opposed to educated ministers. "It is a good thing in its place, and forms no objection to the character or qualifications," the group's historian explained. God did not depend on human education, for "God calls a man to a knowledge of Christ . . . without human learning or with it."[22]

Primitive Baptists also sparred bitterly with other denominations. Methodists in the Holston Conference, comprising East Tennessee and southwestern Virginia, organized tract, missionary, and Bible societies, in addition to Sunday schools, and raised funds for Sunday school libraries. All of this stirred up the ire of the Primitives.[23] The year 1843 was particularly contentious. A Knoxville pamphlet circulated a fifty-six-page sermon by Reverend Creed Fulton, a Methodist who preached in Grayson County and was well known to the Cooleys. Fulton attacked the Reformed, or Calvinist, doctrines professed by Primitive Baptists, defending his own Methodist Arminian worldview against the Primitives' determinism. "The foreknowledge of God has no influence upon either the freedom or certainty of human actions, for this plain reason," he wrote, "that it is knowledge and not influence." Creed went on to defend free grace and conditional election.[24]

In August of that year, the *Monthly Miscellany* of Monroe County, Tennessee, printed an account of a public debate held between a Baptist and a Methodist preacher. The editor charged the Baptist with having the mind of "a pygmy." "Several Baptist preachers in East Tennessee have, for the last two or three years, been making uncalled for and [un]provoked attacks upon the Methodist Discipline," he wrote. "In the spring of 1841 a very large Baptist gun fired off . . . in Knox County, which created quite a panic, but after two days were spent in adjusting the difficulties, in the way of a public debate, the excitement was quelled." The Methodists thought the matter had been settled, but a visitor reported that "a Baptist popgun was popping away at our Discipline" in the region ten miles east of Knoxville. "As is common in such cases," the editor scoffed, "the two wads scarcely raised blood blisters."[25]

Primitive Baptists were against many things, but they were enthusiastically in favor of the printed word. Printed declarations, sermons, minutes, and proceedings were essential to their work, as were their three nationally circulated journals, two from New York and one from North Carolina. The *Signs of the Times,* founded by Gilbert Beebe in New York in 1832, continued publication into the late twentieth century, championing both the sovereignty of God and the radical separation of church and state. A second New York paper, the *Christian Doctrinal Advocate and Spiritual Monitor,* was published from 1837 to 1845. Both made their way into the southern states, but the North Carolina journal, simply titled the *Primitive Baptist,* was the uncontested voice of Primitives in the region. It began semimonthly publication in Tarborough, North Carolina, seat of the influential Kehukee Association, in 1836, and continued until 1879. "We wish to have it distinctly understood, that we are not inimical to Masonry, Temperance, the distribution of the Bible, or the spread of the Gospel—but we do condemn the mingling of professors and non-professors of religion in societies. . . . Believing that Theological schools, Bible, Missionary, Tract, and Sunday School Union Societies are the same in principle—unscriptural . . . we are opposed to them."[26]

In 1826 a widely distributed pamphlet called "The American Telescope by a Clodhopper of North Carolina" laid down some of the group's convictions. The clodhopper was the self-educated minister Joshua Lawrence (1778–1843), leader of the congregation in Tarborough, who printed the pamphlet in Philadelphia at his own expense. His scorn for the mixing of money and religion knew no bounds. He bluntly denounced mission work proposed by Baptists among the Indians in his region, not because he was against evangelizing them, but because he opposed paying the missionaries. "No man could be found . . . to comply with the command of Christ to take neither gold, nor silver, nor scrip. . . . And go into all the world and preach the Gospel," he wrote. "Why, money! Money! Let the people give us their money and the mighty work can be done!" Lawrence chided.[27]

In the Blue Ridge, Primitive Baptists organized the Fisher's River Primitive Baptist Association, in which Jennie Speer's uncle, James J. Speer, was ordained an elder in 1849. Primitives, like all the other denominations, were eager to get their association minutes into print. Fisher's

River took up a collection at their meetings and enlisted a printer to produce several hundred copies of the minutes, along with a copy of the association's "circular letter." Their minutes were printed by Blum & Sons in Salem, North Carolina, the printing office closest to Surry County. In 1847 Blum printed 250 copies of the four-page pamphlet (a single folded sheet) for $5.00. During the 1850s, the minutes were printed in Wytheville, Virginia, where 300 copies cost $8.66.[28]

Temperance and Antitemperance

Primitives could bluster about almost any topic in print, but one of their favorite targets was temperance. The Speers—at least Aquilla, Elizabeth, and their daughters—were fierce temperance advocates who were certain that the issue had eternal consequences. "I dreamed a horrible dream about Noah Reece," Ann wrote to her mother from Jonesville. "I dreamed *Old Scratch* [the devil] came and carried him off alive, and I saw him take a big knife and cut Noah's heart out and chop it up into bits. And he said it was because Noah had been a member of the church, and had gone to stilling to ruin the souls of his fellow men."[29]

On Jennie Speer's twenty-second birthday in 1850, she attended a celebration of the Sons of Temperance in the "new Methodist church" in Greensboro. The speaker was Philip S. White, a Kentucky native born in 1807. Of Whiggish inclination at least from his twenties, he practiced law from Florida to Wisconsin to Pennsylvania before he became a committed member of the Sons in the early 1840s. In 1850, he toured eastern Tennessee, southwestern Virginia, and North Carolina for almost a year. He spoke in nearly every county in North Carolina, delivering some three hundred speeches that brought judges, presidents, college and university professors, and pastors into the Sons' fold. The notoriously argumentative Whig and Methodist preacher W. G. "Parson" Brownlow of Knoxville found his views persuasive.[30]

White arrived in the Blue Ridge during a period of agitation over temperance. "The temperance cause is creating a great excitement in the country," Ann Speer wrote. "The papers are filled with accounts. . . . Lecturers are traveling the State to enlist people in the heavenly work."[31] In the Holston Conference of the Methodist Episcopal Church South alone (extending from Wytheville west through Abingdon and into eastern Tennessee), two hundred men enlisted in the Sons after listening to White. "His speech far exceeded anything I have ever heard on the subject of temperance," Jennie Speer gushed.[32] A portly balding man with bushy whiskers, White showered his venues with printed notices publicizing his work. He may have inspired Jennie's mentor at Greensboro Female College, Charles Force Deems, to begin publishing a small temperance paper in 1853 called the *Ballot Box*, of which no copies survive. Jennie's father, too, was a devoted temperance man. In the spring of 1855, Strong Thomasson heard Aquilla Speer speak at a temperance meeting at Providence church before he passed around the pledge. Speer probably helped found the chapter Thomasson attended. Jennie's gift to her father, an elaborately bound copy of *The National Temperance Offering, and Sons and Daughters of Temperance Gift* (1850), survives in the collection of the Boonville Public Library.[33]

Philip White's success in the Blue Ridge demonstrated what all reformers knew: print was crucial to disseminating their ideas. The Sons of Temperance relied on rousing speeches but they also understood the power of print to spread their message. During the height of Sons' fever, several periodicals devoted to temperance began publishing in North Carolina and Virginia, among them the *Fire Bell* in the office of the *Spirit of the Age* in Raleigh, and the *Southern Era* in Richmond. In the Blue Ridge, Thomas Boyles, a zealous temperance man in Hillsville (the Carroll County seat), proposed the establishment of a temperance weekly. In the fall of 1852 Boyles, a Son himself, circulated a prospectus for the newspaper as far as the northern Virginia Piedmont and perhaps even farther. His paper, he assured his "brothers," would be devoted only to the "great Temperance reformation" and would remain neutral in politics and religion, although his columns would be "open to gentlemen of all parties and denominations for the discussion of any moral or agricultural questions." A temperance journal was sorely needed in southwestern Virginia, he claimed, where the Sons of Temperance were being "insulted, misrepresented, abused, and vilified." He despaired of the "absurd, disgusting, undermining, mean and

contemptible efforts . . . to crush our Order in this section of the country."
The worst enemy of all, he thought, was a certain North Carolina editor.
"There is a blackguard, obscene sheet, published in Raleigh, North Carolina, the avowed aim of which is to oppose our Order, which is taken extensively in this county," he wrote. "It is edited by an old Baptist Preacher, and
is called the 'Freedom's Blade.'" Although the despised *Freedom's Blade*
was printed for at least two years after Boyles wrote, no copies have survived.[34] Success apparently eluded Boyles; there is no indication that his
paper was ever printed. More than a thousand subscribers would have been
needed to support the printing and distribution of a weekly newspaper.

Even so, temperance literature and its advocates had more success
in the southern states than has been recognized. In the Deep South, the
movement unfolded in ways remarkably similar to those in northern states,
albeit often initiated by slaveholders rather than abolitionists.[35] Most of
those in the Blue Ridge sympathetic to the cause were probably Methodists. Both the Primitive Baptists and some teetotaling Missionary Baptists rejected the legitimacy of reform societies organized independently
of churches. Thus, the Mountain Baptist Association of North Carolina
declared in 1851 that, although God decreed temperance to be obligatory,
any man who was a member of the Sons of Temperance should be barred
from church membership. It was the "peculiar task of the church" to im-
pose temperance, they argued. "Secret societies" such as the Sons would
weaken the church.[36]

Holiness

Aquilla Speer's advocacy of temperance was deeply rooted in his Methodism. He faced sectarian opposition even within his own family. Two of his
brothers preached in other churches — one was a Disciple of Christ and the
other a Primitive Baptist — and at least one Speer cousin married a Quaker.[37]
A major point of disagreement in his generation was the doctrine known
as "holiness." This was a complicated vein of Protestant conviction in the
nineteenth century that found advocates across several denominations, including Presbyterians, Methodists, Baptists, Quakers, Episcopalians, and

Congregationalists. The Calvinists Charles Finney and Asa Mahan of Oberlin College preached the holiness doctrine of sanctification, as did Stephen Olin, president of Methodist Wesleyan University, Nathan Bangs, editor of the *New York Christian Advocate,* and the Quaker Hannah Whitall Smith, author of the widely read *Christian's Secret of a Happy Life.* At the heart of the holiness movement was a primitivist impulse to restore the purity of the early New Testament church. Holiness was essentially a call to reform, but holiness advocates were pietists, not separatists. They intended to purify established churches from within.

The true home of holiness was within Methodism. Like the Speer family, Methodists disagreed sharply among themselves. Memorably called "a kind of plain man's transcendentalism," holiness focused on the emotional consequences of faith, fusing perfectionism, revivalism, and pietism. Its advocates decried the bureaucratization of Methodism, calling for a restoration of early practices such as the class meeting. They celebrated the possibility of entire sanctification, or perfection, that was rooted in the teachings of John Wesley, the founder of Methodism. This required a "second blessing" after an initial conversion experience, which would free the believer from the inner disposition to willful sin and fill her with divine love. "Entire sanctification or Christian perfection is neither more nor less than pure love," one holiness advocate wrote. "The Refiner's fire purges out all that is contrary to love." The signs of a predilection for holiness are often difficult to trace, but language that emphasized the heart, the grace of the Lord, and beauty were all characteristic of the tradition.[38]

Jennie Speer was raised among holiness advocates. The movement generally got little traction in the southern states until the 1870s because its doctrines advocated a "social holiness" that usually included abolition. For the Speers, who were known for their antislavery sympathies, this was an advantage. When she was just fifteen, the year after she experienced a camp meeting conversion, Jennie heard a sermon by Reverend Peter Doub, the aged founding father of North Carolina Methodism. Doub was known for giving special prominence to holiness of heart and life. He urged his audience to pursue "a full assurance of acceptance with God." Two years later, Jennie continued to mull over the doctrine. "I have been studying much of late on the subject of heart holiness," she wrote at Jonesville Academy, "and have been led to examine my own heart." This was Jennie's explicit desire for sanctification, or the second blessing. Phoebe Palmer, a leader in the movement, explained: "So soon as you come believingly, and make the required sacrifice, it will be done unto you according to your faith." Yet it eluded Jennie. A few years later, she was still distressed not to have experienced it. "When shall my heart be made perfect? . . . Now, my Lord, I would ask for Jesus' sake that thou wouldst make me every whit whole. Thou hast the power, if thou wilt, thou canst make clean."[39]

Jennie Speer's mentors at Greensboro Female College, Frances Bumpass and Charles Deems, were devoted holiness Methodists. Frances Bumpass was the widow of a Methodist minister and editor who lived with her four children in a Greek Revival home on Piety Hill next to the college. Bumpass took over editorship of a small newspaper, the *Weekly Message,* upon her husband's death in late 1851. Charles Force Deems, president of the college, was also a keen believer in holiness. Both Bumpass and Deems published extensively and they encouraged Jennie Speer's own ambitions to publish. As a woman editor and former schoolteacher, Bumpass was a particularly important role model for Jennie, who was a frequent visitor in the household. Jennie eventually published several anonymous articles in the *Weekly Message.*

The fortunes of the holiness movement were closely tied to print. Holiness language emphasized feeling over thought, drawing deeply from English romanticism. It was a movement that was naturally inclined toward written expression, particularly as it was birthed in an era dominated by sentimental literature. Leaders and laypeople alike were drawn to vivid and poetic language in their hymnbooks, devotions, and descriptions of their lives and the world in which they lived.[40] The emergence of the movement was marked by the appearance of a journal, Rev. Timothy Merritt's *Guide to Christian Perfection,* in 1839, and the published writings of Phoebe Palmer were key to its spread before the Civil War. Palmer was the wife of a Methodist layman, physician, and publisher. She held a weekly "Meeting for the Promotion of Holiness" in her New York parlor that drew many influential Protestants. The meetings were copied by enthusiasts in other cities in

Rev. Charles F. Deems, c. 1865, by Mathew Brady. Courtesy of Wikimedia Commons.

the Northeast by the 1840s, and by the mid-1880s, there were more than two hundred such groups across North America and in Europe. Three of Palmer's four most significant books appeared before Jennie's death—*The Way of Holiness* (1845), *Faith and Its Effects* (1852), and the *Incidental Illustrations of the Economy of Salvation* (1855). Oddly, Jennie never mentioned Palmer's writings, yet she undoubtedly knew them, as her mentor Frances Bumpass featured them in her paper.[41]

Bumpass was an especially ardent holiness advocate.[42] Not long after her husband's sudden death from typhoid fever in 1851, she experienced what she had long yearned for: the second blessing. While the holiness movement was associated nationally with abolitionist sentiment, Bumpass never wavered from her support of slavery. In June 1852, she received a request from a Buffalo, New York, publisher, who enclosed two dollars to pay for an advertisement for Harriet Beecher Stowe's recent novel, *Uncle Tom's Cabin.* She returned both the letter and the money.[43] She was an important confidante and mentor to the young women at the college, offering them hospitality and leading prayer meetings at which she prayed and exhorted seekers and sinners alike. In the fall of 1852, Bumpass attended a camp meeting where she spoke to a woman who was so deeply convinced of her sin that she lay prone on the ground, unmoving, with fixed eyes. "The Lord enabled me to speak a word in season to her . . . and a ray of hope lighted her countenance," Bumpass reported. In the fall of 1854 Bumpass wrote: "I was sent for to attend a prayer meeting at the College. Expected to be asked to speak to the girls. Left the matter wholly with the Lord praying to him, who has all hearts in his hands." She eventually did speak and claimed afterward that she had been filled with the Holy Spirit.[44]

Bumpass's newspaper, the *Weekly Message,* had at least 1,500 subscribers and probably twice as many readers across North Carolina and beyond. Two friends who were missionaries in China subscribed, as did many outside the state. The paper, which Bumpass called her "pet Dove," bore the image of a white dove, symbol of the Holy Spirit, in its masthead, explicitly claiming allegiance to holiness doctrines. The paper drew only lukewarm interest from the North Carolina Conference, suggesting the controversial nature of holiness doctrines for most southern Methodists. Yet Bumpass's enthusiasm was undiminished. Even before her husband's death, the newspaper reflected the couple's devotion to holiness. In 1852 Bumpass published a piece by "T." (possibly Bumpass's good friend Tryphena Mock) which assured readers that God "commanded them to go on to perfection."[45]

Charles Force Deems (1820–1893) was also a fervent holiness advocate. When Jennie Speer met him in 1850, he had just been elected president of Greensboro Female College.[46] Four years later, she told him in a farewell letter that she owed more to him than to "any living man" except her father. Deems was not only a coworker, but also a brother, she wrote, for whom her regard was "almost unbounded."[47] Jennie had been welcomed into his family circle. He and his wife had six children, one of whom was born while Jennie was at college. His eldest son was later killed at the Battle of Gettysburg; Deems opposed secession but supported the Confederacy once the war began. Ruled by fierce ambition and much given to work, he demanded obedience and loyalty from his students and apparently won it from many. "When Mr. Deems says he desires anything it is as if he had commanded it," one of his "girls" reported. "Every absence from church and recitation was recorded and publicly read at Commencement along with their standing in scholarship."[48] "Meals must be on the minute; if you were late it was your hard luck but the *Work* took precedence. When he rested for fifteen minutes before dinner all messages and thrilling family news must wait; he was resting for the *Work*." Sunday evening meals in his home were marked by lively conversation about current events, and he had a great sense of humor, according to his daughter-in-law. His wife, a small, quiet woman, was called "Little Mother." Born in New York City in 1816, she was four years older than her husband.[49] She apparently eschewed adornment of any kind, even forgoing a wedding ring. She took no leadership in church work, but often read aloud "books of philosophy, theology and economics, which she did not pretend to understand." When Jennie was preparing to leave the college in the spring of 1854, she noted, "I shall not regret to say 'good-bye' to Mrs. Deems."[50]

It is difficult to recover a balanced picture of Deems from the cloying adoration of his sons' biography, but even that source suggests that he was more remarkable for his ambition than his humility. A sure sign of this was his eagerness to write for publication. Deems exemplified the penchant of clergy in all denominations to publish their way to the highest levels of their profession.[51] It was not a coincidence that he received an honorary Doctor of Divinity after he had authored a flurry of sermons, temperance and Bible society addresses, and manuals on domestic life. The Methodism that encouraged Charles Deems's interest in publication also fueled Jennie Speer's aspiration to see her own words in print. While Deems's publications brought money and advanced his career, Jennie's ambitions were constrained by her place as a single woman. Even so, she set her mind on teaching and writing, and her conviction that it was the correct path grew over time. "Being desirous to do something that will be beneficial to mankind, I have thought about writing a book, but I know that I am not competent to the task," she wrote in July 1848. Two years later, she had resolved to do just that. "Since I have determined to make efforts to become an authoress, I feel like I have some definite object for which to live."[52]

Starting early on, Deems tied his own fortunes to print. When he was nineteen he set out for New York City, where he secured the anonymous publication of his poems, *The Triumph of Peace and Other Poems* (1840), with the printer Daniel Fanshaw.[53] A year later, he made his way to North Carolina as an agent of the American Bible Society, where he not only sold and distributed tracts and books in Caswell and Iredell Counties, but had one of his own addresses published and compiled a hymnbook. The slim volume of hymns, *Devotional Melodies,* included hymns he wrote himself, along with suggested tunes. "No family that professes to be engaged in cultivating the heart's finer feelings should neglect the important duty of . . . appreciating the 'modulation of sweet sounds' to Him who teaches the happy ones in Heaven the song of Redemption," Deems wrote.[54] As he had hoped, his publishing and skill in the pulpit brought him to the attention of college administrators, and he was invited to teach first at the University of North Carolina in Chapel Hill, where he stayed for five years, and later at Randolph-Macon College, the flagship school of the powerful Virginia Methodist Conference. Hired to teach natural science—a topic Deems admitted he knew nothing about—he left shortly after a protracted and bitter public quarrel with the college president that cost him the support of many of his peers.[55]

By now a married man with a growing family, Deems turned to publication for financial support. "I immediately projected the 'Southern Methodist Pulpit,' a periodical intended to assist me," he recalled. The journal, published by the office of the *Richmond Christian Advocate,* apparently did bolster the family's income for the next few years.[56] He also lectured widely at churches and Odd Fellows' halls, publishing these addresses along with his poems in newspapers and magazines. "The total number of my discourses to the close of the year is one thousand and thirty-six," he sighed in 1853. "Oh, how deeply I feel my feebleness!"[57]

The trustees of Greensboro Female College, one of the oldest women's colleges in the United States, elected Deems to the presidency in 1850. Founded just over a decade earlier, the school was in decline when Deems arrived. He reorganized the college and hired new teachers, arguing that his administrative post made it impossible for him to teach. The average student, he wrote, paid $60 per year. Deems himself was paid $1,000, a professor at the college $800, and smaller salaries were allotted to the other teachers, who were all women. When Jennie returned to teach at the school after her year at Mount Holyoke, she earned a salary of $300 at the "head of the list" of the lady teachers. "You know the whole history of my coming here," Deems wrote to a friend whom he invited to take up a professorship at the college. "I think I hate humbugging. I am determined to elevate the standard of scholarship in the Institution."[58]

A New York firm published two books by Deems while Jennie was at the school: *What Now? A Present for Young Ladies* and *The Home Altar: An Appeal on Behalf of Family Worship with Prayers and Hymns for Family Use.* Both remained in print for the rest of the century.[59] They suggest the ease with which a man like Deems could couple a genuine interest in women's intellectual accomplishment with a determination to promote the domestic sphere. Deems's views of women seem to have been liberal for his time. After the Civil War, in an essay called "How to Manage a Wife," Deems wrote: "Manage? What is that? Does it mean to control? We manage horses. . . . But a wife is not a horse. When two persons are well married, the wife is as superior to her husband in many respects as he is superior to her in others."[60] He encouraged his students to become teachers, missionaries, Sunday school teachers, temperance reformers, and social workers among the poor to the end that they would do useful work. No doubt these views endeared him to Jennie.

What Now? A Present for Young Ladies appeared in a small edition bound in gilt-stamped cloth with an elaborate flowered spine in 1852. Dedicated to the graduating class, it might have been written for Jennie Speer, so thoroughly did she embody the ideal Deems laid out. More than once he

praised Mary Lyon — founder of Mount Holyoke — as one of the era's greatest educators. He urged his students to read her biography and follow her
example. If necessary, he argued, they should put off marriage until they
found an educated man who looked favorably on their calling to a useful
piety. Reading was at the heart of his exhortation, as it would mold young
women to be of "great usefulness, to do much good, to do much more
than the uneducated." He advised readers to build a good library, including
works by "modern" men such as William Hazlitt and Thomas Babington
Macaulay, but also by "older and greater men." He urged them to read tasteful periodicals and works of science, works of the American Tract Society,
and biographies of great and pious women. This list of recommendations
was essentially a summary of the books Jennie and Ann Speer knew.[61]

He also encouraged the students to read his own books, including,
no doubt, *The Home Altar: An Appeal in Behalf of Family Worship with
Prayers and Hymns. The Home Altar* was a kind of Methodist missal, with a
schedule of readings for daily prayer. He urged the sympathetic and kindly
treatment of slaves, whom he called "servants." "A servant is always to be
made known his place, but he is not to be excluded from the Christian
sympathies of the other members of the family. Prayerless brother, do you
know why your servants are so faithless to you? . . . In a word, have you not
taught them to be faithless to their earthly master, by your faithlessness to
our heavenly Master?"[62]

When Jennie Speer began teaching in Greensboro, she and her mentors agreed that much good could be accomplished by those who published. Reform-minded people in their generation believed in the boundless
ability of print to persuade people to change their lives and walk the narrow
path of genuine Christian piety, temperance, and chastity. Yet the literature of reform was countered by an equally mountainous body of print that
advocated sectarianism. Furious arguments made on the page — by Mormons, Primitive Baptists, Wesleyan Methodists, and Universalists among
others — sparked and maintained the acrimonious sectarian debates that
characterized the South. Verbal debates argued fine points of doctrine, but
so did words on the page, and by the time Jennie Speer died, many people

thought the page was far more effective. As her mentor Charles Deems observed in his own monthly magazine, "Who would not seize the opportunity to print a four-page pamphlet which should be read in every hamlet in the country, which should live when he was dead, and be preaching to scores of generations?"[63]

A Literate South

One of the effects of the last two centuries of the naturalization of print is
that the essential history of this major transformation is overlooked.
— Raymond Williams

I am inclined to think that the South is . . . as good a place
as any to fashion different understandings.
— Michael O'Brien

WHAT DO WE GAIN BY REMEMBERING THAT print was ubiquitous in rural neighborhoods before emancipation?

First, print circulated freely across regional borders. Of course, printed texts could, and did, deepen the divide between slave and free states. The shrill voices that, by 1861, argued on podium and page alike that reconciliation of these differences was hopeless have been exhaustively studied. Yet beneath this angry veneer lay a shared body of stories, songs, religious doctrines, poetry, and jokes, spread by word of mouth and in print. The orthodoxy that the South was bereft of print because publishers congregated in northeastern cities ignores how the publishing industry was organized. It underestimates the hunger for printed matter among southern readers, the continued output of small printing offices (much of which has not survived), and the creative ways this burgeoning industry met its customers' demands.

For all its social, economic, and political influence, slavery failed to create a coherent or cohesive culture in the South. Not only was this true for intellectuals, as Michael O'Brien has exhaustively demonstrated, but it was also true for more ordinary people. The work of creating a Confederate culture had to begin almost entirely from scratch, and the brief life of the nation did not provide what was needed to sustain it. What came to be known as southern literary culture took hold only in the toxic nostalgia that prevailed after the failure of Reconstruction.

Second, the experience of readers in the Old South underscores the fluidity of literacy in the nineteenth century. Literacy was not yet a noun or an ideology, much to the chagrin of school reformers. Schooled literacy was available to relatively few children before the Civil War, regardless of where they lived. Most rural people taught themselves to read and write, or learned from relatives, employers, or friends as they found they needed to, and their literacy learning customarily extended well into adulthood. Reformers condemned such ways of learning, but their complaints were self-serving. They colonized reading and writing, remaking these skills into an ideology called literacy that fused reading with republican values, nationalism, capitalism, and native Protestantism. Slaves and free black people sought the citizenship and social power that the ideology of literacy promised yet failed to deliver.

Finally, the circulation of print in the southern states is a reminder of how the history of what has been termed the print revolution was written by partisans. Writers and editors, and others who stood to benefit the most from new printing technology, heralded the steam press and chromolithography. Yet human speech and the work of human hands remained (and remain) the primary channel of human memory. For all it offered, print was a poor substitute for the creative works it inspired. From the stories and couplets of the King James Bible and Isaac Watts's *Hymns and Spiritual Songs,* enslaved people sang spirituals into being that survive two centuries on. From magazine images of Parisian bonnets and shawls, the Cooley sisters adapted designs to stitch their own black bobinet veils and fine delane capes. Rhetorics explained how to arrive at a tasteful turn of phrase, but the Speer sisters poured out their vision and experience into their compositions and declamations. The only surviving physical traces of the Cooleys, Jincy, and the Speers are some carved tombstones, fragile manuscripts, tintypes, and a few lines of sterile descriptions in public records and newspapers. Handwriting, not print, preserved their stories. We remember these women because of the memories and work of their descendants. The story of readers in the Blue Ridge, then, warns us against the banality of technological determinism. Culture is made by human memories, human voices, and human hands. No machine can reproduce this richness.

Abbreviations

AAS	American Antiquarian Society
AJCR	Journal of Amanda Jane Cooley Roberts, Virginia Historical Society
AMS	Diary of Annis "Ann" Melissa Speer, Speer Family Papers, privately held
EACM	Journal of Elizabeth "Betsy" Ann Cooley McClure, Virginia Historical Society
HBA1	A History of the Book in America, vol. 1, *The Colonial Book in the Atlantic World*, edited by Hugh Amory and David D. Hall (Chapel Hill: University of North Carolina Press, 2007)
HBA2	A History of the Book in America, vol. 2, *An Extensive Republic: Print, Culture, and Society in the New Nation, 1790–1840*, edited by Robert A. Gross and Mary Kelley (Chapel Hill: University of North Carolina Press, 2010)
HBA3	A History of the Book in America, vol. 3, *The Industrial Book: 1840–1880*, edited by Scott E. Casper, Jeffrey D. Groves, Stephen W. Nissenbaum, and Michael Winship (Chapel Hill: University of North Carolina Press, 2007)
HSP	Historical Society of Pennsylvania
LCP	Library Company of Philadelphia
LVA	Library of Virginia
NJS	Diary of Nancy Jane "Jennie" Speer, Speer Family Papers, privately held
SFP	Speer Family Papers, privately held
SHC	Southern Historical Collection, University of North Carolina at Chapel Hill
SOP	Allen Paul Speer with Janet Barton Speer, *Sisters of Providence: The Search for God in the Frontier South (1843–1858)* (Johnson City, TN: Overmountain Press, 2000)
VHS	Virginia Historical Society

Notes

Preface

1. AJCR, February 20, 1842, and May 20, 1854.
2. NJS, April 19, 1854.
3. Only Scotland, Prussia, and the free states had higher rates of literacy in 1850. Beth Barton Schweiger, "The Literate South: Reading Before Emancipation," *Journal of the Civil War Era* 3 (September 2013): 331–59.
4. Richard Allen, *A Collection of Spiritual Songs and Hymns, Selected from Various Authors* (Philadelphia, 1801).
5. Roger D. Abrahams, *Everyday Life: A Poetics of Vernacular Practices* (Philadelphia: University of Pennsylvania Press, 2005); Raymond Williams, *The Country and the City* (New York: Oxford University Press, 1973), 289; Richard Hoggart, *The Uses of Literacy* (Harmondsworth, UK: Penguin, 1958), 22–26. On print and oral tradition, Richard M. Dorson, "Print and American Folktales," *California Folklore Quarterly* 4 (No. 3, 1945): 207–15, reprinted in Dorson, *American Folklore and the Historian* (Chicago: University of Chicago Press, 1971) and Stuart H. Blackburn, *Print, Folklore, and Nationalism in Colonial South India* (Delhi: Permanent Black, 2003).
6. "The southerner generally lacked the motives for literacy commonly found in the North . . . [and] had little need to explore new patterns of existence through self-culture." Ronald J. Zboray, *A Fictive People: Antebellum Economic Development and the American Reading Public* (New York: Oxford University Press, 1993), 198. Exceptions among historians include Michael O'Brien, *Conjectures of Order: Intellectual Life and the American South, 1810–1860*, 2 vols. (Chapel Hill: University of North Carolina Press, 2004) and Jonathan Daniel Wells, *Women Writers and Journalists in the Nineteenth-Century South* (New York: Cambridge University Press, 2011). Among literary scholars, see especially Christopher Hager, *Word by Word: Emancipation and the Act of Writing* (Cambridge, MA: Harvard University Press, 2013) and *I Remain Yours: Common Lives in Civil War Letters* (Cambridge, MA: Harvard University Press, 2018).
7. Hinton Rowan Helper, *The Impending Crisis of the South: How to Meet It* (New York: Burdick Brothers, 1857), 406; Michael O'Brien, "The Nineteenth-

Century American South," *Historical Journal* 24 (September 1981): 751–63, reprinted as "Modernization and the Nineteenth-Century South," in *Rethinking the South: Essays in Intellectual History* (Baltimore, MD: Johns Hopkins University Press, 1988), 128. One historian writes that "the Civil War pitted against each other two of the most literate societies on earth." An estimated 90 percent of slaves could not read, but because they comprised just one-third of the population in the slave states, census takers recorded a large majority of literate people overall. William Gilmore-Lehne, "Literacy," in *Encyclopedia of American Social History,* Mary Kupiec Cayton et al., eds. (New York: Charles Scribner's Sons, 1993), 2421–22; Schweiger, "The Literate South."

8. Similarly, Elizabeth McHenry has shown that newspapers were the primary sites for African American reading and publication. *Forgotten Readers: Recovering the Lost History of African American Literary Societies* (Durham, NC: Duke University Press, 2002).

9. Hoggart, *Uses of Literacy;* Raymond Williams, *Culture and Society, 1780–1950* (London: Chatto and Windus, 1958).

10. Raymond Williams, "Culture is Ordinary," in *The Raymond Williams Reader,* John Higgins, ed. (Malden, MA: Blackwell Publishers, 2001), 10–24; Williams, *The Country and the City* (London: Chatto and Windus, 1973), esp. chapter 2, "The Problem of Perspective."

11. Raymond Williams, "Literature and Rural Society," in John Higgins, ed., *The Raymond Williams Reader* (Malden, MA: Blackwell Publishers), 112.

12. Harvey J. Graff, *The Literacy Myth: Literacy and Social Structure in the Nineteenth-Century City* (New York: Academic Press, 1979); Harvey J. Graff, "The Literacy Myth at Thirty," *Journal of Social History* 43 (Spring 2010): 635–61.

13. Bernard Bailyn, *Education in the Forming of American Society: Needs and Opportunities for Study* (New York: W.W. Norton, 1960).

14. *OED Online,* s.v. "literacy, n.," accessed August 29, 2018, http://0-www.oed .com.library.uark.edu/view/Entry/109054?redirectedFrom=literacy ().

15. Michael Winship, " 'The Tragedy of the Book Industry'?: Bookstores and Book Distribution in the United States to 1950," *Studies in Bibliography* 58 (2007–2008): 145–84.

16. Robert Darnton, "First Steps Toward a History of Reading," *The Kiss of Lamourette: Reflections in Cultural History* (New York: W.W. Norton, 1990), 174–77.

17. James A. Secord, *Victorian Sensation: The Extraordinary Publication, Reception, and Secret Authorship of Vestiges of the Natural History of Creation* (Chicago: University of Chicago Press, 2000), 3.

18. Raymond Williams, *Keywords: A Vocabulary of Culture and Society* (1976; New York: Oxford University Press, 1983), 87–93.

19. Abrahams, *Everyday Life;* Shirley Brice Heath, *Ways with Words: Language, Life, and Work in Communities and Classrooms* (New York: Cambridge University Press, 1983); D. F. McKenzie, *Bibliography and the Sociology of Texts* (New York: Cambridge University Press, 1999); Donald G. Mathews, *Religion in the Old South* (Chicago: University of Chicago Press, 1977); David E. Whisnant, *All That Is Native and Fine: The Politics of Culture in an American Region* (Chapel Hill: University of North Carolina Press, 1983); Eileen Southern, *The Music of Black Americans: A History* (New York: W.W. Norton, 1971).

20. Joseph Levinson quoted in Lawrence W. Levine, *Black Culture and Black Consciousness: Afro-American Folk Thought from Slavery to Freedom* (New York: Oxford University Press, 1977), ix; Daniel Wickberg, "What Is the History of Sensibilities? On Cultural Histories, Old and New," *American Historical Review* 112 (June 2007): 661–84.

21. AJCR, March 7, 1847.

22. AJCR, March 25, 1847.

23. Benjamin Franklin Cooley probate inventory, Will Book I, 140–42, Carroll County, Virginia, June Term 1847, LVA.

24. AJCR, May 28, 1847.

25. Holly V. Izard, "Random or Systematic? An Evaluation of the Probate Process," *Winterthur Portfolio* 32 (Summer–Autumn, 1997): 147–67. On estate inventories as a source of book history, William J. Gilmore, *Reading Becomes a Necessity of Life: Material and Cultural Life in Rural New England* (Knoxville: University of Tennessee Press, 1989), 405–9.

Introduction

1. John Bigland, *A Natural History of Animals* (Philadelphia, PA: John Grigg, 1828). In 1848, a female domestic laborer in Wythe County, Virginia, earned 75 cents to one dollar per week, a female farm laborer earned about 50 cents a day. Mary B. Kegley, "Women's Wages in the 1840s," *Wythe County Historical Review* 54 (July 1998): 18; AJCR, November 5, 1843.

2. Michael O'Brien, *Conjectures of Order: Intellectual Life and the American South, 1810–1860* (Chapel Hill: University of North Carolina Press, 2004), 488.

3. Gabriel Zaid, *So Many Books: Reading and Publishing in an Age of Abundance* (Philadelphia, PA: Paul Dry Books, 2003), 21; George Eliot, *Middlemarch,* vol. 1 (New York: E.P. Dutton, 1930), 51. The unrivaled collections of the American Antiquarian Society (AAS) fall far short of being comprehensive

for the period after 1820 and "are undoubtedly weighted toward publications from New England." Robert A. Gross, "Bibliography and the AAS Catalog: A Note on Tables," HBA2, 546.

4. "Preliminary Checklist for Abingdon [VA] 1807–1876," John Cook Wyllie, comp. (Richmond: Virginia State Library, 1945), 5.

5. Edwin Wolf 2nd, *American Song Sheets, Slip Ballads and Poetical Broadsides, 1850–1870; A Catalogue of the Collection of The Library Company of Philadelphia* (Philadelphia, PA: The Library Company of Philadelphia, 1963); E. L. Rudolph, *Confederate Broadside Verse: A Bibliography and Finding List of Confederate Broadside Ballads and Songs* (New Braunfels, TX: The Book Farm, 1950).

6. "Rules of the Clear Creek Camp Meeting," September 14, 1826, and "Bunker Hill Camp Meeting," August 15, 1856, Hawkins County, TN, Holston Conference Archives, Emory & Henry College; Charles A. Johnson, *The Frontier Camp Meeting: Religion's Harvest Time* (Dallas, TX: Southern Methodist University Press, 1955), 143, 214–15.

7. Solomon Lea (1807–1897), first president of Greensboro Female College and later head of Somerville Female Institute in Leasburg, Caswell County, NC, had regular custom with Kay & Troutman of Philadelphia for books and supplies for his students. Account Book, 1856–1859, Solomon Lea Family Papers, 1856–1936, SHC.

8. Scott E. Casper, "The Census, the Post Office, and Governmental Publishing," HBA3, 187.

9. John McCullagh, *The Sunday School Man of the South* (Philadelphia: American Sunday-School Union, 1889), 67–68, 58–61.

10. Aquila Johnson Peyton (1837–1875) diary, 1859–1861, VHS.

11. Christopher H. Owen, *The Sacred Flame of Love: Methodism and Society in Nineteenth-Century Georgia* (Athens: University of Georgia Press, 1998), 46, 75; A[llen] Turner, Account Book, 1822–1826, Rubenstein Rare Book and Manuscript Library, Duke University.

12. Candy Gunther Brown, *Word in the World: Evangelical Writing, Publishing, and Reading in America, 1789–1880* (Chapel Hill: University of North Carolina Press, 2004), 53; Durwood Dunn, *The Civil War in Southern Appalachia* (Knoxville: University of Tennessee Press, 2013), 19.

13. *Minutes of the Holston Annual Conference of the Methodist Episcopal Church, 1836–37* (Knoxville, TN: Ramsey and Craighead, Printers, n.d.), 14–15; *Minutes of the Holston Annual Conference of the Methodist Episcopal Church, 1841–42* (Asheville, NC: J.H. Christy & Co., Printers, n.d.), 8; "Appendix, Course of Study," *Annals of Southern Methodism for 1855*, ed. Rev. Charles F. Deems, DD (New York: J. A. Gray's Fire-Proof Printing Office, 1856), n.p.

14. The American Antiquarian Society (AAS) in Worcester, Massachusetts, stopped collecting schoolbooks decades ago.

15. Beth Barton Schweiger, "A Social History of English Grammar in the Early United States," *Journal of the Early Republic* 30 (Winter 2010): 533–55.

16. "American Text-Books," *American Journal of Education* 30 (Hartford, CT, March 1863): 209–22; *American Journal of Education* 31 (Hartford, CT, June 1863): 401–8; *American Journal of Education* 32 (Hartford, CT, September 1863): 626–40; *American Journal of Education* 37 (Hartford, CT, December 1864): 753–77; *American Journal of Education* 36 (Hartford, CT, September 1864): 601–7; *American Journal of Education* 40 (Hartford, CT, September 1865): 540–75.

17. Charles Monaghan and E. Jennifer Monaghan, "Schoolbooks," HBA2, 305.

18. Frederick Douglass, *My Bondage and My Freedom* (New York: Miller, Orton & Mulligan, 1855), 265.

19. William J. Edwards, *Twenty-Five Years in the Black Belt* (Boston: The Cornhill Co., 1918), 30.

20. *Supplemental Check List of Kentucky Imprints, 1788–1920, including the initial printing of the original Kentucky copyright ledger, and the first account of the run of Baptist minutes in the collection of Mr. Henry S. Robinson,* John Wilson Townsend, ed. (Louisville: Historical Records Survey, 1942); Manfred Gorlach and Ian Michael, *Annotated Bibliography of Nineteenth-Century Grammars of English* (Philadelphia: John Benjamins, 1998).

21. *Annual Catalogue of Jonesville Male and Female Academies, 1855–56* (Salisbury, NC: Bell & James Printers, 1855), 14–15; *The Kentucky Farmers' Almanac* (Lexington, KY: Charles Marshall, 1846); "For Sale at the Milton Bookstore," *Milton* [NC] *Gazette and Roanoke Advertiser,* February 6, 1823, 4.

22. O. A. Roorbach, *List of Booksellers in the United States and the Canadas, collected since May last, by direct communication with every city and town on the list* (New York: O. A. Roorbach, 1859). On the book trade in southern states, see Michael Winship, "The American Book Trade and the Civil War," in *A History of American Civil War Literature,* Coleman Hutchison, ed. (New York: Cambridge University Press, 2016), 17–32.

23. Jerome Blair Collection, Cherry Grove Store, Grayson County, VA. Day Account Book, 13 March 1856–31 December 1856, Kegley Library, Wytheville Community College Library, Wytheville, VA. In 1856, ½ dozen spellers sold for 75 cents retail.

24. "Negro Book," Pocket Memorandum Book, 1854. Hutson's Creek Store, Wythe County, Jerome Blair Collection Set Ib7, Kegley Library, Wytheville Community College Library, Wytheville, Virginia; "Book for Colored Per-

sons," 1859. Daniel B. Barkley & Company, and "Freedman's Book," General Store, Cedar Grove, Washington County, Tennessee, 1866–67, Brabson Family Papers, 1829–1941, Archives of Appalachia, East Tennessee State University.

25. "Turner & Hughes have just received at the N. Carolina Book Store . . . ," *Raleigh Register,* March 12, 1838, in Charles Lee Coon, ed., *North Carolina Schools and Academies, 1790–1840: A Documentary History* (Raleigh, NC: Edwards & Broughton, 1913), 798.

26. Kenneth W. Noe, *Southwest Virginia's Railroad: Modernization and the Sectional Crisis* (Urbana: University of Illinois Press, 1994), 4–18, 37.

27. Arthur Freeling, *The Young Bride's Book, An epitome of the domestic duties and social enjoyments of woman, as wife and mother* (New York: Wilson and Company, 1849).

28. Paul D. Escott, ed., *North Carolina Yeoman: The Diary of Basil Armstrong Thomasson, 1853–1862* (Athens: University of Georgia Press, 1996), 107.

29. John Fea, *The Way of Improvement Leads Home: Philip Vickers Fithian and the Rural Enlightenment in Early America* (Philadelphia: University of Pennsylvania Press, 2008); Catherine E. Kelly, *In the New England Fashion: Reshaping Women's Lives in the Nineteenth Century* (Ithaca, NY: Cornell University Press, 1999); William J. Gilmore, *Reading Becomes a Necessity of Life: Material and Cultural Life in Rural New England, 1780–1835* (Knoxville: University of Tennessee Press, 1989).

30. Brian Stock, *The Implications of Literacy: Written Language and Models of Interpretation in the Eleventh and Twelfth Centuries* (Princeton, NJ: Princeton University Press, 1983), 528–29.

31. Lee Soltow and Edward Stevens, *The Rise of Literacy and the Common School in the United States: A Socioeconomic Analysis to 1870* (Chicago: University of Chicago Press, 1981), 159. The census suggests that in many cases, marshals most likely did not carefully query free black people in their district in 1850 and after.

32. "Instructions to Marshals and Assistants," 1870 Census, quoted in *Measuring America: The Decennial Censuses From 1790 to 2000* (Washington, DC: U.S. Department of Commerce, 2002), 15. The contrast is clear in the published compendium of the Ninth Census. *The Statistics of the Population of the United States . . . compiled from the original returns of the Ninth Census,* vol. 1 (Washington, DC: Government Printing Office, 1872), 396–97.

33. *Ninth Census,* vol. 1 of *The Statistics of the Population of the United States* (Washington, DC: Government Printing Office, 1872), 397. The standard account of nineteenth-century US literacy never clarifies how "illiterate" is defined in relation to the separate skills of reading and writing. Soltow and Stevens, *Rise of Literacy,* 148–92; on higher rates of illiteracy in 1870, see 155–56.

34. U.S. Census Bureau. Census 1840 and 1850. Literacy (Free Population Age 20 and Over). Prepared by Social Explorer, https://www.socialexplorer.com /tables/Census1850/R11807618.

35. E. Jennifer Monaghan, *Learning to Read and Write in Colonial America* (Amherst: University of Massachusetts Press, 2005).

36. *OED Online,* s.v. "literacy," accessed February 8, 2017, http://0-www.oed.com .library.uark.edu/view/Entry/109054?redirectedFrom=literacy.

37. Randal L. Hall, *Mountains on the Market: Industry, the Environment, and the South* (Lexington: University Press of Kentucky, 2012); David E. Whisnant, *All That Is Native and Fine: The Politics of Culture in an American Region* (Chapel Hill: University of North Carolina Press, 1983).

38. As used by folklorists and landscape architects, "vernacular" embraces both the traditional and innovative, the highbrow and the popular. I use "ordinary" in reference to culture and "vernacular" to refer to native language. Roger D. Abrahams, *Everyday Life: A Poetics of Vernacular Practices* (Philadelphia: University of Pennsylvania Press, 2005), 12; John Brinckerhoff Jackson, *Discovering the Vernacular Landscape* (New Haven, CT: Yale University Press, 1984), xii. Also, Henry Glassie, "Architects, Vernacular Traditions, and Society," *Traditional Dwellings and Settlements Review* 1 (1990): 9-21.

39. Both counties were divided within the period of this study. Carroll County was created from the eastern end of Grayson in 1842; Yadkin County was created from the southern half of Surry County in 1850.

40. AJCR, July 9, 1843.

41. NJS, no date [early 1843]. Portions of the Speers' diaries have been published in Allen Paul Speer with Janet Barton Speer, *Sisters of Providence: The Search for God in the Frontier South (1843-1858)* (Johnson City, TN: Overmountain Press, 2000).

42. At least one letter with Jane's signature survives, but she may have dictated it to her daughter, Julia Ann. The sign literacy rate (the people who could sign their name as opposed to an X on a document) among women in Carroll County before 1815, at 64 percent, was equal to that of urban New England women in the same period. Gladys D. Ganley, "The Female Settlers of Carroll County, Virginia: An Examination of Their Historical Documents," master's thesis, Harvard University, 1987, 171.

43. On the ordinary road in the eighteenth century, Monaghan, *Learning to Read and Write in Colonial America,* 13.

44. EACM, June 30, 1844.

45. Elizabeth referred to popular British authors Frederick Marryat (1792-1848) and Edward Bulwer-Lytton (1803-1873). EACM, September 4, 1842.

46. In 1842, Carroll County had three post offices. By 1850, there were eight; by

1860, there were fifteen. "A Guide to the Counties of Virginia; Carroll County," *The Virginia Genealogist* 7 (January–March 1963), no author, 34–35.

47. Nila Banton Smith, *American Reading Instruction* (New York: Silver, Burdett, 1934), 41.

48. AMS, January 29, 1853.

49. Jennie was the only woman from North Carolina to attend Mount Holyoke Seminary before the Civil War. NJS, November 3 and 17, 1850; Jennie Speer, January 7, 1844, quoted in SOP, 41, 30.

50. NJS to "My own dear precious mother," [Elizabeth Ashby Speer], January 26, 1854.

51. NJS, November 20, 1850; September 5, 1845; May 6, 1847.

52. Heath, *Ways with Words;* Edward Sapir, *Language: An Introduction to the Study of Speech* (New York: Harcourt, Brace, 1921), 220. The ways that language can express an indefinite number of thoughts within established grammatical and syntactic norms and rules offers an important model for understanding human creativity. See "Introduction," *Common Places: Readings in American Vernacular Architecture,* Dell Upton and Michael Vlach, eds. (Athens: University of Georgia Press, 1985), xxii; Noam Chomsky, *Aspects of the Theory of Syntax* (Cambridge, MA: Massachusetts Institute of Technology Press, 1965), 6.

53. Escott, ed., *North Carolina Yeoman,* 115–18.

54. AJCR, May 21, June 5, June 18, 1843; Amanda Jane (Cooley) Roberts, Commonplace Book, 1843–1854, VHS.

55. Lawrence Levine, "William Shakespeare and the American People," *Journal of American History* 89 (February 1984): 50; Escott, ed., *North Carolina Yeoman,* 119.

56. Whitney Phillips and Ryan M. Milner, eds., *The Ambivalent Internet: Mischief, Oddity, and Antagonism Online* (New York: Polity Press, 2017).

57. Richard M. Dorson, "Print and American Folktales," *California Folklore Quarterly* 4 (No. 3, 1945): 207–15, reprinted in Dorson, *American Folklore and the Historian* (Chicago: The University of Chicago Press, 1971), 174.

58. Raymond Williams, *Culture and Society, 1780–1950* (1958; Harmondsworth, UK: Penguin, 1977), 297.

Part I. A Good English Education

1. Basil Lanneau Gildersleeve, "The Necessity of the Classics," in *All Clever Men Who Make Their Way: Critical Discourse in the Old South,* ed. Michael O'Brien (Fayetteville: University of Arkansas Press, 1982), 398–419.

Chapter 1. Spellers

1. EACM, November 5, 1843. A portion of Betsy's journal was published as "From Virginia to Missouri in 1846: The Journal of Elizabeth Ann Cooley [McClure]," Edward D. Jervey and James E. Moss, eds., *Missouri Historical Review* 60 (January 1966): 162–208.
2. S. Bruce Jones, "Introduction," (March 15, 1935), typescript of the journal of Elizabeth Ann Cooley McClure, [in author's possession].
3. John C. Inscoe, *Mountain Masters, Slavery and the Sectional Crisis in Western North Carolina* (Knoxville: University of Tennessee Press, 1989), 88.
4. EACM, March 31, 1844. Her purchase suggests she may have sold some of the goods she made.
5. Randal L. Hall, *Mountains on the Market: Industry, the Environment, and the South* (Lexington: University Press of Kentucky, 2012), 16.
6. AJCR, December 29, 1848.
7. AJCR, July 16, 1847.
8. John Perry Alderman, *Carroll 1765–1815: The Settlements: A History of the First Fifty Years of Carroll County, Virginia* (Hillsville, VA: Alderman Books, 1985), 7.
9. AJCR, December 25, 1853; January 4 and January 8, 1854.
10. Kenneth W. Noe, *Southwest Virginia's Railroad: Modernization and the Sectional Crisis* (Urbana: University of Illinois Press, 1994), 67–79.
11. Inscoe, *Mountain Masters, Slavery, and the Sectional Crisis*, 62.
12. AJCR, November 2, 1847.
13. AJCR, November 26, 1846; August 29, 1847; September 5, 12, 1847; March 26, 1849; May 15, 1849.
14. AJCR, August 5, 1849.
15. AJCR, October 5, 1850; Richard O. Currey, *A Geological Visit to the Virginia Copper Region* (Knoxville, TN, 1859), 60.
16. AJCR, April 14, 1846.
17. David Henkin, *The Postal Age: The Emergence of Modern Communications in Nineteenth-Century America* (Chicago: University of Chicago Press, 2007), 2.
18. John M. Washington, "Memorys of the Past," in David W. Blight, ed., *A Slave No More: Two Men Who Escaped to Freedom* (New York: Harcourt), 169–75.
19. B. A. Botkin, ed., *Lay My Burden Down: A Folk History of Slavery* (New York: Dell Publishing, 1973), 194.
20. Botkin, *Lay My Burden Down*, 179.
21. Janet Cornelius, *When I Can Read My Title Clear: Literacy, Slavery, and Religion in the Antebellum South* (Columbia: University of South Carolina Press, 1991); Botkin, *Lay My Burden Down*, 61.

22. Steven Shapin and Barry Barnes, "Head and Hand: Rhetorical Resources in British Pedagogical Writing, 1770–1850," *Oxford Review of Education* 2 (1976): 231–54.

23. Carlo Ginsburg, *The Cheese and the Worms: The Cosmos of a Sixteenth-Century Miller,* trans. John Tedeschi and Anne Tedeschi (New York: Routledge, 1980); David D. Hall, *Worlds of Wonder, Days of Judgment: Popular Religious Belief in Early New England* (Cambridge, MA: Harvard University Press, 1989).

24. Raymond Williams, *The Long Revolution* (London: Chatto & Windus, 1961); Carl Kaestle, *Pillars of the Republic: Common Schools and American Society, 1780–1860* (New York: Hill & Wang, 1983), 75–103; Bernard Bailyn, *Education in the Forming of American Society* (New York: Vintage Books, 1960), 48.

25. E. Jennifer Monaghan, "Literacy Instruction and Gender in Colonial New England," in *Reading in America: Literature and Social History,* ed. Cathy N. Davidson (Baltimore, MD: Johns Hopkins University Press, 1989), 53–80.

26. This important change has been overlooked in the definitive account of American literacy. Lee Soltow and Edwards Stevens, *The Rise of Literacy and the Common School in the United States: A Socioeconomic Analysis to 1870* (Chicago: University of Chicago Press, 1981), 155–56.

27. Devereux Jarratt, *The Life of the Reverend Devereux Jarratt, Rector of Bath Parish, Dinwiddie County, Virginia. Written by Himself, in a series of letters addressed to the Rev. John Coleman, one of the ministers of the Protestant Episcopal Church, Maryland* (Baltimore, MD: Warner and Hanna, 1806), 14–15.

28. Caleb Bingham, *The Columbian Orator,* David Blight, ed. (New York: New York University Press, 1998).

29. E. Jennifer Monaghan, "Reading for the Enslaved, Writing for the Free: Reflections on Liberty and Literacy," *Proceedings of the American Antiquarian Society* 108 (October 1998), 309–41.

30. David Blight, "Introduction," in Bingham, *Columbian Orator,* xxi.

31. Elizabeth Keckley, *Behind the Scenes, Or Thirty Years a Slave and Four Years in the White House* (New York, 1868), 25. On the authoritarian nature of schooling, Michael B. Katz, *The Irony of Early School Reform: Educational Innovation in Mid-Nineteenth Century Massachusetts* (Cambridge, MA: Harvard University Press, 1968).

32. Monaghan, "Reading for the Enslaved, Writing for the Free," 309–41; Thomas D. Morris, *Southern Slavery and the Law, 1619–1860* (1996; Chapel Hill: University of North Carolina Press, 1999); Heather Williams, *Self-Taught: African American Education in Slavery and Freedom* (Chapel Hill: University of North Carolina Press, 2007), Appendix, "African Americans, Literacy, and the Law in the Antebellum South," 203–14.

33. Tammy K. Byron, "A Catechism For Their Special Use: Slave Catechisms in the Antebellum South," PhD diss., University of Arkansas, 2008.

34. David Vincent, *The Rise of Mass Literacy: Reading and Writing in Modern Europe* (Cambridge: Polity Press, 2000), 29.

35. Paul J. Finkelman, ed., *Encyclopedia of African American History, 1619–1895,* vol. 1 (New York: Oxford University Press, 2006), 451; Hilary J. Moss, *Schooling Citizens: The Struggle for African American Education in Antebellum America* (Chicago: University of Chicago Press, 2009), chapters 3 and 4.

36. Quoted in Eugene D. Genovese, *Roll Jordan Roll: The World the Slaves Made* (New York: Pantheon Books, 1974), 565, 566; Frederick Douglass, *Narrative of the Life of Frederick Douglass* (1845; New York: Library of America, 2000), 308.

37. Botkin, *Lay My Burden Down,* 61.

38. Kenneth Cmiel, *Democratic Eloquence: The Fight Over Popular Speech in Nineteenth-Century America* (New York: William Morrow and Company, 1990).

39. *Autobiography, Sermons, Addresses and Essays of Bishop L. H. Holsey, DD* (Atlanta, GA: The Franklin Printing and Publishing Co., 1898), 18.

40. Charles H. Nichols, *Many Thousand Gone: The Ex-Slaves' Account of Their Bondage and Freedom* (Bloomington: Indiana University Press, 1969), 70.

41. Genovese, *Roll, Jordan, Roll,* 439.

42. E. Jennifer Monaghan, *A Common Heritage: Noah Webster's Blue-Back Speller* (Hamden, CT: Archon Books, 1983); Charles Hoole, quoted in Nila Banton Smith, *American Reading Instruction* (New York: Silver, Burdett, 1934), 32.

43. Works Progress Administration, Historical Records Survey, 1935–1942, Arkansas, File F, Questionnaire for Baxter County, Benton County, Boone County, Bradley County, Carroll County, Crawford County, Cross County, Franklin County, Grant County, and Yell County, Special Collections, Mullins Library, University of Arkansas, Fayetteville.

44. William H. Heard, *From Slavery to Bishopric in the AME Church: An Autobiography* (Philadelphia: A.M.E. Book Concern, 1928), 33.

45. *Autobiography, Sermons, Addresses and Essays of Bishop L. H. Holsey,* 17.

46. Noah Webster, *A Grammatical Institute of the English Language* (Hartford, CT: Hudson and Goodwin, 1783), 5.

47. Monaghan, *Common Heritage,* 35–36.

48. EACM, August 21, 1843.

49. AJCR, January 18, 1846.

50. John W. Carroll, *Autobiography and Reminiscences of John W. Carroll* (Henderson, TN, 1898), 10; Rebecca Latimer Felton, *Country Life in Georgia in the Days of My Youth* (Atlanta, GA: Index Printing, 1919), 59; EACM, March 26, 1842.

51. "Autobiography of Gideon Lincecum," quoted in Arthur Palmer Hudson, ed., *Humor of the Old Deep South* (New York: Macmillan, 1936), 387–88.

52. William E. Barton, "The Strength of the Hills," *The Christian Register* 77 (July 14, 1898): 788.

53. David Vincent, "Reading Made Strange: Context and Method in Becoming Literate in Eighteenth and Nineteenth-Century England," in *Silences and Images: The Social History of the Classroom,* Ian Grosvenor, Martin Lawn, and Kate Rousmaniere, eds. (New York: Lang, 1999), 188.

54. Joel Benton, quoted in Monaghan, *Common Heritage,* 193.

55. Dan A. Rudd and Theo Bond, *From Slavery to Wealth: The Life of Scott Bond* (Madison, AR: The Journal Printing Company, 1917), 26.

56. AJCR, March 5 and March 10, 1842.

57. AJCR, March 19, 1848; May 12 and 25, 1852.

58. AJCR, February 7, 1852.

59. Kaestle, *Pillars of the Republic,* 13; Sun Go and Peter Lindert, "The Uneven Rise of American Public Schools to 1850," *Journal of Economic History* 70 (March 2010): 4. The 1850 census counted 558,000 rural common school students to 24,000 urban common school students. See also Sarah L. Hyde, *Schooling in the Antebellum South: The Rise of Public and Private Education in Louisiana, Mississippi, and Alabama* (Baton Rouge: Louisiana State University Press, 2016).

60. U.S. Census Bureau, 1850 Census. Data prepared by Social Explorer, https://www.socialexplorer.com/tables/Census1850/R11807826; Yadkin County School Records, 1853–1878, C.R. 106.926.1, North Carolina State Archives, Raleigh. Census records do not show any free black students in any of the three counties.

61. AJCR, March 5, 1851; October 6, 1844; May 8, 1851.

62. *The Star* (Raleigh, NC), March 2, 1809, 3.

63. Ellin Lee Rogers, "History of the Paper Mill at Salem, North Carolina, 1789–1873," master's thesis, Wake Forest University, 1982, 15–16, 58; Jon F. Sensbach, *A Separate Canaan: The Making of an Afro-Moravian World in North Carolina* (Chapel Hill: University of North Carolina Press, 1998), 162–63.

64. *Minutes of the Fisher's River Baptist Association of the Primitive Faith* (Salem, NC: Blum & Son, 1847).

65. Little work has been done on paper manufacturing in the southern states. Rogers, "History of the Paper Mill at Salem, North Carolina," 36–37; Lyman Horace Weeks, *A History of Paper-Manufacturing in the United States, 1690–1916* (New York: Burt Franklin, 1916), 167–69, 269; John Bidwell, *American Paper Mills, 1690–1832: A Directory of the Paper Trade* (Hanover, NH: Dartmouth College Press, 2013).

66. Belinda Hermence, ed., *My Folks Don't Want Me to Talk about Slavery* (Winston-Salem, NC: John F. Blair, 1984), 75–80.

67. David Warren Steel, "John Wyeth and the Development of Southern Folk Hymnody," in *Music from the Middle Ages through the 20th Century: Essays in Honor of Gwynn McPeek*, Carmelo P. Comberiati and Matthew C. Steel, eds. (London: Gordon and Breach, 1988), 1; Rachel Augusta Brett Harley, "Ananias Davisson: Southern Tunebook Compiler, 1780–1857," PhD diss., University of Michigan, 1972, 13–14.

68. Williams, *Self-Taught*, Appendix, "African Americans, Literacy, and the Law in the Antebellum South," 204.

69. This is the "absolute minimum." E. Jennifer Monaghan, *A Common Heritage: Noah Webster's Blue-Back Speller* (Hamden, CT: Archon Books, 1983), 215–20.

70. Joan R. Sherman, ed., *The Black Bard of North Carolina: George Moses Horton and His Poetry* (Chapel Hill: University of North Carolina Press, 1997), 2.

71. Janet Cornelius, "'We Slipped and Learned to Read': Slave Accounts of the Literacy Process, 1830–1865," Harvey J. Graff, ed., *Literacy and Historical Development: A Reader* (Carbondale: Southern Illinois University Press, 2007), 332, n. 28; Monaghan, *A Common Heritage*, 194.

72. David Micklethwait, *Noah Webster and the American Dictionary* (Jefferson, NC: McFarland and Company, 2000), 76–79, 94.

73. James N. Green, "The Rise of Book Publishing," HBA2, 114; Hellmut Lehmann-Haupt, *The Book in America: A History of the Making and Selling of Books in the United States* (New York: R.R. Bowker, 1952), 80–82.

74. Emily Ellsworth Ford Skeel, comp., *A Bibliography of the Writings of Noah Webster* (New York: New York Public Library, 1958), 35–133, Appendix K.

75. Monaghan, *A Common Heritage*, 141–42.

76. Monaghan, *A Common Heritage*, 217.

77. Noah Webster, *The Elementary Spelling Book, being an Improvement on the American Spelling Book* (Charleston, SC: S. Babcock, 1837).

78. On Cooledge, see H. L. Mencken, *The American Language*, 4th ed. (New York: Alfred A. Knopf, 1960), 385. On Appleton, see Monaghan, *Common Heritage*, 192.

79. Monaghan, *A Common Heritage*, 147–51; Emily Ellsworth Fowler Ford, comp., Emily Ellsworth Ford Skeel, ed., *Notes on the Life of Noah Webster* (New York, 1912), 514–16.

80. Charles L. Coon, *North Carolina Schools and Academies, 1790–1840, A Documentary History* (Raleigh, NC: Edwards and Broughton Printing Company, 1915).

81. James Gilreath, "Mason Weems, Matthew Carey and the Southern Booktrade, 1794–1810," *Publishing History* 10 (1981): 27–49, citation on 42.

82. Henry C. Carey, May 25, 1854, quoted in Edwin T. Freedley, *Philadelphia and Its Manufactures: A Hand-Book* (Philadelphia: Edwards Young, 1859), 157.

83. Edwin T. Freedley, *Philadelphia and Its Manufactures, A Handbook* (Philadelphia: Edward Young, 1859), 162. Lippincott was licensed to print *The Elementary Spelling Book* in 1848, for example, by George F. Cooledge of New York.

84. Skeel, *A Bibliography of the Writings of Noah Webster,* 106.

85. Rogers, "History of the Paper Mill at Salem," 77.

86. Keith Whitescarver, "School Books, Publishers, and Southern Nationalists: Refashioning the Curriculum in North Carolina Schools, 1850–1861," *North Carolina Historical Review* 79 (January 2002): 28–49.

87. Rev. Robert Fleming, *The Revised Elementary Spelling Book, Revised and Adapted for the Youth of the Southern Confederacy Interspersed with Bible Readings on Domestic Slavery* (Atlanta, GA: J. J. Toon, 1863).

Chapter 2. Grammars

1. AJCR, February 20, 1842, August 20, 1843; EACM, August 6, 1843.

2. David Walker, *Appeal to the Coloured Citizens of the World* (1829; University Park, PA: Penn State University Press, 2000), 32.

3. Daniel Alexander Payne, *Recollections of Seventy Years,* ed. C. S. Smith (Nashville, TN, 1888), 21–22; Stephen Weeks, "John Chavis Antebellum Negro Preacher and Teacher," *The Southern Workman* 43 (February 1914): 101–8, quote on 106; Brantley York, *The Autobiography of Brantley York* (Durham, NC: The Seeman Printery, 1910), 60; Paul D. Escott, ed., *North Carolina Yeoman: The Diary of Basil Armstrong Thomasson, 1853–1862* (Athens: University of Georgia Press, 1996), 124.

4. Kenneth Cmiel, *Democratic Eloquence: The Fight Over Popular Speech in Nineteenth-Century America* (New York: William Morrow and Company, 1990), 54; Abraham Lincoln, "Autobiography Written for Campaign," in *Lincoln: Selected Speeches and Writings* (New York, 1992), 266.

5. "Language is not a neutral medium that passes freely and easily into the private property of the speaker's intentions. . . forcing it to submit to one's own intentions and accents, is a difficult and complicated process." Mikhail Bahktin, *Speech Genres and Other Late Essays,* trans. Vern W. McGee (Austin: University of Texas Press, 1986), 294.

6. York, *Autobiography,* 10; John Carroll, *Autobiography and Reminiscences of John W. Carroll* (Henderson, TN, 1898), 10.

7. Rollo Laverne Lyman, *English Grammar in American Schools Before 1850* (Washington, DC: Government Printing Office, 1922), 9; Clifton Johnson, *Old-*

Time Schools and School-books (1904; New York: Dover Publications, 1963), 363.

8. Joseph E. Worcester, *A Universal and Critical Dictionary of the English Language* (Boston: Wilkins, Carter, and Company, 1846), 318; Joseph E. Worcester, *A Dictionary of the English Language* (Boston: Hickling, Swan and Brewer, 1860), 634.

9. "Preface," Allen M. Scott, *A New Southern Grammar of the English Language, Designed for the Use of Schools or Private Learners* (Memphis, TN: Hutton and Freligh, 1861).

10. Beth Barton Schweiger, "A Social History of English Grammar in the Early United States," *Journal of the Early Republic* 30 (Winter 2010): 533–55; Lyman, *English Grammar in American Schools Before 1850*, 9; Samuel Kirkham, *English Grammar in Familiar Lectures* (Rochester, NY: Marshall, Dean & Co, 1833), 11; "Editor's Book Table—Frost's Practical English Grammar," *Godey's Lady's Book* (Dec. 1842), 307.

11. Lucille M. Schultz, *The Young Composers: Composition's Beginnings in Nineteenth-Century Schools* (Carbondale, IL: Southern Illinois University Press, 1999).

12. William Gilmore, *Reading Becomes a Necessity of Life: Material and Cultural Life in Rural New England, 1780–1835* (Knoxville: University of Tennessee Press, 1989); Monaghan, "Reading for the Enslaved, Writing for the Free: Reflections on Liberty and Literacy," *Proceedings of the American Antiquarian Society* 108 (October 1998): 309–41.

13. Kirkham, *English Grammar*, 2.

14. *OED Online*, s.v. "literacy," accessed February 14, 2017, http://0-www.oed.com.library.uark.edu/view/Entry/109054?redirectedFrom=literacy ().

15. *The Social Construction of Literacy*, Jenny Cook-Gumperz, ed. (New York: Cambridge University Press, 1986), 1.

16. William F. Woods, "The Evolution of Nineteenth-Century Grammar Teaching," *Rhetoric Review* 5 (Fall 1986): 5.

17. EACM, August 21, 1843.

18. Charles Monaghan, *The Murrays of Murray Hill* (Brooklyn: Urban History Press, 1998), vii, 130–34; Edward Hitchcock, *The Power of Christian Benevolence Illustrated in the Life and Labors of Mary Lyon* (Northampton, MA: Hopkins, Bridgman, and Company, 1852), 290; Cmiel, *Democratic Eloquence*, 75; Ingrid Tieken-Boon van Ostade, "Introduction," and Kayoko Fuami, "Lindley Murray and the Introduction of English into Japan," in van Ostade, ed., *Two Hundred Years of Lindley Murray* (Munster, Germany: Nodus Publikationen, 1996), 10, 125; Lyman, *English Grammar in American Schools Before 1850*,

80; Ian Michael, *The Teaching of English: From the Sixteenth Century to 1870* (New York: Cambridge University Press, 1987), 327; Percival Leigh, *The Comic English Grammar* (London: R. Bentley, 1840), and Alfred Crowquill (pseud. Alfred Henry Forrester), *The Pictorial Grammar* (London: Harvey and Darton, 1842). Leigh's book appeared in several American editions.

19. Murray, *English Grammar*, 13, 41, 137; G. P. Quackenbos, *English Grammar* (New York: D. Appleton and Company, 1863), 7.

20. Murray, *English Grammar*, 251, 257.

21. Cmiel, *Democratic Eloquence*, 89.

22. Lyman, *English Grammar in American Schools Before 1850*, 80–82.

23. Monaghan, *Murrays of Murray Hill*, 130–37; Lyman, *English Grammar in American Schools Before 1850*, 81; Cmiel, *Democratic Eloquence*, 75.

24. Book Trades Collection, Mss. Boxes B, Box 2, Folders 6 and 12, AAS.

25. Weems quoted in James N. Green, " 'The Cowl knows best what will suit in Virginia': Parson Weems on Southern Readers," *Printing History* 17 (1995): 26–34, quote on 30.

26. Lyman, *English Grammar in American Schools Before 1850*, 92, 100.

27. Edgar W. Knight, *Public School Education in North Carolina* (Boston: Houghton Mifflin Company, 1916), 198–99.

28. James Pyle Wickersham, *A History of Education in Pennsylvania, Private and Public, Elementary and Higher* (Lancaster, PA: Inquirer Publishing, 1886), 193.

29. Lyman, *English Grammar in American Schools Before 1850*, 82–92; *Annual Report of the State Commissioner of Common Schools for the Year 1854* (Columbus, OH, 1855), 74–77.

30. *Alexandria (VA) Herald*, April 14, 1823, 3; April 23, 1823, 2; September 1, 1823, 3.

31. J[oseph] H[ervey] Hull, *English Grammar by Lectures* (Hagerstown, MD, 1823); *English Grammar by Lectures*, 7th ed. (Maysville, KY, 1833).

32. "Mr. Shalrman's Scholars," *City Gazette* [Charleston SC], February 26, 1823, 3; "Mr. Ingersoll proposes," *Augusta Chronicle and Georgia Advertiser*, January 31, 1824, 3; "English Grammar," *Baltimore Patriot and Mercantile Advertiser*, July 6, 1831, 1; "School opposite Episcopal church," *The Civilian and Galveston* [Texas] *City Gazette*, August 20, 1842, 3; "Professor Bronson," [New Orleans] *Times-Picayune*, January 22, 1846, 2.

33. Jeremiah Greenleaf, *Grammar Simplified; or An Ocular Analysis* (Brattleborough, Vermont, 1819).

34. Kirkham, *English Grammar in Familiar Lectures*, 11.

35. Seth T. Hurd, *A Grammatical Chart, or Private Instructor of the English Language* (Boston: John Marsh, 1827); J. Knowlton, *A Compilation of Ideas Partly*

Original and Partly Collected from Different Authors on the Science of Grammar (Salem, MA: Damon's Press, 1843); George Freidenburg, *A Lecture Containing the Principles of Grammar* (Watertown, NY? s.n., 184?); Jeremiah Greenleaf, *The Self-Taught Grammarian, or Family Grammar* (New York, 1821); J. S. Muzzy, *Temperance and Grammar* (Cincinnati: Shepherd and Co., 1844). Greenleaf also produced maps, gazetteers, two grammars under different titles, and a Latin grammar. All broadsides are in the collection of the AAS.

36. York, *Autobiography,* 19.

37. Tomlinson Store Ledger B (1834–1848), 85, Randolph County, NC, Rubenstein Rare Book and Manuscript Library, Duke University.

38. Tomlinson Store Ledger B (1834–1848), 56.

39. SOP, 34.

40. NJS, October 8, 1846.

41. "Testimonials," in Brantley York, *The Illustrative and Constructive Grammar of the English Language* (Salisbury, NC: Carolina Watchman Press, 1854), v–viii.

42. York, *Autobiography,* 61.

43. York, *Illustrative and Constructive Grammar;* York, *Autobiography,* 67.

44. York, *Autobiography,* 65.

45. York, *Autobiography,* 80; F. P. Julian to "Pres. Peacock," April 15, 1895, Brantley York Papers, Rubenstein Rare Book and Manuscript Library, Duke University.

46. John J. Gumperz, "Interactional Sociolinguistics in the Study of Schooling," in *The Social Construction of Literacy,* ed. Cook-Gumperz, 46; Watts, *Improvement of the Mind,* Joseph Emerson, rev. (Boston, 1833), 226.

47. Robert J. Connors, *Composition-Rhetoric: Backgrounds, Theory, and Pedagogy* (Pittsburgh, PA: University of Pittsburgh Press, 1997), 115–16.

48. Locke, *An Essay Concerning Human Understanding,* Roger Woolhouse, ed. (1690; New York: Penguin Books, 1997), 147–52.

49. On faculty psychology, Daniel Walker Howe, *Making the American Self: From Jonathan Edwards to Abraham Lincoln* (Cambridge, MA: Harvard University Press, 1997); Goold Brown, *The Grammar of English Grammars,* 10th ed. (New York: William Wood, 1872), iv–v.

50. William F. Woods, "Nineteenth-Century Psychology and the Teaching of Writing," *College Composition and Communication* 36 (February 1985): 20–41; *Annual Report of the State Commissioner of Common Schools for the Year 1854* (Columbus, OH, 1855), 57.

51. David Vincent, *The Rise of Mass Literacy: Reading and Writing in Modern Europe* (Cambridge: Polity Press, 2000), 29.

52. Woods, "Evolution of Nineteenth-Century Grammar Teaching," 9–10.

53. Murray, *English Grammar,* 195–96.

54. Brown, *Grammar of English Grammars,* 65; James L. Golden and Edward P. J. Corbett, *The Rhetoric of Blair, Campbell, and Whately* (Carbondale: Southern Illinois University Press, 1990), 30.

55. Dell Upton, ed., *Madaline: Love and Survival in Antebellum New Orleans* (Athens: University of Georgia Press, 1996), 35; Basil Armstrong Thomasson, March 9, 1856, in Escott, ed., *North Carolina Yeoman,* 129; John Joseph, *The Life and Sufferings of John Joseph* (May 22, 2003) (http://docsouth.unc.edu /neh/jjoseph/jjoseph.html).

56. *OED Online,* http://0-www.oed.com.library.uark.edu/view/Entry/224855.

57. Cmiel, *Democratic Eloquence;* Michael P. Kramer, *Imagining Language in America: From the Revolution to the Civil War* (Princeton, NJ: Princeton University Press, 1992); Dennis E. Baron, *Grammar and Good Taste: Reforming the American Language* (New Haven, CT: Yale University Press, 1982); R. H. Robins, *A Short History of Linguistics* (Bloomington: Indiana University Press, 1967).

58. Jonathan Steinberg, "The Historian and the Questione della Lingua," in *The Social History of Language,* ed. Peter Burke and Roy Porter (Cambridge: Cambridge University Press, 1987), 198–209, esp. 206; Alessandro Duranti, *Linguistic Anthropology* (New York: Cambridge University Press, 1997), 2–3.

59. Murray, *English Grammar,* 13.

60. On dress and manners, Karen Halttunen, *Confidence Men and Painted Women: A Study of Middle Class Culture in America, 1830–1870* (New Haven, CT: Yale University Press, 1982), esp. 110–11, 118–22.

61. David R. Sewell, *Mark Twain's Languages: Discourse, Dialogue, and Linguistic Variety* (Berkeley: University of California Press, 1987), 25, 16.

62. Adiel Sherwood, *Gazetteer of the State of Georgia* (Charleston, SC: W. Riley, 1827), 138–39; Adiel Sherwood, *Gazetteer of the State of Georgia,* 3rd ed. (Washington, DC: P. Force, 1837), 72. More than 140 letters written by plantation overseers in North and South Carolina from the 1810s into the 1850s used nonstandard spellings and ungrammatical expressions throughout. Edgar W. Schneider and Michael B. Montgomery, "On the Trail of Early Nonstandard Grammar: An Electronic Corpus of Southern US Antebellum Overseers' Letters," *American Speech* 76 (Winter 2001): 388–410.

63. Jonathan Swift, quoted in Harry Levin, "The Wages of Satire," in *Literature and Society,* ed. Edward W. Said (Baltimore, MD: The Johns Hopkins University Press, 1980), 1–14, quote on 7.

64. AJCR, August 13, 1843.

65. Downing "created no little amusement from Maine to Georgia, to say nothing of the other side of the Atlantic." "Notices of New Works — Powhatan; A Metrical Romance in Seven Cantos by Mr. and Mrs. Seba Smith," *Southern Literary Messenger* 7 (July 1841): 587–88.

66. Walter Blair, *Horse Sense in American Humor* (New York: Russell and Russell, 1942), 61, 62.

67. Seba Smith, *The Select Letters of Major Jack Downing* (Philadelphia, 1834), 9.

68. Eugene Current-Garcia, "Newspaper Humor in the Old South, 1835–1855," *Alabama Review* 2 (April 1949): 102–21.

69. Henry Prentice Miller, "The Background and Significance of Major Jones' Courtship," *Georgia Historical Quarterly* 4 (December 1946): 267–96, quote on 287. Thompson was influenced by Smith's Downing letters. The Jones letters appeared as *Major Jones' Courtship* (Madison, GA, 1843).

70. Nelle Smither, "Library of American Humorous Works: A Bibliographical Study," master's thesis, Columbia University, 1936, 19–21.

71. Current-Garcia, "Newspaper Humor."

72. Smith, *Letters of Major Jack Downing*, v.

73. Professor Larrabee, "Miscellaneous Sketches," *Ladies Repository* 6 (March 1846), 66.

74. *Southern Literary Messenger* 3 (April 1837): 222.

75. U.S. Census Bureau. Census 1850. Literacy (Free Population Age 20 and Over). Prepared by Social Explorer. (https://www.socialexplorer.com/tables /Census1850/R11803229).

76. "Skitt," [Harden E. Taliaferro], *Fisher's River (North Carolina): Scenes and Characters* (1859; New York: Arno Press, 1977), [facsimile edition] 17–18, 187.

77. EACM, November 30, 1845.

78. Guy Bailey, "When Did Southern American English Begin?" in *Englishes Around the World: Essays in Honour of Manfred Görlach*, ed. Edgar W. Schneider, v. 1 (Philadelphia: John Benjamins Publishing Company, 1997), 255–75.

79. EACM, May 14, 1843.

80. William Ellery Channing, *Self-Culture*, facsimile ed. (1838; New York, 1969), 44–45.

Chapter 3. Rhetorics

1. AMS, January 1, 1853.

2. Steven Shapin and Barry Barnes, "Head and Hand: Rhetorical Resources in British Pedagogical Writing, 1770–1850," *Oxford Review of Education* 2 (1976): 231–53, esp. 231–35.

3. Robert J. Connors, *Composition-Rhetoric: Backgrounds, Theory, and Pedagogy* (Pittsburgh: University of Pittsburgh Press, 1997), 51–52.

4. Forten quoted in Suzanne L. Bunkers and Cynthia Anne Huff, eds., *Inscribing the Daily: Critical Essays on Women's Diaries* (Amherst: University of Massachusetts Press, 1996), 140.

5. NJS, December 3, 1850.

6. EACM, November 5, 1843; "Advertisement for Cory's Bookstore and Printing Office," July 3, 1823, *Milton Gazette and Roanoke Advertiser*, 1; David Henkin, *The Postal Age: The Emergence of Modern Communications in Nineteenth-Century America* (Chicago: University of Chicago Press, 2008), 101–16; Konstantin Dierks, *In My Power: Letter Writing and Communications in Early America* (Philadelphia: University of Pennsylvania Press, 2011). Dilworth essentially copied Samuel Richardson's *Familiar Letters on Important Occasions* (London, 1741).

7. John Todd, quoted in Deirdre M. Mahoney, " 'More Than an Accomplishment': Advice on Letter Writing for Nineteenth-Century American Women," *Huntington Library Quarterly* 66 (2003): 411–23, quotes on 415, 417.

8. Henkin, *Postal Age,* 3.

9. Dierks, *In My Power,* 235–79. On Civil War letters, Christopher Hager, *I Remain Yours: Common Lives in Civil War Letters* (Cambridge, MA: Harvard University Press, 2018) and Robert E. Bonner, *The Soldier's Pen: Firsthand Impressions of the Civil War* (New York: Hill and Wang, 2006).

10. Scott M. Stephan, "Reconsidering the Boundaries of Maternal Authority in the Evangelical Household: The Davis Family of Antebellum Murfreesboro," *North Carolina Historical Review* 83 (April 2006): 165–92.

11. Tamara Plakins Thornton, *Handwriting in America: A Cultural History* (New Haven, CT: Yale University Press, 1996), 92–122.

12. Blair, *Lectures on Rhetoric,* 418.

13. Sue Walker, "The Manners of the Page: Prescription and Practice in the Visual Organization of Correspondence," *Huntington Library Quarterly* 66 (2003): 307–29.

14. R. Turner, *Parlour Letter-Writer* (Philadelphia: Thomas, Cowperthwait and Co., 1847), 20, 31.

15. Turner, *Parlour Letter-Writer,* 26, 25, 98–99, 261.

16. James L. Golden and Edward P. J. Corbett, *The Rhetoric of Blair, Campbell, and Whately* (Carbondale: Southern Illinois University Press, 1990), 23–25.

17. Blair, *Lectures on Rhetoric,* 37; Ann Speer, "Soliloquizing in the Wild Wood," November 3, 1854, SFP.

18. Golden and Corbett, *Rhetoric of Blair, Campbell, and Whately,* 53.

19. Wordsworth, "Lines Composed a Few Miles above Tintern Abbey," lines 89–99.

20. AMS, January 5, January 6, 1853.

21. S. F. Cary, ed., *The National Temperance Offering, and Sons and Daughters of Temperance Gift* (New York: R. Vandien, 1850). Aquilla Speer's copy is in the Boonville Community Library, Boonville, NC.

22. Hugh Blair, "Lecture II—Taste," in *The Rhetoric of Blair, Campbell, and Whately,* ed. Golden and Corbett, 37–40; Alonzo Potter, "Influence of Literature on the Moral Sentiments," in *The Christian Keepsake and Missionary Annual,* ed. John A. Clark (Philadelphia, 1838), 281–92, quote on 282.

23. Karen Lystra, *Searching the Heart: Women, Men, and Romantic Love in Nineteenth-Century America* (New York: Oxford University Press, 1989), 8; Beth Barton Schweiger, "Reading the Bible in a Romantic Era," in *The Bible in American Life,* ed. Philip Goff, et al. (New York: Oxford University Press, 2017), 69–80.

24. AMS, March 25, 1853.

25. Rufus W. Clark, *Lectures on the Formation of Character, Temptations and Mission of Young Men* (Boston, 1853), 99.

26. *Jonesville (NC) Enterprise,* June 4, 1858. Only two issues of this paper are extant.

27. Ruby Bray Canipe and Brenda Moxley Couch, *Early Elkin-Jonesville History and Genealogy* (Jonesville, NC: Tarheel Graphics, 1981), 87–100.

28. *Annual Catalogue of Jonesville Male and Female Academies* (Salisbury, NC: Bell and James, Printers, 1855), 12–13, 15. No image of the school survives.

29. J. Graham Ramsay, DD, "An Address Delivered before the Students of Jonesville Academy, Yadkin Co., NC June 10th AD 1853," J. G. Ramsay Papers, 1784–1855, Series 3, Folder 118, SHC; David Jaffee, "The Village Enlightenment in New England, 1760–1820," *William and Mary Quarterly* 47 (July 1990): 327–46.

30. *Annual Catalogue of Jonesville Male and Female Academies,* 10; S. A. LaRoche to Iveson Brookes, October 27, 1845, quoted in Heidi Maria Schultz, "Southern Women Learn to Write: 1830–1860," PhD diss., University of North Carolina at Chapel Hill, 1996, 22.

31. Canipe and Couch, *Early Elkin-Jonesville,* 89; Z. H. Dixon, "Jonesville Male and Female Academies, 1845–1860," *The North Carolina Teacher,* vol. 4 (January 1928): 143, 153.

32. "Annual Catalogue of the Trustees, Officers and Students of Jonesville Male and Female Academies for 1853–54," in *Early Elkin-Jonesville History and Genealogy,* ed. Ruby Bray Canipe and Brenda Moxley Couch (Jonesville, NC: Tarheel Graphics, 1981), 91–96.

33. "Notice. On Friday, June 11th 1858," *Jonesville (NC) Enterprise,* June 4, 1858, 4.

34. Robert J. Connors, *Composition-Rhetoric: Backgrounds, Theory, and Pedagogy* (Pittsburgh, PA: University of Pittsburgh, 1997), 79.

35. Lucille M. Schultz, *The Young Composers: Composition's Beginnings in Nineteenth-Century Schools* (Carbondale: Southern Illinois University Press, 1999), 96.

36. Canipe, *Early Elkin-Jonesville History,* 88; Yadkin County Tax Register, 1850–1861, microfilm, Yadkinville Public Library; W. L. VanEaton, "Important Sale! having determined to go West," broadside, Jonesville, NC, October 1868, Rubenstein Rare Book and Manuscript Library, Duke University.

37. NJS, December 2, 1845.

38. "Improved System of Teaching," Brantley York Papers, Rubenstein Rare Book and Manuscript Library, Duke University.

39. *Jonesville (NC) Enterprise,* June 4, 1858, 1.

40. NJS, "Harmony of Nature," June 29, 1848, SFP.

41. *Circular of Greensboro Female College, Greensboro, North Carolina for the Scholastic Year ending June 5, 1853* (Richmond, VA: Charles H. Wynne, Printer, 1853), 15.

42. Charles Lee Smith, *The History of Education in North Carolina* (Washington, DC: Bureau of Education, 1888), 121; Mary Beall, quoted in Christie Anne Farnham, *The Education of the Southern Belle: Higher Education and Student Socialization in the Antebellum South* (New York: New York University Press, 1994), 147–48.

43. NJS, December 6, 1850.

44. NJS, December 8, 1850.

45. NJS, April 29, 1851.

46. Deems probably paid the tuition costs.

47. Amanda Porterfield, *Mary Lyon and the Mount Holyoke Missionaries* (New York: Oxford University Press, 1997), 33; Jennie Speer diary, March 23, 1853, and March 30, 1853, quoted in SOP, 166, 169.

48. Appendix, *Seventeenth Annual Catalogue of the Mount Holyoke Female Seminary, 1853–54* (Northampton, MA: Hopkins, Bridgman, 1854); Elizabeth Allen Green, *Mary Lyon and Mount Holyoke: Opening the Gates* (Hanover, NH: University Press of New England, 1979), 226–27; NJS, October 22, 1852.

49. Porterfield, *Mary Lyon,* 32.

50. Julia Tolman, December 14, 1846, quoted in Green, *Mary Lyon,* 247.

51. Suzanne B. Spring, "Forming Letters: Mount Holyoke, Emily Dickinson, and Nineteenth-Century Epistolary Compositions," PhD diss., University of Michigan, 2005, 110.

52. Jennie Speer, "Mount Holyoke Female Seminary," n.d., SFP; Spring, "Forming Letters," 85–87. Jennie wrote a report on her experience at Mount Holyoke for Charles Deems that has apparently not survived.

53. Heidi Maria Schultz, "Southern Women Learn to Write: 1830–1860," PhD diss., University of North Carolina at Chapel Hill, 1996, 95.

54. NJS, "Untitled—Saturday February 5, 1853, Mt Holyoke," SFP.

55. NJS, "The Beautiful Lies in the Depths of the Soul," June 11, 1853, Mt Holyoke, SFP.

56. SOP, 14.

57. No title, no date, SFP.

58. AMS, February 13, 1853.

59. Ann Douglas, *The Feminization of American Culture* (New York: Alfred A. Knopf, 1977).

60. Sheila M. Rothman, *Living in the Shadow of Death: Tuberculosis and the Social Experience of Illness in American History* (Baltimore, MD: Johns Hopkins University Press, 1995), 16–17.

61. Rothman, *Living in the Shadow*, 18–21.

62. Kay K. Moss, *Southern Folk Medicine, 1750–1820* (Columbia: University of South Carolina Press, 1999), 58–62; Jennie to "My Mother," March 23, 1854, SFP; AMS, August 25, 1857.

63. Aaron Clinton Speer edited the weekly *Tennessee Patriot* from 1853 to 1854 in Lawrenceburg, Tennessee, before moving on to edit *The Boonville Missourian* in Boonville, Missouri, and then to open a school in Independence, ninety-five miles further west. Allen Paul Speer, *Voices From Cemetery Hill: The Civil War Diary, Reports, and Letters of Colonel William Henry Asbury Speer (1861–1864)* (Johnson City, TN: The Overmountain Press, 1997), 16.

64. Rothman, *Living in the Shadow*; Katherine Ott, *Fevered Lives: Tuberculosis in American Culture since 1870* (Cambridge, MA: Harvard University Press, 1996).

65. Rothman, *Living in the Shadow*, 4.

66. Edward Johnson, MD, *Life, Health, and Disease* (New York: John Wiley, 1850), 109–11, quotes on 109, 110.

67. Barbara Miller Solomon, *In the Company of Educated Women: A History of Women and Higher Education in America* (New Haven, CT: Yale University Press, 1985), 56.

68. Harvey Lindsly, "Observations on the Ill Health of American Women," *Southern Literary Messenger* (February 1839): 89–94, quote on 93; Joseph Ray, "The Health of Teachers," *The Ladies Repository* (July 1852): 274–75, quote on 274.

69. Caroline Lee Hentz, *The Planter's Northern Bride* (Philadelphia: T. B. Peterson and Brothers, 1854), 147.

70. AJCR, October 29, 1852.

71. AJCR, April 30, 1852, and February 13, 1853.

72. AJCR, November 17, 1852, and April 9, 1853.

73. AJCR, July 11, 1853, and April 30, 1854. The $220 may have represented her contributions to the household through her teaching, weaving, and sewing. The amount of the allowance for James is not known because the page is torn.

74. "No. 1 The Time to Die," N. J. Speer, Mt. Holyoke Female Seminary, November 9, 1852, SFP.

75. NJS, April 22, 1853, and March 2, 1854.

76. NJS, March 13, 1854, April 29, 1854, and September 1, 1856.

77. AMS, August 25, 1857, September 20, 1857, August 25, 1857. The best treatment of family and Methodism is A. Gregory Schneider, *The Way of the Cross Leads Home: The Domestication of American Methodism* (Bloomington: Indiana University Press, 1993).

Part II. A Musical, Literary, and Christian Miscellany

1. Richard M. Dorson, *American Folklore and the Historian* (Chicago: University of Chicago Press, 1971), 185.

Chapter 4. Songs

1. Cecil J. Sharp, "Introduction," *English Folk Songs from the Southern Appalachians: Comprising 122 Songs and Ballads, and 323 Tunes,* Olive Dame Campbell and Cecil J. Sharp, eds. (New York: G.P. Putnam's Sons, 1917), viii; EACM, June 4, 1843.

2. Cecilia Conway, *African Banjo Echoes in Appalachia: A Study of Folk Traditions* (Knoxville: University of Tennessee Press, 1995), 121–59.

3. The incident unleashed a violent campaign against suspected abolitionists and lived on in local memory into the next century, when an account was enclosed in the cornerstone of a white Methodist church built in 1902 in Fries, Virginia, on the New River. Elizabeth Willets Crooks, *Life of Rev. A. Crooks, A.M.* (Syracuse, NY: Wesleyan Methodist Publishing House, 1875), 18, 47; B. F. Nuckolls, *Pioneer Settlers of Grayson County Virginia* (Bristol, TN: The King Printing Company, 1914), 12–15; Randal L. Hall, *Mountains on the Market: Industry, the Environment, and the South* (Lexington: University Press of Kentucky, 2012), 76–79.

4. AJCR, November 2, 1851. The phrase "launched into eternity" was a cliché in print of the period. Kenneth Cmiel, *Democratic Eloquence: The Fight Over*

Popular Speech in Nineteenth-Century America (New York: William Morrow and Company, 1990), 111.

5. W. E. B. Du Bois, *The Souls of Black Folk, Essays and Sketches,* 2nd ed. (Chicago: A.C. McClurg, 1903), 255; J. B. T. Marsh, *The Story of the Jubilee Singers; With Their Songs,* rev. ed. (New York: S.W. Green's Son, 1883), 136; Lawrence W. Levine, *Black Culture and Black Consciousness: Afro-American Folk Thought from Slavery to Freedom* (New York: Oxford University Press, 1977), 38.

6. Stephen Marini, "Hymnody as History: Early Evangelical Hymns and the Recovery of American Popular Religion," *Church History,* 71 (June 2002): 273–306, n. 14, 279.

7. Phillips Barry, "The Transmission of Folk-Song," *Journal of American Folklore* 27 (January–March 1914): 67. Twentieth-century collectors who searched for a "pure" oral tradition found songs that had been circulated by print or phonograph recording before they re-entered the oral tradition. David C. Rubin, *Memory in Oral Traditions: The Cognitive Psychology of Epic, Ballads, and Counting-out Rhymes* (New York: Oxford University Press, 1995), 264–65.

8. George Pullen Jackson, *White Spirituals in the Southern Uplands: The Story of the Fasola Folk, Their Songs, Singings, and "Buckwheat Notes"* (Chapel Hill: University of North Carolina Press, 1933); Irving Lowens, "A Northern Precursor of Southern Folk-Hymnody," in *Music and Musicians in Early America* (New York, W.W. Norton, 1964), 138–55.

9. Richard Hulan, "'Our Creed in Metre': The Hymnology of the Restoration Movement to 1835," master's thesis, Vanderbilt University, 1971; Hulan, "Camp-Meeting Spiritual Folksongs: Legacy of the 'Great Revival in the West,'" PhD. diss., University of Texas, 1978; David Warren Steel, "John Wyeth and the Development of Southern Folk Hymnody," in *Music from the Middle Ages through the 20th Century: Essays in Honor of Gwynn McPeek,* Carmelo P. Comberiati and Matthew C. Steel, eds. (London: Gordon and Breach, 1988), 357–74; Kay Norton, *Baptist Offspring, Southern Midwife–Jesse Mercer's 'Cluster of Spiritual Songs' (1810): A Study in American Hymnody* (Warren, MI: Harmonie Park Press, 2002); Kay Norton, "Who Lost the South?" *American Music* (Winter 2003): 391–411; Steel, *Makers of the Sacred Harp;* Harry Eskew, "William Walker's 'Southern Harmony': Its Basic Editions," *Latin American Music Review* 7 (Autumn–Winter, 1986): 137–48.

10. Norton, "Who Lost the South?" 405.

11. James E. Kirby, Russell E. Richey, and Kenneth E. Rowe, *The Methodists* (Westport, CT: Greenwood Press, 1996), 193, n. 19.

12. David Warren Steel with Richard Hulan, *The Makers of the Sacred Harp* (Urbana: University of Illinois Press, 2010), 50.

13. Eileen Southern, *The Music of Black Americans: A History*, 2nd ed. (New York: W.W. Norton, 1983); Dena Epstein, *Sinful Tunes and Spirituals: Black Folk Music to the Civil War* (Urbana: University of Illinois Press, 2003); William H. Tallmadge, "The Black in Jackson's White Spirituals," *The Black Perspective in Music* (Autumn 1981): 139–60.

14. Albert J. Raboteau, *Slave Religion: The "Invisible Institution" in the Antebellum South* (New York: Oxford University Press, 1978), 239; Levine, *Black Culture, Black Consciousness*, 37, 36.

15. Eileen Southern, "An Origin for the Negro Spiritual," *The Black Scholar* 3 (June 1972), 11. See also Southern, *Music of Black Americans*, 75–79, 167–77.

16. Southern, *Music of Black Americans*, 79. Lawrence Levine's influential 1977 *Black Culture and Black Consciousness* did not cite Southern. Her full statement on Allen's influence appeared in 1983, but earlier articles stated her view on the question.

17. J. Roland Braithwaite, "Originality in the 1801 Hymnals of Richard Allen," in *New Perspectives on Music: Essays in Honor of Eileen Southern*, Josephine Wright, ed. (Detroit, MI: Harmonie Park Press, 1992), 71–91.

18. Braithwaite, "Originality in the 1801 Hymnals of Richard Allen," 73–80.

19. "The New Hymn Book," *Quarterly Review of the Methodist Episcopal Church, South* 1 (January 1848): 69–130; James Penn Pilkington, *The Methodist Publishing House, A History*, 2 vols. (Nashville, TN: The Abingdon Press, 1968), 1:147–48; Nathan Bangs, *A History of the Methodist Episcopal Church*, 4th vol. (New York: G. Lane and P.P. Sandford, 1841), 433.

20. Anne Dhu Shapiro, "Black Sacred Song and the Tune-Family Concept," in *New Perspectives on Music: Essays in Honor of Eileen Southern*, ed. Josephine Wright (Warren, MI: Harmonie Park Press, 1992), 101–15.

21. Anne Dhu McLucas, *The Musical Ear: Oral Tradition in the USA* (Burlington, VT: Ashgate, 2010), 83, n.7. "Lining out" is still used in congregational singing, especially among Primitive Baptists.

22. Samuel Davies to "J. F." August 26, 1768, quoted in Epstein, *Sinful Tunes and Spirituals*, 104.

23. James M. Simms, *The First Colored Baptist Church in North America* (Philadelphia, J.B. Lippincott, 1888), 42–43.

24. Christopher H. Owen, *The Sacred Flame of Love: Methodism and Society in Nineteenth-Century Georgia* (Athens: University of Georgia Press, 1998), 81.

25. Joan R. Sherman, *The Black Bard of North Carolina: George Moses Horton and His Poetry* (Chapel Hill: University of North Carolina Press, 1997), 2.

26. William T. Dargan, *Lining Out the Word: Dr. Watts Hymn Singing in the Music of Black Americans* (Berkeley: University of California Press, 2006), 181.

27. EACM, May 18, 1846.

28. EACM, April 15, 18; May 15; June 7, 10, 13, 18, 1846.

29. Frederick Douglass, *My Bondage and My Freedom* (New York: Miller and Orton, 1857), 97.

30. Charles Colcock Jones quoted in Southern, *Music of Black Americans,* 146.

31. William T. Dargan, "Texts from Lloyd's Hymn Book in the Quiltwork of African American Singing Styles," in *Benjamin Lloyd's Hymn Book: A Baptist Song Tradition,* ed. Joyce H. Cauthen (Montgomery, AL: Alabama Folklife Association, 1999), 29–47.

32. Marini, "Hymnody as History," 279, n. 14; Elizabeth Cornetti, "Some Early Best Sellers in Piedmont North Carolina," *Journal of Southern History* 16 (August 1950): 327; Selma Lewis Bishop, *Isaac Watts's Hymns and Spiritual Songs (1707): A Publishing History and a Bibliography* (Ann Arbor, MI: Pierian Press, 1974); *The Psalms and Hymns of Dr. Watts Arranged by Dr. Rippon, Corrected and Improved by Rev. C. G. Sommers and Rev. John L. Dagg* (Philadelphia: Clark and Lippincott, 1837); J[ames] C[ephas] Derby, *Fifty Years Among Authors, Books, and Publishers* (New York, 1884), 387. The correspondence between Philadelphia printer William W. Woodward and his preacher-peddlers is in the Simon Gratz Collection, HSP.

33. McLucas, *The Musical Ear,* 83.

34. "Extract of a Letter from Rev. John Evans Findley," *Methodist Magazine* 26 (1803), quoted in Ellen Eslinger, *Citizens of Zion: Social Origins of Camp Meeting Revivalism* (Knoxville: University of Tennessee Press, 1999), 227.

35. Benjamin St. James Fry, *"Early Methodist Song Writers,"* 407; Steel, *Makers of Sacred Harp,* 58–59; Dickson Bruce, *And They All Sang Hallelujah: Plain-Folk Camp Meeting Religion, 1800–1845* (Knoxville: University of Tennessee Press, 1977), 100–101.

36. Roger Robins, "Vernacular American Landscape: Methodists, Camp Meetings, and Social Respectability," *Religion and American Culture* 4 (Summer 1994): 165–91; Bruce, *And They All Sang Hallelujah,* 89.

37. Hulan, "Camp-Meeting Spiritual Folksongs," 175–80.

38. Lemuel Birkitt, quoted in Guion Griffis Johnson, *Antebellum North Carolina: A Social History* (Chapel Hill: University of North Carolina Press, 1937), 395, n. 110.

39. Thomas Hinde, *The Pilgrim's Songster* (1810; Chillicothe, OH, 1815), quoted in Hulan, "Frontiers of the American Hymn," in Steel, *Makers of the Sacred Harp,* 64–69, quote on 69. The first edition of Hinde's songster is lost. Granade's printer Daniel Bradford also printed a lost work by Joshua Morris, simply called *A Collection of Spiritual Songs* in 1804.

40. Richard Hulan, "John Adam Granade: The 'Wild Man' of Goose Creek," *Western Folklore* 33 (January 1974): 77–87, esp. 82–83; Hulan, "Frontiers of the American Hymn," 66.

41. Eileen Southern, "A Camp-Meeting Spiritual," in *Themes and Variations: Writings on Music in Honor of Rulan Chao Pian* (Cambridge, MA: Harvard University Department of Music, 1994), 59–81.

42. Benjamin St. James Fry, "The Early Camp-Meeting Song Writers," *Methodist Quarterly Review* 4th. ser., 11 (1859): 401–13; Charles A. Johnson, *The Frontier Camp Meeting: Religion's Harvest Time* (Dallas, TX: Southern Methodist University Press, 1955), 193, 194; *Autobiography of Elder Matthew Gardner, A Minister in the Christian Church Sixty-Three Years* (Dayton, OH: Christian Publishing Association, 1874), 61, 66–67; Thomas Cleland, DD, *Evangelical Hymns* 3rd ed. (Lexington, KY: T.T. Skillman, 1829); *Western Luminary* (Lexington, KY), August 24, 1825, 112. Gardner did not offer a name of his hymnbook.

43. Steel, *Makers of the Sacred Harp,* 59–60; *The Rise of Methodism in the West,* William Warren Sweet, ed. (New York: The Methodist Book Concern, 1920), 56–57; Theophilus Armenius [Thomas S. Hinde], "Account of the Rise and Progress of the Work of God in the Western Country," *Methodist Magazine* 2 (1819), 273; Epstein, *Sinful Tunes and Spirituals,* 176; Russell E. Richey, *Early American Methodism* (Bloomington: Indiana University Press, 1991), 47–64; Robins, "Vernacular American Landscape," 169; Johnson, "Camp Meeting Hymnody," 114.

44. For one example, James Latta, *A Discourse on Psalmody; in which it is clearly shewn, that it is the duty of Christians to take the principal subjects and occasions of their psalms, hymns, and spiritual songs from the Gospel of Christ* (Philadelphia: William W. Woodward, 1794).

45. Eslinger, *Citizens of Zion,* 172–73.

46. AMS, April 11, 1853.

47. Fry, "Early Camp Meeting Song Writers," 412.

48. William Parkinson, "Preface," *A Selection of Hymns and Spiritual Songs in Two Parts* (New York, c1817), n.p.; John P[oage] Campbell, "A Sermon on Sacred Music: Preached Before a Public Concert in Washington" (Washington, KY: Hunter and Beaumont, 1797), 32.

49. Cushing Biggs Hassell and Sylvester Hassell, *History of the Church of God: From the Creation to A.D. 1885* (Middletown, NY, 1886), esp. 547.

50. Oliver C. Weaver, Jr., "Benjamin Lloyd: A Pioneer Primitive Baptist in Alabama," in *Benjamin Lloyd's Hymn Book: A Primitive Baptist Song Tradition,* ed. Joyce H. Cauthen (Montgomery, AL: Alabama Folklife Association, 1999), 49–55.

51. Kay Norton, *Baptist Offspring, Southern Midwife: Jesse Mercer's Cluster of*

Spiritual Songs (1810), A Study in American Hymnody (Warren, MI: Harmonie Park Press, 2002), 83; Joey Brackner, "Elder Benjamin Lloyd and His Hymn Book," in *Benjamin Lloyd's Hymn Book,* 57–76.

52. Steel, *Making of the Sacred Harp,* 65; Barton Stone, "Answer to a Letter of Enquiry," *Christian Messenger* 9 (October 1835), quoted in Hulan, "Our Creed in Metre," 8.

53. "Bibliography and Index of Baptist Hymnals," in *"I Will Sing the Wondrous Story": A History of Baptist Hymnody in North America,* ed. David W. Music and Paul A. Richardson (Macon, GA: Mercer University Press, 2008); Andrew Broaddus, *Collection of Sacred Ballads* (Caroline County, VA, 1790); NJS quoted in SOP, 32. The *Dover Selection of Spiritual Songs* (1828) and the *Virginia Selection of Psalms* (1836) circulated Broaddus's work across the southern states into the latter decades of the century.

54. Marini, "Hymnody as History," n. 2, 275; Rosalind Remer, "Preachers, Peddlers, and Publishers: Philadelphia's Backcountry Book Trade, 1800–1830," *Journal of the Early Republic* 14 (Winter 1994): 505–6; Robert B. Semple to William W. Woodward, September 17, 1817, Ferdinand J. Dreer Autograph Collection, HSP.

55. Jesse Mercer to W. W. Woodward, January 7, 1823, Gratz Collection, HSP.

56. Mercer's account book 1822–24, quoted in C. Ray Brewster, *The Cluster of Jesse Mercer* (Macon, GA: Renaissance Press, 1983), 43, 223, n. 10.

57. Brewster, *The Cluster,* 16. Brewster found eight imprints from 1810 to the fifth edition in 1835; Kay Norton identified eleven editions, of which she located nine with imprints in Augusta, Philadelphia, and New York. Mercer's nineteenth-century biographer located only five editions. Brewster, *Cluster,* 217–18; Norton, *Baptist Offspring,* 77; C. D. Mallary, *Memoirs of Elder Jesse Mercer* (New York, 1844), 85–86.

58. Norton, *Baptist Offspring,* 44, 59.

59. Norton, *Baptist Offspring,* 75.

60. Steel, "John Wyeth and the Development of Southern Folk Hymnody," 1; Irving Lowens, *Music and Musicians in Early America.*

61. Jackson, *White Spirituals,* 23; Augusta Brown in the *Musician and Intelligencer of Cincinnati* (1848), quoted in Buell E. Cobb, Jr., *The Sacred Harp: A Tradition and Its Music* (Athens: University of Georgia Press, 1978), 63; Constance Rourke, *The Roots of American Culture and Other Essays* (New York: Harcourt, Brace, 1942), 177–94, quote on 185.

62. D. W. Krummel, *Bibliographical Handbook of American Music* (Urbana: University of Illinois Press, 1987), 15; Brett Sutton, "Shape-Note Tune Books and Primitive Hymns," *Ethnomusicology* 26 (January 1982): 24.

63. Steel, *Making of the Sacred Harp,* 42, 45 ff.; Table I, Tune Books Compiled

by Southerners, 1816–1860 in David Warren Steel, "Lazarus J. Jones and 'The Southern Minstrel' (1849)," *American Music* 6 (Summer 1988): 123–57, table on 124. On new findings, see Marion Hatchett, "The Shape-Note Tunebooks of Andrew W. Johnson of Tennessee," in *Hymnology in the Service of the Church: Essays in Honor of Harry W. Eskew,* ed. Paul R. Powell (St. Louis: Morningstar Music Publishers, 2008), 36.

64. Eskew, "William Walker's 'Southern Harmony.'"

Chapter 5. Stories

1. EACM, May 8, 1842.
2. Leslie Mitchell, *Bulwer Lytton: The Rise and Fall of a Victorian Man of Letters* (London: Hambledon and London, 2003), esp. xv–xxi, 109–29.
3. EACM, May 8, 1842.
4. *The Ladies Repository and Gatherings of the West* 1 (January 1841): 26.
5. L. L. Hamline, "Reading," *The Ladies Repository and Gatherings of the West* 1 (January 1841): 2–7, quotes on 2, 3.
6. F. G. Hibbard, *Biography of Leonidas L. Hamline, DD* (Cincinnati, OH: Hitchcock and Walden, 1880).
7. *Graham's American Monthly Magazine of Literature and Art* 41 (July 1852): 7–12.
8. Brian Stock, *The Implications of Literacy: Written Language and Models of Interpretation in the Eleventh and Twelfth Centuries* (Princeton, NJ: Princeton University Press, 1983), 528–29.
9. *A Catalogue of Chapbooks in the New York Public Library,* comp. Harry B. Weiss (New York: New York Public Library, 1936), 6; Victor E. Neuberg, *The Penny Histories* (New York: Harcourt, Brace & World, 1969), 47. For a list of printers known to have produced chapbooks, see Victor E. Neuberg, *Chapbooks: A Guide to Reference Material on English, Scottish and American Chapbook Literature of the Eighteenth and Nineteenth Centuries,* 2d. ed. (London: Woburn Books, 1972), 70–74.
10. Louis B. Wright, *Culture on the Moving Frontier* (New York: Harper & Row, 1955), 53; Joseph Doddridge, *Notes on the Settlement and Indian Wars of the Western Parts of Virginia and Pennsylvania from 1863 to 1783* (Albany, NY: Joel Munsell, 1876), 124.
11. Elizabeth Cornetti, "Some Early Best Sellers in Piedmont North Carolina," *Journal of Southern History* 16 (August 1950): 324–37.
12. William H. Robinson, *From Log Cabin to Pulpit, or Fifteen Years in Slavery* (Eau Claire, WI: James H. Tifft, 1913), 158–59.

13. Inventory of John J. Trigg's estate in 1817, in Mary B. Kegley, *Early Adventurers in the Town of Evansham, the County Seat of Wythe County, Virginia, 1790–1839* (Wytheville, VA: Kegley Books, 1998), 328.

14. *Catalogue of Chapbooks,* 19, 44.

15. SOP, 10, 8.

16. L. H. Sigourney, *Pocahontas and Other Poems* (New York: Harper and Brothers, 1841), 19. Marryat, a former British naval officer, wrote popular maritime adventures.

17. "Missouri Intelligencer," 1829, quoted in Carle Brooks Spotts, "The Development of Fiction on the Missouri Frontier (1830–1860), *Missouri Historical Review* 28 (July 1934): quote on 276; Lewis E. Atherton, "James and Robert Aull—A Frontier Missouri Mercantile Firm," *Missouri Historical Review* 30 (October 1935): 3–7; Bernard Cresap, "The Muscle Shoals Frontier: Early Society and Culture in Lauderdale County," *The Alabama Review* 9 (July 1956): 188–213; James O. Knauss, "Education in Florida, 1821–1829," *The Quarterly* 3 (April 1925): 34.

18. Clarence S. Brigham, "Report of the Librarian—An Account of American Almanacs and Their Value for Historical Study," *Proceedings of the American Antiquarian Society* 35 (October 1925): 194–209, quote on 209. On religious readers of eighteenth-century almanacs, T. J. Tomlin, *A Divinity for All Persuasions: Almanacs and Early American Religious Life* (New York: Oxford University Press, 2014).

19. *Grenville's Georgia Almanac* (Augusta, GA: Charles E. Grenville, 1847). This copy is held by the AAS.

20. *Grenville's Georgia Almanac;* Douglas C. McMurtrie, *A Check-List of Kentucky Almanacs, 1789–1830* (Frankfort, KY: 1932).

21. James A. Bear, Jr. and Mary Caperton Bear, *A Checklist of Virginia Almanacs, 1732–1850* (Charlottesville: Bibliographical Society of the University of Virginia, 1962), viii; *The Kentucky Farmer's Almanac for the Year of Our Lord 1846* (Lexington, KY: Charles Marshall, 1845).

22. *The Christian Farmer's Almanack for the Year of Our Lord 1829* (Louisville, KY: Morton, 1828).

23. *The Franklin Almanac for 1821* (Richmond, VA: N. Pollard, 1821), 48.

24. S. S. Steele, *The Louisiana Almanac; 1845, Calendar of Useful Knowledge, Containing A World of Important Facts* (New Orleans, LA: S. Woodall, 1844).

25. *Kentucky Farmers' Almanac; The Western and Southern Almanac for the Year of Our Lord 1847* (Louisville, KY: G.H. Monsarrat, 1846); *Minutes of the Union Baptist Association* (Natchez, MS: William C. Grissam, 1827).

26. Christensen, *Edward Bulwer-Lytton,* 223–24; David S. Reynolds, *Beneath the*

American Renaissance: The Subversive Imagination in the Age of Emerson and Melville (Cambridge, MA: Harvard University Press, 1988), 228.

27. William Charvat, *The Origins of American Critical Thought, 1810–1835* (1936; New York: A.S. Barnes and Company, 1961), 11, 15, 152–53; Webster quoted in Karen Halttunen, *Murder Most Foul: The Killer and the American Gothic Imagination* (Cambridge, MA: Harvard University Press, 1998), 61.

28. Bulwer-Lytton, quoted in Mitchell, *Bulwer-Lytton*, 116.

29. Michael O'Brien, *Conjectures of Order: Intellectual Life and the American South, 1810–1860*, 2 vols. (Chapel Hill: University of North Carolina Press, 2004), 744–45.

30. Cathy N. Davidson, *Revolution and the Word: The Rise of the Novel in America* (New York: Oxford University Press, 1986), 110.

31. "Professor Larrabee," "Miscellaneous Sketches," *Ladies Repository* 6 (March 1846): 66–69, quote on 66.

32. NJS, April 14, 1844; Leonard Woods, D.D., *A Sermon Preached at Haverhill, Massachusetts in Remembrance of Mrs. Harriet Newell*, 4th ed. (Boston: Samuel T. Armstrong, 1814); *Memoirs of Mrs Harriet Newell, Wife of the Rev. S. Newell, American Missionary to India, Who Died at the Isle of France, Nov. 30, 1812. Aged Nineteen Years* (Edinburgh: Andrew Jack and Co., 1821).

33. *Memoirs of Mrs Harriet Newell*, 9.

34. Davidson, *Revolution and the Word*, 38–54.

35. Christensen, *Edward Bulwer-Lytton*, 225.

36. Emily B. Todd, "Walter Scott and the Nineteenth-Century American Literary Marketplace: Antebellum Richmond Readers and the Collected Editions of the Waverley Novels," *Papers of the Bibliographical Society of America* 93 (December 1999): 495–517.

37. Taylor's "The Oakland Stories," included at least four titles that appeared between 1860 and 1865. George Boardman Taylor, *Claiborne* (New York and Boston, 1860); *Cousin Guy* (New York and Boston, 1863); *Coster Grew* (American Baptist Publication Society, n.d.); *Gustave* (New York, 1865); Sallie E. Hughes, *Lucy Hall; or, Responsibility Realized* (Charleston, SC: Southern Baptist Publication Society, 1860). On moral fiction by northern Protestants, see Candy Gunther Brown, *The Word in the World: Evangelical Writing, Publishing, and Reading, 1789–1880* (Chapel Hill: University of North Carolina Press, 2004), esp. 95–105.

38. Little is known about how print was distributed across the country, and especially in the southern states. Michael Winship, " 'The Tragedy of the Book Industry?': Bookstores and Book Distribution in the United States to 1950," *Studies in Bibliography* 58 (2007–2008): 145–84; Michael Winship, "The

American Book Trade and the Civil War," in *A History of American Civil War Literature,* ed. Coleman Hutchison (New York: Cambridge University Press, 2016), 17–32.

39. Paul D. Escott, ed., *North Carolina Yeoman: The Diary of Basil Armstrong Thomasson, 1853–1862* (Athens: University of Georgia Press, 1996), 127.

40. Edward Bulwer-Lytton, *The Pelham Novels* (Boston: Charles Gaylord, 1837).

41. James J. Barnes, "Edward Bulwer Lytton and the Publishing Firm of Harper and Brothers," *American Literature* 38 (March 1966): 35–48, quote on 36.

42. James J. Barnes, *Authors, Publishers and Politicians: The Quest for an Anglo-American Copyright Agreement, 1815–1854* (Columbus: Ohio State University Press, 1974), 1–29.

43. EACM, January 29, 1843.

44. *Brother Jonathan* 3 (October 1, 1842), 134.

45. Constance Rourke, *American Humor: A Study of the National Character* (1931; New York: New York Review of Books, 2004), 21–26, quotes on 21–22 and 23.

46. Quoted in Harper, *House of Harper,* 77. See also Ronald J. Zboray, *A Fictive People: Antebellum Economic Development and the American Reading Public* (New York: Oxford University Press, 1993), chapter 2, "The Publisher's Market."

47. *Brother Jonathan* 3 (November 12, 1842), 314.

48. Barnes, *Authors, Publishers and Politicians,* 6–7.

49. Frank Luther Mott, *Golden Multitudes: The Story of Best Seller in the United States,* 3rd ed. (New York: R.R. Bowker, 1966), 76–79; Eugene Exman, *The Brothers Harper: A Unique Publishing Partnership and Its Impact Upon the Cultural Life of America from 1817 to 1853* (New York: Harper and Row, 1965); J. Henry Harper, *The House of Harper: A Century of Publishing in Franklin Square* (New York: Harper & Brothers, 1912), 63–65, 76–77.

50. "A New Cheap and Popular Periodical," *Hillsborough Recorder,* Hillsborough, NC (Orange County), November 28, 1832, 1.

51. Merle M. Hoover, *Park Benjamin, Poet and Editor* (New York: Columbia University Press, 1948), 127, n. 9.

52. Frank Luther Mott, *History of American Magazines, 1741–1850,* vol. 1 (New York: D. Appleton and Company, 1930), esp. 359–61, 513–14, and 523–24; Hoover, *Park Benjamin,* chapter 6, "The New World, 1839–1845," and Appendix, "The Extra Numbers."

53. William J. Gilmore, *Reading Becomes a Necessity of Life: Material and Cultural Life in Rural New England, 1780–1835* (Knoxville: University of Tennessee Press, 1989), 185–86; J. H. Scruggs, Jr., comp., *Alabama Postal History* (Birmingham, 195-), [Unpaginated]; David A. Rawson, "News in the Valley:

Periodical Subscribers at the New Market Post Office, 1804–1844," in *After the Backcountry: Rural Life in the Great Valley of Virginia, 1800–1900,* ed. Kenneth E. Koons and Warren R. Hofstra (Knoxville: University of Tennessee Press, 2000), 252.

54. Richard B. Kielbowicz, "Mere Merchandise or Vessels of Culture? Books in the Mail, 1792–1942," *Papers of the Bibliographical Society of America* 82 (June 1988): 169–200.

55. Kielbowicz, "Mere Merchandise or Vessels of Culture?" 171; Jonathan Daniel Wells, *Women Writers and Journalists in the Nineteenth-Century South* (New York: Cambridge University Press, 2011), 66.

56. Ensign and Thayer's *Travellers' Guide Through the States of Ohio, Michigan, Indiana, Illinois, Missouri, Iowa, and Wisconsin* (Buffalo, NY: Ensign & Thayer, 1850); EACM, January 29, 1843.

57. William D. Cooley [Independence, Jackson County, Missouri] to "Dear Father & Mother, Brother and Sisters," August 22, 1841, Cooley Family Papers, VHS; EACM, January 29, 1843.

58. Joseph Doddridge, *Notes on the Settlement and Indian Wars of the Western Parts of Virginia and Pennsylvania* (Wellsburgh, VA: Office of the Gazette, 1824); Joseph Doddridge, *Logan: The Last of the Race of Shikellemus Chief of the Cayuga Nation* (Buffaloe Creek, Brooke County, VA: Buffaloe Printing Office, 1823), 47.

59. Doddridge, *Notes on the Settlement,* 146.

60. Doddridge, preface to the "Dialogue" in *Logan: The Last of the Race,* n.p.

61. Richard M. Dorson, "Print and American Folktales," in *American Folklore and the Historian* (Chicago: University of Chicago Press, 1971), 177; *OED Online,* s.v. "folklore," accessed March 09, 2017, http://0-www.oed.com.library.uark .edu/view/Entry/72546?redirectedFrom=folklore ().

62. Constance Rourke, *American Humor: A Study of the National Character* (1931; New York: New York Review of Books, 2004), 39–40.

63. William Harvey Miner, *Daniel Boone, Contribution Toward a Bibliography of Writings Concerning Daniel Boone* (1901; New York: Burt Franklin, 1970).

64. Timothy Flint, *Biographical Memoir of Daniel Boone, the First Settler of Kentucky* (Cincinnati, OH, 1833). Flint reportedly interviewed Boone himself, although he also included apocryphal stories. John Ervin Kirkpatrick, *Timothy Flint: Pioneer, Missionary, Author, Editor, 1780–1840* (Cleveland, OH, 1911).

65. J. M. Peck, *Life of Daniel Boone,* Library of American Biography, vol. 13 (Boston, 1847).

66. Carl J. Weber, "Introduction," *A Bibliography of Jacob Abbott* (Waterville, ME: Colby College Press, 1948).

67. Lincoln to Harper and Brothers, quoted in Harper, *House of Harper*, 77–78.

68. Ira Bruce Nadel, *Biography: Fiction, Fact and Form* (London: Macmillan, 1984), chapter 1, "Biography as Institution."

69. *Obituary Addresses on the occasion of the death of the Hon. Henry Clay* (Washington, DC: United States Congress, 1852), 9.

70. Brown, *Word in the World*, 88–95.

71. Christopher Tolley, *Domestic Biography: The Legacy of Evangelicalism in Four Nineteenth-Century Families* (Oxford: Clarendon Press, 1997), esp. chapter 3.

72. Joan Jacobs Brumberg, *Mission for Life: The Story of the Family of Adoniram Judson* (New York: The Free Press, 1980), 1–19.

Chapter 6. Doctrines

1. Russell E. Miller, *The Larger Hope: The First Century of the Universalist Church in America, 1770–1870* (Boston: Unitarian Universalist Association, 1979), 311–19.

2. Miller, *The Larger Hope,* 728; AJCR, April 11, 1847.

3. Sarah Mendell and Margaret Hosmer, *Notes on Travel and Life By Two Young Ladies* (New York: published for the authors, 1854), 240–41.

4. David Paul Nord, *Faith in Reading: Religious Publishing and the Birth of Mass Media in America* (New York: Oxford University Press, 2004); Candy Gunther Brown, *The Word in the World: Evangelical Writing, Publishing, and Reading in America, 1789–1880* (Chapel Hill: University of North Carolina Press, 2004).

5. Gaylord P. Albaugh, *American Religious Periodicals and Newspapers Established from 1730 through 1830* (Worcester, MA: American Antiquarian Society, 1994), xi–xxi; Douglas C. McMurtrie, *Early Printing in Tennessee: With a Bibliography of the Issues of the Tennessee Press, 1793–1830* (Chicago: Chicago Club of Printing House Craftsmen, 1933).

6. AJCR, July 2, 1843.

7. David Rice McAnally, *Life and Times of the Rev. S. Patton, D.D. and Annals of the Holston Conference* (St. Louis, MO: Methodist Book Depository, 1859), 232.

8. Guion Griffis Johnson, *Antebellum North Carolina, A Social History* (Chapel Hill: University of North Carolina Press, 1937), 347.

9. Durwood Dunn, *The Civil War in Southern Appalachia* (Knoxville: University of Tennessee Press, 2013), 19–30.

10. Johnson, *Antebellum North Carolina,* 368.

11. John Perry Alderman, *Carroll 1765–1815: The Settlements: A History of the First*

Fifty Years of Carroll County, Virginia (Hillsville, VA: Alderman Books, 1985), 309.

12. AJCR, September 7, 1852.

13. Stephen B. Weeks, *Southern Quakers and Slavery: A Study in Institutional History* (Baltimore, MD: Johns Hopkins University Press, 1896), 243.

14. Letter from Jamestown, NC to the Rev. L. Lee, October 25, 1845, quoted in Lucius C. Matlack, *The History of American Slavery and Methodism from 1780–1849* (New York, 1849), 361.

15. Claude R. Rickman, "Wesleyan Methodism in North Carolina, 1847–1902," master's thesis, University of North Carolina, 1952, 20; *Annual Report of the American and Foreign Anti-Slavery Society*, May 6, 1851 (New York: American and Foreign Anti-Slavery Society, 1851), 77.

16. Randal L. Hall, *Mountains on the Market: Industry, the Environment, and the South* (Lexington: University Press of Kentucky, 2012), 77; *Annual Report of the American and Foreign Anti-Slavery Society* (New York: American Foreign and Anti-Slavery Society, 1851), 77.

17. Rickman, "Wesleyan Methodism," 21–32.

18. Patrick Q. Mason, *The Mormon Menace: Violence and Anti-Mormonism in the Postbellum South* (New York: Oxford University Press, 2011), 10–11; *Wilford Woodruff: History of His Life and Labors Recorded in His Daily Journals,* ed. Matthias F. Cowley (Salt Lake City, UT: The Deseret News, 1909), 46–63.

19. Mason, *Mormon Menace*, 28, 21, 20, 27, 26, 30.

20. Noah Carlton Baldwin diary, July 12, 1858, Virginia Baptist Historical Society, Richmond; Catherine Harwood, "Rev. Noah Carlton Baldwin" (Abingdon, VA: Washington County Historical Society, 1945).

21. Baldwin diary, April 1, 1855; June 20, 1850; introduction, 4.

22. Cushing Biggs Hassell, *History of the Church of God from Creation to AD 1885* (Middletown, NY: Beebe's Sons Publishers, 1886), 704–5.

23. August 26, 1844, Blountville Circuit, Holston Conference of the Methodist Episcopal Church, Stewards' Quarterly Conference Records, 1841–1886, Archives of Appalachia, East Tennessee State University, 31; *Minutes,* Holston Conference of the Methodist Episcopal Church (Knoxville, TN: Knoxville Republican Office, 1833), 15.

24. Reverend Creed Fulton, "A Discourse on Foreknowledge, Predestination, and Election Delivered in the Methodist Episcopal Church in Knoxville, Tenn. February 1843" (Knoxville, TN: James C. Moses, 1843), 10.

25. Debate between Reverend Israel Robards and Timothy Sullens, [Monroe County, Tennessee] *Monthly Miscellany* 1 (August 1843).

26. "Proposals for Publishing in the Town of Tarborough, N.C. A semi-monthly

paper, Entitled the Primitive Baptist," October 3, 1835, in *The Formation of the Primitive Baptist Movement,* ed. Jeffrey Wayne Taylor (Kitchener, ON: Pandora Press, 2004), 169; Joseph Biggs, *A Concise History of the Kehukee Baptist Association From Its Original Rise to the Present Time* (Tarborough, NC: Office of the Tarborough Free Press, 1834), 249.

27. "The American Telescope by a Clodhopper of North Carolina," [Joshua Lawrence] (Philadelphia, PA, 1825), 3–4.

28. Ashburn, *History of Fisher's River Primitive Baptist Association,* 27–29, 37; *Minutes of the Fisher's River Baptist Association of the Primitive Faith, Surry County, North Carolina,* October 1847 (Salem: Blum and Son, 1847).

29. Ann Speer to "My dear affectionate Mother," May 14, 1854, SFP.

30. NJS, October 8, 1850; James M. Edney, "Philip S. White," *American Temperance Magazine and Sons of Temperance Offering* 1 (1851), 263–67.

31. AMS, January 25, 1853.

32. NJS, October 8, 1850.

33. Paul D. Escott, ed., *North Carolina Yeoman: The Diary of Basil Armstrong Thomasson, 1853–1862* (Athens: University of Georgia Press, 1996), 24, 68; S. F. Cary, ed., *The National Temperance Offering, and Sons and Daughters of Temperance Gift* (New York: R. Vandien, 1850).

34. "Prospectus of the 'Wednesday Messenger' (Hillsville, VA)," September 24, 1852; *Freedom's Blade* began printing c1852; it is listed in W. T. Coggeshall, *The Newspaper Record* (Philadelphia: Lay and Brother, 1856), 43.

35. John W. Quist, *Restless Visionaries: The Social Roots of Antebellum Reform in Alabama and Michigan* (Baton Rouge: Louisiana State University Press, 1998), 463.

36. J. F. Fletcher, *A History of Ashe County North Carolina and New River Virginia Baptist Associations* (Raleigh: Commercial Printing Company, 1935), 25.

37. James Jones Speer was a Baptist preacher, and Joshua Kennerly Speer became a preacher in the Christian tradition founded by Alexander Campbell. NJS, November 3 and 17, 1850.

38. Timothy L. Smith, *Revivalism and Social Reform: American Protestantism on the Eve of the Civil War,* 8; Melvin E. Dieter, *The Holiness Revival of the Nineteenth Century* (Metuchen, NJ: Scarecrow Press, 1980), 4; Charles Edwin Jones, *Perfectionist Persuasion: The Holiness Movement and American Methodism, 1867–1936* (Metuchen, NJ: Scarecrow Press, 1974); Randall J. Stephens, *The Fire Spreads: Holiness and Pentecostalism in the American South* (Cambridge, MA: Harvard University Press, 2008); A. Gregory Schneider, *The Way of the Cross Leads Home: The Domestication of American Methodism* (Bloomington: University of Indiana Press, 1993).

39. Christopher Owen, *The Sacred Flame of Love: Methodism and Society in Nineteenth-Century Georgia* (Athens: University of Georgia Press, 1998), 54–55, 259; L. S. Burkhead, *Centennial of Methodism in North Carolina* (Raleigh, NC: John Nichols, Book and Job Printer, 1876); "Letter to Mr. M. by Mrs. Palmer, *Weekly Message* (Greensboro, NC), December 18, 1852, 1; NJS, April 8, 1843; March 1, 1846; June 11, 1848.

40. Steven D. Cooley, "The Possibilities of Grace: Poetic Discourse and Reflection in Methodist/Holiness Revivalism," PhD diss., University of Chicago, 1991.

41. "An Extract from the Way of Holiness, by Mrs. Palmer," *Weekly Message*, October 16, 1852, 1.

42. Cheryl Fradette Junk, " 'Ladies Arise! The World Has Need of You': Frances Bumpass, Religion, and the Power of the Press, 1851–1860," PhD diss., University of North Carolina, 2005.

43. *Weekly Message,* June 10, 1852, 2.

44. Frances Bumpass diary, September 30, 1854; September [n.d.] 1852, SHC.

45. Junk, "Ladies Arise!" 78, 79.

46. "Charles Force Deems," in *Dictionary of North Carolina Biography*, vol. 2, ed. William S. Powell (Chapel Hill: University of North Carolina Press, 1986), 49–50; John B. Weaver, "Charles F. Deems: The Ministry as Profession in Nineteenth-Century America," *Methodist History* 21 (April 1983): 156–69; Edward M. Deems and Francis M. Deems, *Autobiography of Charles Force Deems, D.D., LL.D.* (New York: Fleming H. Revell Company, 1897).

47. Jennie to "My dear Mr. Deems," May 3, 1854, transcription, SFP.

48. Charles C. Weaver, "G. F. C. Before the War," Trinity Archive, November 1896, quoted on undated note, Deems File, Brock Museum, Greensboro College.

49. Virginia Price Deems, "A Word-Picture of Mrs. Charles F. Deems," in Samuel Bryant Turrentine, *A Romance of Education: A Narrative Including Recollections and Other Facts Connected with Greensboro College* (Greensboro, NC: Piedmont Press, 1946), 56.

50. Virginia Price Deems, "Of Dr. Deems' Descendants," April 21, 1837, Deems File, Brock Museum, Greensboro College; NJS, April 5, 1854.

51. Beth Barton Schweiger, *The Gospel Working Up: Progress and the Pulpit in Nineteenth-Century Virginia* (New York: Oxford University Press, 2000), 68–69.

52. NJS, July 15, 1848; November 23, 1850.

53. [Charles F. Deems] *The Triumph of Peace and Other Poems* (New York: D. Fanshaw, 1840). Deems sold his book of poetry at Methodist bookstores. Undated clipping, interleaved in copy of *Speech of the Rev. C. F. Deems, D.D., on the Trial of Rev. Wm. A. Smith, D.D., for Immorality, Before the Virginia Confer-

ence, December, 1855 (Wilmington, NC, 1858), North Carolina Collection, University of North Carolina Special Collections.

54. Deems, *Devotional Melodies* (Raleigh, NC: Thomas Jefferson Lemay, 1841), vi. Deems dedicated this volume to the Rev. Edmund S. Janes of the American Bible Society.

55. Deems defended himself in a closely argued 150 page pamphlet account of the trial of Smith before the Virginia Conference of the Methodist Episcopal Church, South. *Speech of the Rev. C. F. Deems; Proceedings of the Virginia Conference in the Trial of W. A. Smith, D.D.* (Richmond, VA: 1856).

56. Deems, *Autobiography*, 97.

57. Deems, *Autobiography*, 118.

58. NJS to "My dear Mother," May 23, 1853, SFP; Charles Force Deems to William C. Doub, Esq., June 7, 1851, facsimile in Deems File, Brock Museum, Greensboro College. Doub became Professor of Mathematics and Ancient Languages for the session 1851–52.

59. Charles F. Deems, *What Now? A Present for Young Ladies* (New York: M.W. Dodd, 1852).

60. Charles F. Deems, "How to Manage a Wife," facsimile of handwritten essay, Deems File, Brock Museum, Greensboro College.

61. Deems, *What Now?*, 41–42, 86–87.

62. Charles F. Deems, *The Home Altar: An Appeal in Behalf of Family Worship with Prayers and Hymns* (New York: M.W. Dodd, 1851), 31.

63. *Southern Methodist Pulpit* 9 (March 1849): 150–51.

Index

Numbers in *italics* indicate images.